I0893005

EDWARD LONGSHANKS' FORGOTTEN CONFLICT

EDWARD LONGSHANKS' FORGOTTEN CONFLICT

The Anglo-French War 1294–1303

David Pilling

AMBERLEY

First published 2024

Amberley Publishing
The Hill, Stroud
Gloucestershire, GL5 4EP

www.amberley-books.com

ISBN 978 1 3981 1351 0 (hardback)
ISBN 978 1 3981 1352 7 (ebook)

British Library Cataloguing in Publication Data. A catalogue record for this book is available from the British Library.

1 2 3 4 5 6 7 8 9 10

Typesetting by SJmagic DESIGN SERVICES, India.
Printed in the UK.

CONTENTS

NOTE ON MONEY

Medieval money and coinage is a complicated topic, but some general explanations might be helpful.

Money in this era was divided into two categories: moneys of account and actual coinage. Moneys of account in England, France and Aquitaine were based on the *livre* or pound. These were made up of twenty *sous* or shillings, each worth twelve *deniers* or pennies.

The pound sterling in England, the *livre tournois* or *parisis* in France and the *livre bordelais* in Aquitaine were all made up of 240 pennies. This rate fluctuated in exchange values depending on monetary policy. The mark, worth thirteen shillings and six pence sterling, was another common English money of account. In Aquitaine, especially during the thirteenth century, there were local currencies such as the *livre chipotin* of Bigorre and the *livre morlaas* of Béarn.

The basic unit of coinage was the silver penny, which was also a money of account. The king-dukes of England and Aquitaine carefully guarded their rights to coin and shared profits from the mint at Bordeaux with the archbishop. No French coinage circulated in Aquitaine until after the final conquest of the duchy in 1453.

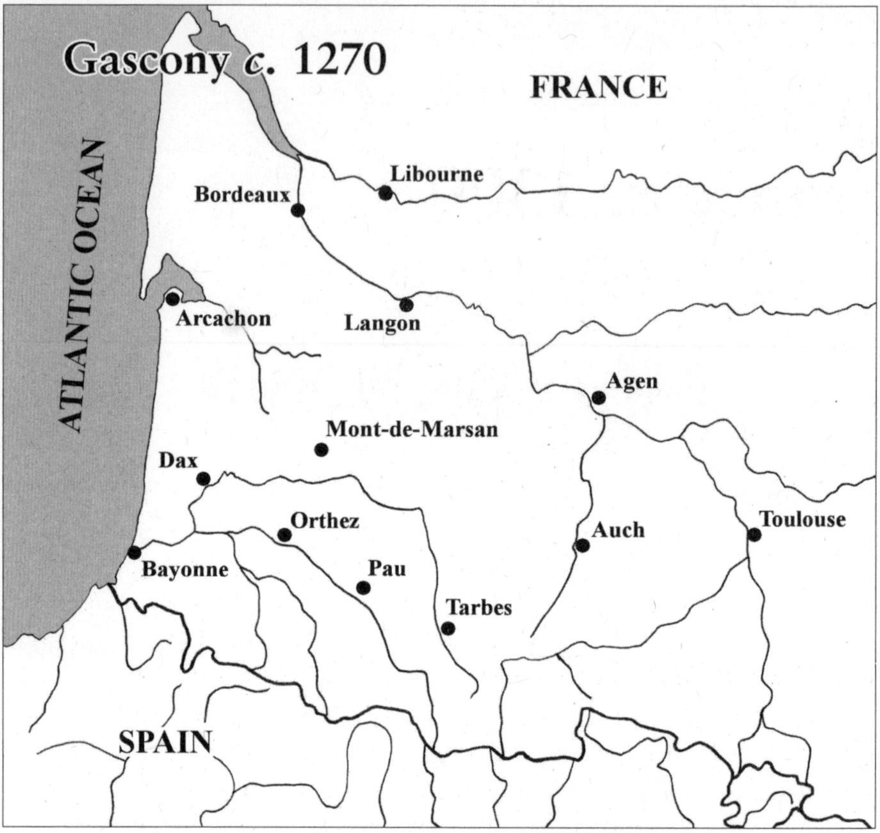
Gascony c. 1270
FRANCE
ATLANTIC OCEAN
Libourne
Bordeaux
Arcachon
Langon
Agen
Mont-de-Marsan
Dax
Orthez
Auch
Toulouse
Bayonne
Pau
Tarbes
SPAIN

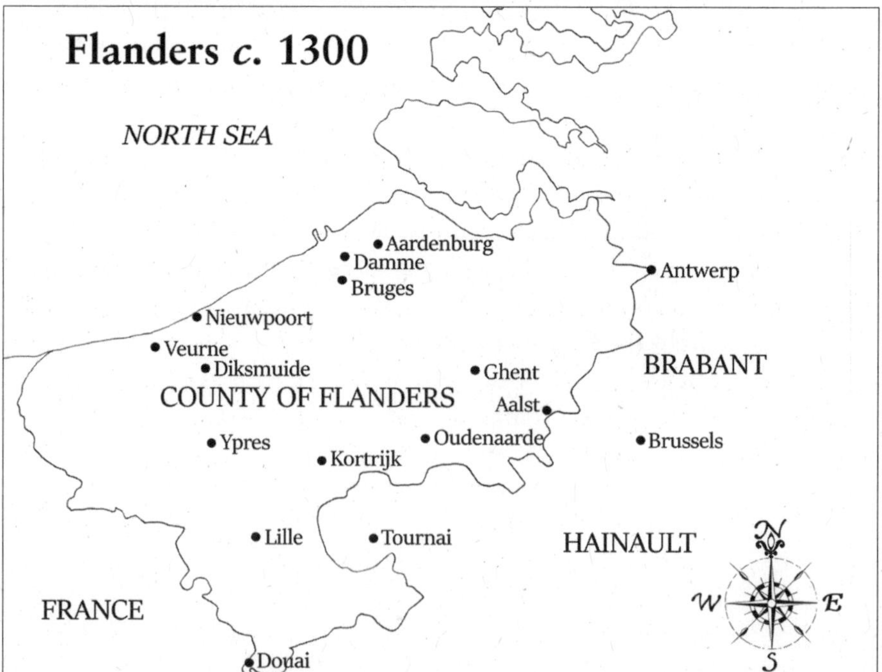
Flanders c. 1300
NORTH SEA
Aardenburg
Damme
Bruges
Antwerp
Nieuwpoort
Veurne
Diksmuide
Ghent
BRABANT
COUNTY OF FLANDERS
Aalst
Ypres
Oudenaarde
Brussels
Kortrijk
Lille
Tournai
HAINAULT
FRANCE
Douai
N
W
E
S

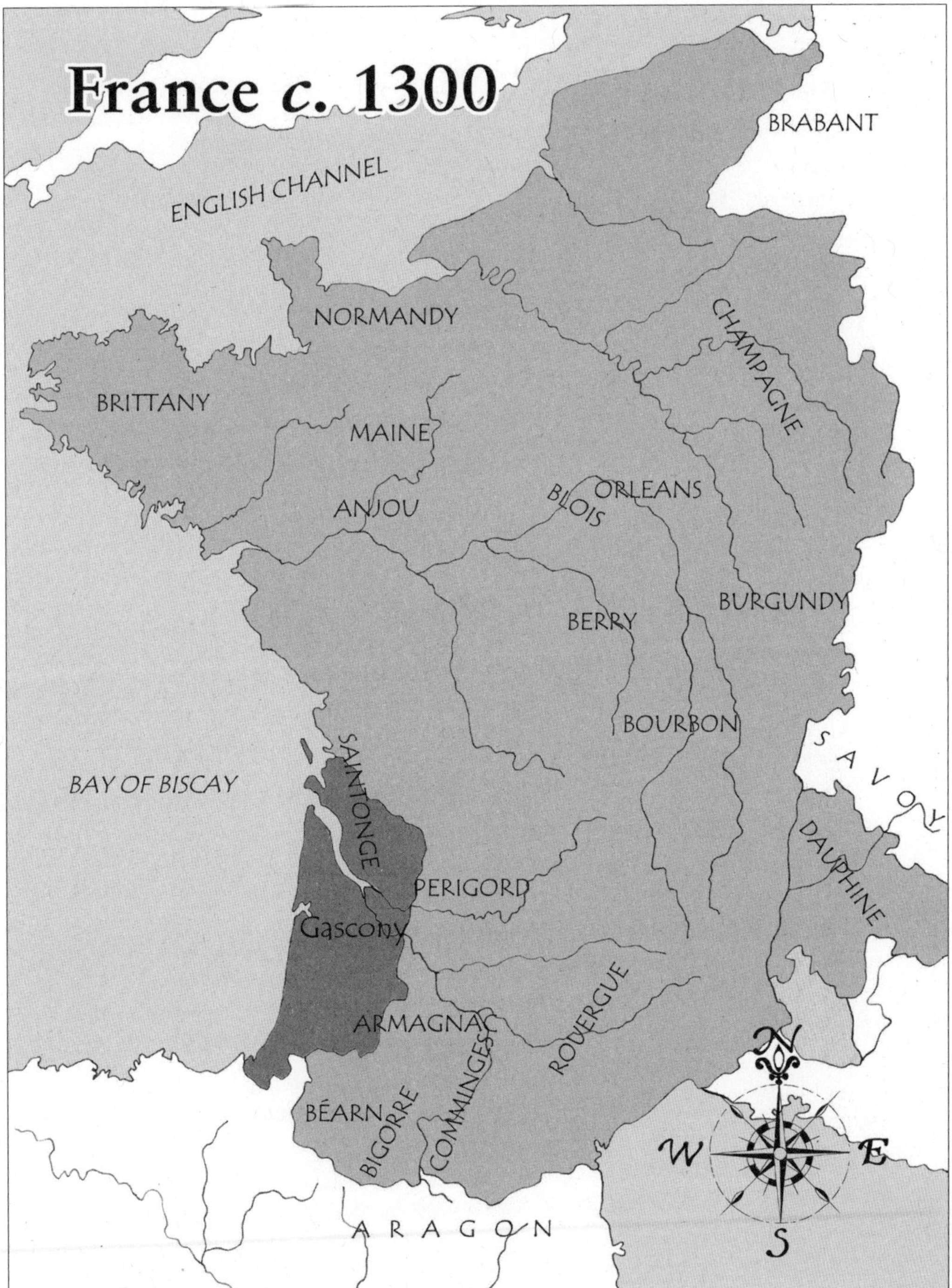
France c. 1300
BRABANT
ENGLISH CHANNEL
NORMANDY
CHAMPAGNE
BRITTANY
MAINE
ORLEANS
BLOIS
ANJOU
BURGUNDY
BERRY
BOURBON
SAVOY
BAY OF BISCAY
SAINTONGE
DAUPHINE
PERIGORD
Gascony
ROVERGUE
ARMAGNAC
COMMINGES
BÉARN
BIGORRE
COMMINGES
N
W
E
S
ARAGON

INTRODUCTION

The Hundred Years War occupies a special place in the popular imagination. This is partially thanks to Shakespeare's glorification of Henry V and his famous victory of Agincourt, though English victories at Crécy and Poitiers are no less renowned. French victories such as those at Formigny and Castillon tend to fall somewhat under the radar, at least on the English side of the Channel.

One might be forgiven for thinking that traditional Anglo-French enmity began in 1337. In fact the roots go back at least two generations further, and have little to do with competing 'national' identities. The Hundred Years War was triggered by a joust over sovereignty between two royal dynasties, both essentially French in culture and outlook. In particular, the war of 1294–1303, long before either the Black Prince or Henry V mounted their first charger, deserves greater attention.

This was an obscure conflict, and from a British perspective overshadowed by Edward I's wars in Wales and Scotland. Yet it was an expensive and wide-ranging affair, at one point involving all the major powers of western Europe. The outcome had severe financial repercussions for England and France, and helped to preserve Scottish independence as well as retain Gascony for the English crown. It also sowed the seeds for the later, much better-known conflict.

For all that, the war of 1294–1303 has been virtually dismissed by some historians as a sideshow, or at best a curiosity. Joseph R. Strayer, the biographer of Philip IV of France, had this to say: 'The war of

Aquitaine (or the Gascon war) was one of the most peculiar conflicts of the Middle Ages. It was not a bloody war; there were no major battles and relatively few skirmishes.'[1] And further, 'From the purely military point of view, the war of Aquitaine hardly deserves notice.'[2]

Strayer was referring to the war in the duchy of Gascony in south-west France, now part of Nouvelle-Aquitaine and in the thirteenth century the last significant fragment of the vast, ramshackle family firm known as the 'Angevin Empire'. The central issue of the war was Gascony (sometimes referred to as Guienne or the province of Aquitaine), though the conflict quickly widened.

Those who fought in Gascony would surely have disagreed with Strayer's remarks. There were plenty of bloody incidents and much hard fighting: the hanging of Gascon prisoners from the walls of Rions in 1295, for instance, or the epic thirteen-week siege of St-Sever. There was also at least one major field engagement, at Bellegarde in February 1297.

When the war spread, engulfing much of northern Europe, the eventual result was 'financial exhaustion and military stalemate'.[3] Nevertheless, it taught the combatants some important lessons for the future:

> ... the conflict taught military and logistical lessons to both sides which demonstrated the problems and difficulties encountered in a war confined to Aquitaine. The widening of the theatre of warfare to embrace Flanders in 1297 was partly an admission that neither side could win a war fought exclusively in south-west France. This lesson, and the precedents of Philip Augustus's reign, combined to shift active warfare towards northern France and the Low Countries. Militarily, the Anglo-French war for Aquitaine may have established guidelines for future strategy at the beginning of the Hundred Years War.[4]

For all these reasons and more (which shall be explored later), this conflict had considerable short- and long-term significance. Yet there has been no full-length study of the war in Aquitaine since Charles Bémont's narrative, written over a century ago.[5] This book seeks to redress the balance, and to offer a fresh perspective on events in Flanders and the Low Countries.

I

FALL OF EMPIRE

At the heart of this conflict lay the rivalry between the Angevin kings of England and the Capetian kings of France. In 1154 Henry II (r. 1154–89), son of Geoffrey of Anjou and the Empress Matilda, became King of England and the head of an enormous cross-Channel realm stretching from the borders of Scotland to the edge of the Pyrenees. Henry and his successors Richard I (r. 1189–99) and John (r. 1199–1216) could convincingly claim to be the most powerful rulers in western Europe.[1]

At the height of Angevin power, their dominions in France consisted of Normandy, Maine, Touraine, Brittany, Anjou, Poitou, Limousin, Saintonge, Périgord, Quercy, Gascony and the Agenais. The dynasty also extended its influence west, deep into Auvergne and the Central Massif.[2] Within this conglomerate there were sharp regional differences in language, law and custom, especially between the people of southern and northern France. Yet a measure of unity was provided by land and seaborne communication routes: 'The sea-ports of western France – Rouen, Nantes, La Rochelle, Bordeaux, Bayonne – were linked in common dependence upon England and the Iberian peninsula.'[3] These sea-ports, in particular Bordeaux and Bayonne, would play a crucial role in the war of 1294–1303.

Almost from the start, the Angevin kings experienced considerable difficulty in defending their 'empire'. In 1173–4 Henry II was faced with the revolt of his wife, Eleanor of Aquitaine, and three of his sons. Eleanor was backed by Louis VII, the Capetian King of France, who sensed an opportunity to break Henry's power in France. The coalition was soon joined by the King of Scotland, the counts of Flanders, Boulogne and Blois and other rebels in Poitou, Normandy and England.

Thanks to his swift action and large-scale hiring of mercenaries, Henry was able to crush the revolt, which ended with the capture of Eleanor and William the Lion, King of Scots. Nevertheless, the events of 1173–4 exposed the weakness in his armour. Apart from Henry's inability to control his own family, the sheer size and unwieldy nature of his realm made it vulnerable to attack from neighbouring powers. There was also the danger of internal rebellion, whereby disgruntled vassals could switch their allegiance to the kings of France or Scotland. For the moment, Henry had averted disaster, but the fault lines were there for all to see.

Nemesis arrived in the shape of Philip Augustus (r. 1180–1223), the Capetian king who made it his mission to destroy Angevin hegemony in France. Gerald of Wales, a half-Welsh clergyman and chronicler, later recited a story of Philip sitting apart from his barons at a council meeting, apparently lost in thought as he chewed on a hazel stick. When asked what was on his mind, Philip replied that he had been wondering whether it was his task to make France great again, just as in the days of Charlemagne.[4] This story, though told in hindsight, was probably meant to reflect the young Philip's determination to humble the Angevins.

Like his father, Louis VII, Philip attempted to turn Henry's sons against their father, only with much more success. In 1189 the old king was finally brought low by the combined assault of Philip and Henry's eldest surviving son, Richard, known as Coeur-de-Lion or the Lionheart. On 4 June 1189, now mortally ill, Henry was forced to accept a humiliating treaty. Two days later, he died at Chinon. The misery of his last hours was made even more wretched by the news that his youngest son, John, in whom he had placed his trust, had joined his enemies. Upon being informed of this, Henry is said to have turned his face to the wall and muttered:

> Now let the world go as it will. I care for nothing more. Shame, shame upon a conquered king.[5]

The brief reign of his successor, Richard I (r. 1189–99), witnessed a plunge in the fortunes of the Angevin lands in France, followed by a spectacular but short-lived revival. In the summer of 1190 Richard and Philip accompanied each other to the Holy Land on the Third Crusade, only to fall out at the siege of Acre. Philip returned early and immediately set about attempting to exploit Richard's absence. In league with the English king's treacherous brother, John, Philip conducted a successful invasion of eastern Normandy. However, John failed to lead a revolt in England and Richard's agents managed to contain an uprising in Aquitaine in the south-west.

Philip's situation was helped by the capture of Richard on his way home from crusade. He was taken prisoner by Leopold of Austria, whom Richard had alienated in the Holy Land, and handed over to the Holy Roman Emperor, Henry VI. The captive monarch was only released in February 1194 upon payment of an enormous ransom, largely raised in England. He also had to agree to resign the kingdom of England to Henry, and then receive it back as a fief of the empire.[6]

Richard's return heralded a dramatic revival of the Angevin cause. For all his skill as a politician, Philip Augustus was no match for his former ally on the battlefield. Between 1194 and 1198 Richard drove his enemy out of Normandy and managed to gain more territory in France than he had inherited. He inflicted a humiliating defeat on Philip at Gisors, where the French king was lucky not to be drowned. When a truce was made in January 1199, Philip offered to restore virtually all his previous gains to Richard. The Lionheart's unexpected death, struck down by a crossbow bolt at Chalus in April, was interpreted by the French as divine aid: 'God, wrote William the Breton, had come to save France.'[7]

The late king's supporters naturally took a different view. To Geoffrey of Vinsauf, who composed a lament in the Lionheart's honour, it came as a terrible shock:

> O death! Do you realise whom you have snatched from us? To our eyes he was light: to our ears melody, to our minds amazement. Do you realise, impious death, whom you have snatched from us? He was the lord of warriors, the glory of

> kings, the delight of the world. Nature knew not how to add any further perfection; he was the utmost she could achieve...[8]

This outpouring of grief was perhaps inspired by a lack of confidence in Richard's successor. To date John (r. 1199–1216) had pursued a distinctly unimpressive career, betraying his father and brother and intriguing with Philip. His revolt in England was a disastrous failure, and he had done very little to suggest he would make an effective king or hold off the French.

John got off to a bad start, with far-reaching consequences. In 1200 he agreed to the Treaty of Le Goulet, whereby he acknowledged Philip as his lord for the fiefs he held in France. In addition he agreed to pay a 'relief' of 20,000 marks to his overlord. This was a customary payment that any feudal lord could demand of a vassal entering upon his inheritance. The significance of this demand lay in the exorbitant fee, as well as the demand itself and John's agreement to pay. Nobody had ever demanded such things from Henry II or Richard I, who went no further than performing the traditional act of homage. John had bowed to the *superioritas* of the French crown, and set a precedent that his heirs would have little choice but to follow.[9]

Matters briefly improved. In August 1201 John pulled off a startling victory at Mirabeau, capturing more than two hundred knights and his nephew Arthur of Brittany, who had joined forces with Philip. His warrior brother Richard had only captured half as many knights at Gisors, so it looked as though John had redeemed himself. However, he proceeded to throw away every advantage. The suspicious disappearance of Arthur, possibly murdered by the king himself in a fit of drunken rage, along with the harsh treatment of other prisoners, alienated the nobility of Poitou, Anjou, Maine and Touraine.

It has been said that John 'could not resist the temptation to kick a man when he was down'.[10] This savage personality flaw had a direct impact upon Angevin fortunes in France. Disgusted by John's behaviour, whole swathes of the aristocracy defected to Philip. By 1204, just three years after his victory at Mirabeau, John's continental inheritance lay in tatters. The surrender of Rouen to Philip in June signalled the loss of the whole of Normandy, including Richard's great castle at Château Gaillard, while the death of Eleanor of Aquitaine triggered mass desertions in Gascony and Poitou. The dire situation only got worse when Gascony was invaded by the armies of Alfonso VIII of Castile. This was the result of a marriage more than thirty years earlier, when Henry II had given Gascony as a dowry to his daughter Eleanor when she was wedded to Alfonso. In 1204, exploiting John's weakness, Alfonso chose to march in and seize his wife's inheritance by force.[11]

John was down, but not quite out. In summer 1205 he and his mercenary captains staged a partial recovery and drove the Castilians out of Gascony and Poitou. John then crossed the Loire and ravaged Anjou, perhaps as a precursor to launching a reconquest of Normandy. When Philip came up with an army, however, John beat a hasty retreat and agreed to a two-year truce. Eight years went by before he set foot again on the Continent.

The nadir of John's fortunes came in 1214. He had spent the intervening years patiently constructing a 'grand alliance' of European princes against Philip – the same strategy that his grandson Edward I would deploy against the French in 1294–98. John mustered an impressive list of allies including the Holy Roman Emperor, the counts of Flanders and Holland and the dukes of Brabant and Lorraine. On 27 July the allied army – John was not present, so the English troops were led by his half-brother William Longespée, Earl of Salisbury – clashed with the French at Bouvines. It was a hard-fought battle, in which Philip was unhorsed and almost killed, but in the end the French triumphed.[12]

Pitched battles were rarely decisive in the medieval era, but Bouvines was an exception. For John it signalled the end of any hope of the recovery of Normandy or his other lands in northern France. He was compelled to return to England, shamed and defeated, with nothing to show for the severe taxes he had imposed on his English subjects to pay for the expedition. In the opinion of the Barnwell chronicler he had become the plunderer of his subjects, and a failed one at that.[13]

John's failure in Normandy was followed by a French invasion of England led by Philip's eldest son, Prince Louis. The outcome was still in the balance when John died in October 1216, leaving as his heir the nine-year-old Henry. For a while the boy-king's prospects looked bleak, but the death of John removed much of the reason for war in England. Many of the English barons started to turn away from Louis, though not before he was formally crowned King of England in London.[14] His forces suffered disastrous defeats on land (at Lincoln in May 1217, a battle known as the Fair of Lincoln) and at sea (off the coast of Sandwich in August 1217). These reverses scuppered Louis's ambitions, and later the same year he gave up and withdrew to France.

The Capetian failure to conquer England did not spell the end of their efforts to destroy the remnants of Angevin power in France. After the death of his father, Philip Augustus, in 1223, Louis took the king as Louis VIII and resumed the offensive. Distracted by the revolt of Fawkes de Bréaute, one of John's old mercenary captains, the minority government in England could do nothing to prevent the French invasion of Poitou. In the summer of 1224 Louis marched in triumph through the territory, taking one town and castle after another. Finally, on 3 August 1224, the last English bastion of La Rochelle surrendered to the French king.[15]

Gascony was next. Stung into action by the humiliating loss of Poitou, the English government finally got into gear and organised an effective response. Richard of Cornwall, Henry III's younger brother, was dispatched along with the Earl of Salisbury to repel the French and crush pro-Capetian supporters in Gascony. Aided by English tax money and large loans from the cities of Bordeaux and Bayonne, they succeeded in driving out the French.[16] Once again, and certainly not for the last time, the duchy was preserved.

Over the next twenty years King Henry made sporadic attempts to recover what his father had lost. In 1230 he mounted an expedition from Brittany to Bordeaux that at least managed to recapture the isle of Oléron, but little else was achieved. Over a decade later his hopes were raised when the pro-Capetian Count of La Marche, Hugh de Lusignan, chose to defy Louis IX of France. Hugh forged an alliance with Henry and in May 1242 the English king landed at Royan to try his luck again. The venture ended in dismal failure. Henry and his allies were routed by the French and Taillebourg and forced to flee south, into Gascony, after which Hugh submitted to Louis on humiliating terms.[17]

So ended yet another disastrous Angevin attempt to recover their lost glories. Henry campaigned once more on the Continent, in Gascony in 1253, this time with more success. He put an end to the threat of Castilian invasion by betrothing his eldest son, Edward, to the King of Castile's daughter, Eleanor. By this stage Henry had given up hope of recovering his lands, and switched to a policy of harmony and co-operation with the French. In 1253–4 he visited Louis peacefully in Paris, as Duke of Aquitaine, to settle a factional dispute at Bordeaux. Finally, the long-standing quarrel between the two dynasties was resolved at the Treaty of Paris in 1259.

Via the terms of this treaty (see Appendix 1 for a full transcript), Henry agreed to surrender his claims to Normandy, Anjou, Maine, Touraine and Poitou. In return he agreed to hold Gascony as a vassal or fiefdom of the French crown, a tremendous concession that would have devastating repercussions. After eighty years of bitter conflict, the feud between the houses of Plantagenet and Capet was over. Or so it seemed.

2

THE LAND OF *OÏL* AND ÒC

The last substantial piece of the Angevin inheritance was a complex land with its own laws, customs (*fors*) and dialects. Part of this complexity lies in terminology. Confusingly, Henry III and his heirs were referred to as dukes of Aquitaine, while the usual description of the territory itself is Gascony. The distinction lies in the historical roots of this land: 'From the earliest days the term Aquitaine has been used primarily to designate a territory which was an administrative unit, while Gascony was basically a land bound by a common language.'[1]

The history of Aquitaine stretched back to the days of the Roman Republic. From the time of Julius Caesar it described a conquered province of Gaul bounded by the Atlantic Ocean, the Garonne River and the Pyrenees. By the end of the fourth century AD the territory had been enlarged and divided into three provinces. These were Aquitania Prima, with its capital at Bourges, east of Limoges and Cahors; Aquitania Secunda, with the capital at Bordeaux; and Novempopulana, which stretched from Bazas in the north to the Pyrenees in the south and east.

Bordeaux, the future capital and staple of the wine trade, was in a favoured position from the start. It lay on the axis of major commercial routes and was home to schools and administration centres. For a time Aquitaine prospered as a centre of learning and culture, but all of this was swept away in the fifth century by the repeated invasions of Franks and Visigoths. These warlike peoples fought over the rich lands of the south-west, and by the end of the sixth century a third challenger arose in the form of the Vascones, a tribe of non-Latinised Iberians. Over the years they firmly established themselves in Aquitaine and imposed their own language, Basque.

The idea of Gascony and Aquitaine as separate entities was already in existence by the time of Charlemagne (742–814). He and his descendants would make sporadic efforts to create a kingdom of Aquitaine, but this was prevented by the rise of feudal lordships within this very large territory. Over the centuries the dukes of Aquitaine gained control of Poitou and the warring barons of the south-west, and eventually the court of Aquitaine became more rich and powerful than the court of the French king in Paris. At the start of the twelfth century they even outshone the king-duke of England and Normandy, Henry I, son of the famous Conqueror.

This brings us onto Eleanor of Aquitaine and her marriage to the future Henry II of England. Her father, Duke William X, died on pilgrimage in 1137 and left Eleanor, aged just sixteen, heiress to all his vast lands. Unsurprisingly, the other princes of Christendom saw her as a rich prize, but the King of France had the controlling interest. As Eleanor's feudal overlord, Louis VI of France (r. 1108–1137) had the disposal of her marriage, and ensured the prize did not slip through his fingers by marrying Eleanor to his son in 1137. A few weeks later the king died, and Louis the Younger, as he was known, became Louis VII.

What kind of land was Eleanor's coveted inheritance? It was a patchwork of various regions, differing from each other in terms of geography as well as dialect and culture. In the twelfth century Aquitaine was a centre of patronage for troubadours and poets: the earliest troubadour poetry arose in Poitou and the Limousin, with Duke William IX of Aquitaine and his neighbour Eble 'the Singer' of Ventadorn. After the death of her father, Eleanor moved north and Poitiers virtually ceased to be a centre of patronage. There was something of a revival in the early thirteenth century, when Savery de Mauléon, King John's Seneschal of Aquitaine, protected troubadours. The powerful counts of Foix in southern Gascony, notably Raimon-Roger (1188–1223) and Roger-Bernard III (1265–1302), also entertained troubadours. This practice was followed by their vassals, such as the counts of Comminges.[2]

Aymery Picaud, a twelfth-century Poitevin priest, provided an eloquent contemporary picture of Aquitaine in his guide for pilgrims along the route to Compostella. As a cultured Poitevin who spoke the *langue d'oil*, Aymery looked down on his southern neighbours and their barbarous speech, the *langue d'oc* (also known as Occitan). These terms were named after their separate words for 'yes': *oïl* and *òc*, respectively. He admitted that the wine of the Bordelais (the region of Bordeaux) was excellent and fish abundant in the rivers, but added that their tongue was crude. It was even worse than the rustic dialect of the men of Saintonge, the region adjacent to his homeland of Poitou.

Nor did he have much good to say about the Gascons themselves. He found them 'verbose, cynical, lecherous, drunkards, and badly clothed', although these unattractive traits were balanced by their skill at arms and hospitality to the poor. The Basque country in particular, on the approach to the Pyrenees and the pass of Roncesvalles, was especially awful. The country was wooded and mountainous, poor in bread and wine, and the people spoke a 'barbarous language'. At least the apple orchards produced good cider, and the reliance on grazing and rearing stock yielded an abundance of milk.

Aymery's prejudices aside, it is true that the uplands of southern Aquitaine, the *pays pyrénéen*, were markedly different to the *pays aquitaine* in the north. In the south, the *montagnards* or mountain people of Béarn had certain similarities with the people of Gwynedd in north Wales. They were both warlike peoples in mountainous upland areas, with their own distinct customs and society. The Béarnais and the north Welsh relied on stock-raising and seasonal transhumance, although the *montagnards* preferred to distance themselves from seigneurial authority. This was in contrast to Gwynedd, where mountain and lowland areas were in close proximity, and the lords of north Wales exercised a tighter jurisdiction.[3]

The lords of southern Gascony had dynastic connections with Aragon, Navarre and Catalonia, the kingdoms beyond the Pyrenees. Gaston VII de Moncada, Viscount of Béarn in the reigns of Henry III and Edward, was heir to the lordships of Moncada and Castelviel in Catalonia; his mother was of Catalonian lineage and, through her, he was a cousin of the King of Aragon.[4] From the perspective of the king-dukes of England, these connections were a potential threat to their hold on Gascony. The kings of Navarre had their own pretensions to suzerainty over lands north of the Pyrenees, and could muster the support of their kinsmen in the duchy.[5] For instance, in 1244 the King of Navarre, Thibaut IV, exploited internal divisions in Gascony to launch an invasion. He was sent packing by Henry III's seneschal, Nicholas de Meules, but many Gascon nobles continued to fight even after Thibaut's withdrawal. Apart from Gaston, these included the viscounts of Gramont, Soules and Tartas.[6]

It is difficult to make generalisations about the Gascon nobility. They were not a homogenous group, and there were hundreds of middling to lesser gentry families. The number multiplied over the generations: from about 1150 to 1300, the noble houses of the Bordelais alone increased from fifty to roughly 200.[7] This trend gave rise to an increase in the number of castles and *maisons-fortes* (fortified manor houses), along with a danger of overcrowding. At times a castle had to be shared between co-heirs, which made for awkward living arrangements. In 1288, the castle of Puy-Calvary in the Agenais was divided between two sons, Raymond-Guillaume and Guillaume de Palazols. They built a common wall to divide their living quarters: Raymond-Guillaume had the hall, while his brother dwelled in the tower. Neither was permitted to molest or disturb the other by making windows through which to observe his rival.[8]

Some of the peculiar local customs of the gentry are contained inside the *Recognitiones Feudorum*, a massive survey of feudal duties owed to the king-duke, drawn up by Edward I in 1274. The services included a family bound to prepare for the king and ten knights a meal consisting of beef, pork, chicken, onion and cauliflower. If one of the family was a knight, he should serve the meal wearing red shoes with silver spurs. Another tenant had to go with the king to a particular oak tree, and set fire to it using firewood drawn by two tail-less oxen. Unless the oxen made their escape, he was to let the tree burn to the ground.[9]

The majority of these nobles lived on very modest means. A valuation of lands held by dispossessed Gascons during the French occupation of 1294–1303 reveals the upper level of annual income was no more than 300 *livres tournois*. For context, a fine warhorse in this era could cost 200 *livres tournois*. A few of the wealthier nobles of the middle rank, such as Pons de Castillon and the Captal de Buch, enjoyed landed incomes of 1,000 *livres tournois*. Most nobles were dependent on serf labour and receipt of rents for their livelihood.[10]

Then there were the great houses of Aquitaine. These were few in number: an early fourteenth-century description of Gascony lists four counts and fifteen viscounts among the upper nobility, set apart from the common mass of gentry.[11] Of the counts, those of Foix and Armagnac were the most powerful in the south, and constantly feuding. In the thirteenth century the house of Foix exploited their ancient privileges to pursue an aggressive policy of expansion. As well as fighting the counts of Armagnac, they successfully absorbed lesser families through marriage, vassalage and inheritance.[12] The allegiance of the Count of Foix would play an important role in the Anglo-French war.

The true strength of Gascony lay in towns and commerce. After the French conquered Poitou and La Rochelle in the reign of Henry III, Bordeaux once again became an important provincial capital. The conquest of La Rochelle removed its main competitor for the wine trade, although there was some competition from upstream towns such as La Réole. Bordeaux had the advantage of controlling the River Gironde, the main waterway of the duchy, and of being able to dominate lesser towns along the River Garonne and on the Dordogne. As the chief exporter of wine to England, the Bordelais had the most to lose if the English connection was broken. To the south, the port of Bayonne provided ships and sailors for Bordeaux's commerce and the transport of wine to England. The Bayonnais also traded with Castile and Navarre, and controlled trade along the River Adour.[13]

Within these towns, competition was fierce over the profits of trade with England. Factions and warring parties developed within Bordeaux and Bayonne, and the Plantagenet regime had to tread carefully in its relations with the noble families. At Bordeaux the most prominent factions were the Colom and the Soler, a medieval Gascon version of the Montagues and the Capulets. Edward I (r. 1272–1307) took the side of the Soler, in an effort to create a single party in the city loyal to his interests.[14]

The above is just a sketch of this rich and complicated land: a thorough overview would (and has) filled many volumes. Now it is time for one of our two main protagonists to take centre stage.

3

A TASTE OF POWER

Henry III's son and heir, Edward – or Sir Edward or the Lord Edward, as he was known – had been granted Gascony by his father in 1254. This was part of a substantial landed endowment for his wedding to Eleanor, daughter of the King of Castile.[1] Edward was just fifteen, and Gascony would provide his first testing ground in war and politics. His control of the duchy was only nominal, since Henry retained the title of Duke of Aquitaine. True authority was exercised by the king's seneschal, Stephen Longespée.[2] This left Edward in an awkward subordinate position, which he resented and did all he could to overcome.

King Henry departed from the duchy in early November 1254. Shortly after his father was gone, Edward showed the direct, hands-on form of government that would later define his style of his kingship. On 2 January 1255, barely two months into his administration, he ordered the mayor of Oléron to appear before him to answer why, and on whose authority, he had received certain men into his community, to its detriment.[3] Less than a fortnight later, Edward promised to bring to judgement in his court at Bergerac before Easter (28 March 1255) one Renaud de Pons and his wife Marguerite. This was another instance of Edward's style of lordship:

> Letters patent promising, at the instance of the mayor, knights and burgesses of Bergerac to bring the case concerning Renaud de

> Pons, Marguerite his wife, Rudell, son of Elie Rudell, and all the other heirs of Elie Rudell, for judgement before Edward's court before the coming Easter. Edward has released Renaud de Pons from captivity in order that he might be freer to prosecute his case, and promises to implement certain testamentary bequests of Elie Rudell, including the assignation of her dowry to Roga, his widow.[4]

This case related to a dispute over the succession to the lordship of Bergerac, which had provided Edward with his first experience of warfare. In 1254 King Henry had briefly laid siege to Renaud de Pons and his supporters at Bergerac. Edward was present at the siege and apparently captured Renaud during the fighting; hence the latter's presence in Edward's prison. The dispute was only settled years later, but reveals his intention to deliver justice and be involved personally in litigation. Traditionally, justice in Gascony was rendered via the four courts of the duchy (Bordeaux, Bazas, Dax and St-Sever). In the case above, Edward set aside this custom and promised to judge the case in his own court.[5]

There are several other instances of Edward's direct justice in Gascony. On 5 May 1255 he instructed Arnaud-Guillame de Marsan to surrender the castle of Roquefort to Raymond de Béarn, so the latter could hold it until Edward's court had decided if the castle should be retained by Edward or Raymond.[6] Shortly afterwards, on 24 May 1255, he ordered Aimar, the squire of Amaubin de Barés, to be delivered from custody so the prisoner could answer complaints against him in Edward's court when required to do so.[7]

All did not go smoothly for Edward in Gascony. His godfather, Simon de Montfort, had previously served as seneschal and warned Henry III of the violent nature of the Gascon gentry: 'One cannot stay such men by an army in the kind of war which they will make, for they will do nothing but rob the land, and burn and plunder, and put the people to ransom, and ride by night like thieves by twenty or thirty or forty in different parts...'[8]

Edward would have been well advised to keep this warning in mind. The duchy's finances were in a poor state, so he decided to levy a tax. This was partially justified as a traditional levy on the occasion of his being knighted. Unfortunately the tax coincided with another imposed by his father to fund a new crusade, and the combined financial strain was too much for the Gascon nobles to bear. They rose in revolt, and in the spring and summer of 1255 Edward found himself at war. He reacted quickly, seizing towns, fortifying castles, ordering the construction of ships and bringing in materials, money and grain from his lordship of Ireland. When the king heard of the revolt, he cancelled a tournament in England and rushed over pre-paid knights to aid his son in Gascony.[9]

The scant records of the campaign suggest Edward coped well enough. In July he laid siege to Gramont Castle after its lord, Arnaud-Guillaume, refused to appear in court to justify his claim to it. Gramont stood near Arraute on the frontiers of the vicomtés of Béarn and Soule, and the kingdom of Navarre; this was a volatile border region, where the local gentry were frequently in revolt against the English crown.[10]

At the end of the month, after several weeks of siege, Arnaud-Guillaume was permitted to sue for peace.[11] This is an example of compromise on Edward's part, as those rebels who did not wish to negotiate were free to depart. The assistance of Gaston de Béarn is notable. Gaston was the viscomte of Béarn, on the southern borders of Gascony, and had caused a deal of trouble for Simon de Montfort and Henry III. He was foremost among the Gascon nobles who rebelled against Henry in 1253, but in 1255 assisted Edward to calm the duchy. This new-found helpful attitude was not to last.

The revolt was over by August, and Edward took the opportunity to reconcile former enemies. At the same time he continued to collect the tax money that had caused the trouble in the first place. On 20 August, for instance, he ordered the delivery of money collected in the bailliage of Lormont as an aid for his knighthood.[12] In October he appointed the former lord of Gramont, Arnaud-Guillaume, as Constable of Gramont. After capturing Gramont in July Edward had taken the castle for himself, and now gave its previous master custody of the place.[13] Here Edward showed a light touch in dealing with his enemies, and another example of a gift for compromise.

Edward took pains to secure his grip on the duchy by strengthening its fortifications. On 23 March he licensed the men of Cocument in the diocese of Bazas to build an enclosure and fortalice; in return they agreed to pay Edward sixpence per annum for each house, and to do customary military service.[14] He also reinforced the town of Fronsac, occupied Guiche and improved the defences of Bayonne, an important sea-port on the south-west coast.[15] This could be taken as an early example of Edward's interest in military architecture, which he would later display to stunning effect in Wales. He also showed a streak of pragmatism by ordering the church at La Réole to be destroyed, since its location threatened the security of the castle. The monks were compensated for their loss.[16]

This early stint in Gascony also revealed Edward's taste for dissimulation, or what might be termed the 'art' of politics. When he was recalled to England, a row blew up between Edward and his father. The cause was a protest made to Edward by Gascon merchants who objected to the extortions of royal officials. King Henry was allegedly furious that the complaint had been put to his son, rather than him, and accused Edward of ingratitude. He even went so far as to recall the way in which Henry II's dearest sons had turned against him.[17]

This dispute fizzled out, only for a more serious one to arise. Henry favoured a policy of mediation between two of the rival families in Bordeaux, the aforementioned Soler and Colom. Edward, however, wanted to ensure loyalty to him in the form of a single party. With this in mind he made a treaty with Gaillard del Soler, though he did not inform his father. In return Gaillard offered to win control of the mayoralty of Bordeaux and build a new castle in the town, meanwhile swearing not to make peace with his enemies without Edward's consent nor make marriage alliances against his interests.[18]

For a while Henry was kept in the dark, and continued his policy of reconciliation between the rival factions. He only discovered the truth when Gaillard returned to Gascony and foolishly boasted of his alliance with Edward. As a consequence he was arrested. Interestingly, even though he had deceived his father, it was Edward who won in the end. Four years later, in 1259, he renewed his treaty with Gaillard, and in the following year Henry dropped all charges against the Gascon.[19]

Edward did not return to Gascony until the autumn of 1260, when he again concerned himself with the feud between the Colom and Soler families in Bordeaux. In October he gained control of the mayoralty, which he had previously planned to do via his secret treaty with Gaillard del Soler. He reformed the coinage, restored law and order in the duchy and put an end to a damaging conflict over the lordship of Soule in southern Gascony. This latter dispute had rumbled on for several years, and required Edward's personal attention.

The War of Mauléon

The viscountcy of Soule, in south-west France on the edge of the Pyrenees, occupied an important strategic position. Mauléon, the chief stronghold of the viscounts, controlled the pass to the Iberian peninsula, and thus occupied the main route between Gascony and the kingdom of Navarre. The viscounts of Soule owed homage to the English crown, but in 1244 Viscount Raymond-Guillaume chose to switch his allegiance to the King of Navarre, and supported a Navarrese invasion of Gascony. When Simon de Montfort became seneschal, Raymond-Guillaume rebelled a second time. In 1252 Simon laid siege to Mauléon, took the viscount prisoner and only released him on payment of a ransom. As an extra precaution, Simon left a garrison in Soule to ensure the viscount's good conduct.[20]

When Edward first came to Gascony, in 1255, he continued Simon's policy. In October of that year, he gave the lord of Tardets, Guillaume-Arnold, command of the men whom Simon had left as guardians of the land of Soule. Friction soon arose between Tardets and the viscount, and a brief war ensued. On 26 September 1256, at Dax, they agreed to make peace, thanks to the mediation of Gaston de Béarn and Henry III's seneschal, Stephen Longespée. Via this agreement, the rival parties swore to observe absolute peace with regard to each other, and with Lord Edward. The terms were stiff. If the viscount of Soule or his sons committed any further violence, their lands would be forfeit and pass into Edward's hands. The viscount also had to agree to send some of his knights, who had killed Tardets' men, on pilgrimage to the Holy Land. If they refused to go, he was obliged to drive them into exile.[21]

This peace did not endure. It seems Edward or his father had decided to take direct control of Soule, probably due to its strategic advantages: in August 1257 one of his loyal barons, the lord of Navailles, swore to obtain the viscountcy of Soule and Mauléon for Henry III and his heir. He and the seneschal, Longespée, then invaded the province and seized the castle of Beloscar. Raymond-Guillaume died in arms at Aroue, defending his land, but resistance continued under his widow, Marquèse, and their sons. The ducal army laid siege to Mauléon, where the town and barbican fell to the attacking forces. Before they could mount an assault on the keep, Gaston de Béarn stepped in again to broker a truce. This time it was agreed that Gaston would take custody of Mauléon, while Longespée occupied Beloscar. In the meantime the new viscount, Augier, would go to England to beg mercy of Henry III and ask him to ratify the treaty. If Augier could not go, he would send deputies in his stead.[22]

Augier had inherited his father's fiery temperament. He refused to accept the terms of the peace, or to go to England. Somehow he regained control of Mauléon, and in the winter of 1258 the ravaged province was again at war. On 12 December one Bernard-Garcia, lord of Osserain, handed over his castle to the custody of the King of England, to be garrisoned against Augier for the duration of the war; he also pledged to help Lord Edward with all his means, offering his property as security.[23]

The young viscount managed to sustain his resistance for three years. Finally, in 1261, Edward himself took charge of the situation. He raised the feudal host of Gascony – '*la convocation de l'ost*' – and marched into Soule to lay siege to Mauléon.[24]

However, instead of forcing a military solution, Edward showed a delicate touch. Augier was allowed to receive messages from the Pope, who urged him to come to terms. The result was a final settlement, sealed outside Mauléon on 3 November 1261. Auger agreed to an act of 'voluntary and spontaneous submission', not done through 'fear or force' of Edward's power. This reads like an attempt to save the viscount's honour, and make the terms appear less humiliating. In exchange for the permanent surrender of Mauléon and Soule, he was granted the townships of Laharie, Saubusse, Saas and Angoume, along with Edward's rights in the parishes of ten further townships.[25] The ubiquitous Gaston de Béarn probably had a hand in these negotiations, since he was among Edward's company at Mauléon.[26]

Augier thus emerged from the affair with dignity intact, but the harsh reality could not be concealed. He had signed away his inheritance forever, and the land of Soule had been absorbed by the English crown. Afterwards the disinherited viscount took service with the King of Navarre. His subsequent history, and that of Soule, shall be included in a later chapter.[27]

Amid all this success, Edward displayed his more arbitrary tendencies by allegedly seizing the temporalities of the archbishopric of Bordeaux. Overall, however, he had done remarkably well. In the autumn Gaillard and another Gascon, Bertrand de Ladills, reported to the king that 'our lord Edward is in a good and prosperous state, and by God's grace his affairs in Gascony are going well'.[28]

The young prince's impressive performance in Gascony stood in contrast to his record in England, where he was suspected of plotting to depose his father.[29] He was also deep in debt, apparently because several members of his household had embezzled funds during his time in the duchy.[30] Edward himself showed no desire to leave Gascony, and had to be pressured by Henry to come home and lead a military expedition to Wales. The prince's estates in north Wales, granted to him as part of his appanage in 1254, were under attack from Llywelyn ap Gruffudd, lord of Gwynedd. As the situation got worse, King Henry wrote a furious letter to Edward reminding him of his responsibilities:

> These things should cause you great concern. This is no time for laziness or boyish wantonness. It is a disgrace to you that Llywelyn spurns the truce which he promised to maintain with us, for I am growing old, while you are in the flower of early manhood, and yet, instigated by some men of my realm, he dares to do it.[31]

Edward duly went home to lead a rather unsuccessful campaign against the Welsh.[32] He spent much of the rest of the 1260s in England, where the tensions between his father and Simon de Montfort dissolved into civil war. The temporary collapse of royal authority in England encouraged Henry's enemies overseas to threaten the borders of Gascony. Gaston de Béarn resumed his intrigues with the King of

Navarre, Theobald II, and started negotiations to marry his daughter, Constance, to the latter's son. Theobald also obtained the homage of the counts of Comminges and d'Astarac. In 1266, growing tensions between Navarrese and Plantagenet supporters erupted into civil war. The partisans of Navarre laid siege to the castle of Lourdes, while the rival factions came to blows in the streets of Bayonne. Arnaud-Guillaume, the troublesome lord of Gramont, renewed his ancient fealty to Navarre and admitted the Navarrese to his castle.[33]

The situation was calmed somewhat by the intervention of King Louis of France, who persuaded the sides to accept a truce in December.[34] Two months later Jean de Grailly, a Savoyard knight favoured by Edward, conducted successful negotiations in Paris. Here it was agreed that Constance de Béarn would be betrothed to Henry of Almaine, son of Richard of Cornwall and Henry III's nephew. This severed her father's alliance with Theobald of Navarre and put an end to the disturbances.[35]

The settlement of Gascony was followed in July 1267 by the defeat of the last Montfortian rebels in England.[36] A few years of relative peace followed, until the unresolved issues of the Treaty of Paris gave rise to more bloodshed and controversy.

4

THE LANDS I OUGHT TO HOLD

The English found it almost impossible to enforce all the clauses of the Paris agreement. One bone of contention was Henry's claim to lands that he held from the dowry of his aunt, Joan of England, mother of Count Raymond VII of Toulouse. The dowry included the lands of Agenais, Quercy and Saintonge. These rights were formally recognised by the treaty, stipulating that if the family of the counts of Toulouse were to be extinguished, those lands would be turned over to the King of England.[1]

Raymond's only child, his daughter Joan, died in August 1271. Thus, in October, Henry sent envoys to Paris to 'ask and receive' the lands he was owed. Another request was sent in January 1272, along with a new objection that certain agents of the King of France were harassing the officers of Henry's son, Edward, about the homage of the city of Limoges.[2]

The new French king, Philip III (called 'the Bold', r. 1270–85), was not minded to fulfil his side of the bargain. Instead he put Henry off with vague answers and went on a tour of his kingdom. For the short time that remained to him, Henry did not press his claims any further. Twice, on 20 May and 5 June, he wrote to Philip excusing himself from coming to Paris to perform the act of homage for Gascony on account of his health. He finally succumbed on 20 November 1272, after a reign of fifty-six years.[3]

Henry's heir, Edward, was still abroad when his father died. He had gone on crusade in 1269 and remained absent for five years. After surviving an attempt on his life by a Syrian assassin, he started the long journey home in September 1272.[4] This proved no less dramatic than his narrow escape from the Holy Land. In July 1273 Edward accepted an invitation to compete in a tournament at Chalons in Franche-Comté that quickly degenerated into a real battle. When he saw the treachery of his opponents, Edward ordered his men to respond in kind:

> He said to his men, 'Spare no-one you set eyes on now, and do the same to them as they are doing to us.' So they began killing the other side, savagely attacking them everywhere with the sword. The men on foot had retreated from the slaughter of their fellows when they saw many of their people fall, but boldly joined the combat of the mounted men; they gutted many of the horses and cut their girths, so that their riders fell to the ground.[5]

At this time Franche-Comté was still part of the Holy Roman Empire, so the bloodbath at Chalons should not be interpreted as part of Anglo-French tensions. Once Edward had vanquished his opponents, he made his way to Paris to do homage for Gascony to King Philip. He did so on 6 August with this form of words: 'Lord king, I do you homage for all the lands which I ought to hold of you.'[6]

This strictly conditional statement clearly referred to the failure of the French to act upon the territorial clauses of the Treaty of Paris. Edward was implying that he could not and would not perform liege homage in full until he was invested with the lands and rights agreed between his father and Philip's father, Louis IX.[7]

Further difficulties arose almost immediately. Another condition of the Treaty of Paris was that Louis IX would cede to Henry III all rights 'that he has and holds in these three bishoprics and in the cities, namely, of Limoges, Cathors and Périgueux, in fief and domain'.[8] Whether the French king had possessed much of worth in these dioceses is doubtful. They were, according to one French historian, 'a complex and varying bundle of rights and jurisdictions, often barely effective, a fruitful source of disputes and appeals'.[9]

Effective or not, the dioceses were yet another bone of contention. Limousin in particular, just north of Gascony, was a disputed land torn by bloody feudal discord. On the one side was the commune of the city of Limoges, on the other the viscountess, Marguerite of Limoges. In 1262 Louis IX had ordered his officers to observe strictly neutrality in such troubled areas, but the court of Philip III had set aside this policy and favoured the viscountess over the commune. This was apparently because the citizens were suspected of being pro-English and wishing to swap their allegiance to the King of England. As one local annalist put it:

> The French seneschal behaved like the court of his master; some excused the person of the King, but injustice was not less obvious. They hated us because of the King of England, because those who had assembled the spirits of the King and of his advisors against us claimed wrongfully that we love the English best.[10]

While his court favoured Marguerite, Philip had forbidden her to take up arms against the commune. She disregarded this order and joined forces with a band of robbers in Chalusset who 'plundered all, mutilated cattle, scattered wheat and did all kinds of wickedness'.[11] In spite of this, the parlement of Paris granted the city to Marguerite, even though the bourgeois of Limoges had declared they were not her men but those of the king. Philip further alienated the bourgeois by ordering them to release some of Marguerite's soldiers they had taken prisoner, while allowing the viscountess to retain her captives.[12]

The men of Limoges fought back. On 5 July they attacked Marguerite's castle at Aixe, where an indecisive engagement was fought with casualties on both sides. Since Philip would not help them, the commune took the extraordinary step of inviting the King of England to be their overlord. On 25 July, the day before Edward arrived in Paris to do homage, his consort, Eleanor of Castile, came to Limoges and was led in procession to St Martial by the citizenry.[13] She was accompanied by the Seneschal of Gascony, Luke de Tany, at the head of an army.

On 7 August – the day after Edward paid homage to Philip in Paris – de Tany engaged the army of the viscountess in open battle:

> In the same year, on the day following the feast of Saint Sixtus, the king of England's seneschal, who had come to the aid of the citizens of Limoges against the viscountess of Limoges, had a great victory over her army, between Aixe and the town of Limoges. He wounded and captured many of them, killing a nobleman and many others, without loss to him or his allies, at which the townsfolk rejoiced greatly. Moreover, they captured the banner of Girbert de Tamines.[14]

Three days later, another engagement was fought. Again, Marguerite's men came off worse:

> On the feast of Saint Laurence following [10 August], one of the viscountess's men was found dead and many horses on both sides too, but the viscountess lost many more. In that same year, the aforesaid burgesses made their oath of fealty to the knight William de Valence, the king of England's uncle and count of Bigorre, for their service of the said king. They sent a warning to the viscountess to desist from harassment of the citizens, which she did not wish to do.[15]

William de Valence, Edward's Lusignan half-uncle, arrived at Limoges with letters from the English king. These requested the inhabitants of Limoges, in spite of their previous allegiance to Philip, to swear homage to Edward as Duke of Aquitaine. The commune agreed, and the rite of oath-swearing took place in the abbey of St Martial on 3 September.[16] Edward thus used the war in Limousin to try and enforce his claim to the city of Limoges, which ought to have ceded to him anyway via the Treaty of Paris. At first he was successful, and his seneschal inflicted two stinging military defeats on the viscountess. He also gained the enthusiastic support of the commune of Limoges.

Meanwhile the fighting continued. On 16 September the bourgeois of the city marched out, with drums and trumpets, to launch a second assault on the castle of Aixe. On the way they plundered a church, which caused some of the bourgeois to fear divine wrath. When they reached the gates of Aixe, panic set in and the bourgeois militia scattered in all directions. The viscountess's cavalry pursued and killed a number of them, including children and clerks. Further skirmishes were fought on 27 September and 2 October. All the while Edward attempted to send assistance. On 23 October he wrote to the seneschals of Gascony and the Limousin, and to the Viscount of Ventadour, and asked them to rescue the town of Limoges.[17]

Philip chose this moment to intervene. His envoys ordered everyone to lay down their arms and to abide by the king's sentence, which was pronounced at the parlement of All Saints' Day (1 November). Edward was ordered to give up the 'brandons' or torches which were the symbol of the oaths of fidelity of the commune of Limoges. If he neglected to do this, the Seneschal of Périgord would force him; he was also to abstain from fighting the viscountess and permit her to do justice in the city. In a personal letter to Edward, the French king went further and ordered his kinsman to remove his bailiff from the city and to recognise Marguerite's right to armed justice in time of rebellion. Edward had been ordered to cease and desist in no uncertain terms, but the sentence of the court was suspended for several months.[18]

As if this wasn't enough, Edward now became embroiled in a separate conflict. While the drama in Limousin unfolded, he was at St-Sever in southern Gascony, overseeing a survey of feudal dues. Here he was made aware of the defiance of Gaston, the volatile Viscomte of Béarn who had caused Edward's father so much trouble. In September Gaston refused the king's summons to come and swear homage at St-Sever along with the rest of the Gascon nobility. When Edward sent an envoy, Géraud de Laur, to demand Gaston's presence, the vicomte's men threw Géraud into prison and tortured him.[19] Gaston was arrested and ordered by the court of St-Sever to submit and deliver his castle of Orthez into the hands of the king-duke. He promised to abide by this judgement, but then fled to his lands and proclaimed defiance.[20]

Edward was careful to act according to the law. Another court was held, and it was decided that the king-duke could move against Gaston if he disobeyed one more summons.[21] This summons was rejected, and Edward assembled an army at the start of November 1273 for his second military campaign in Gascony. Along with the conflict in Limousin, he was now effectively at war at both ends of his duchy.

The king-duke's first action was to march into Marsan, Gaston's lordship in the south of Gascony, and gain the submission of his tenants. Resistance had collapsed by 27 November, when Gaston's daughter Constance agreed to surrender the fortified town of Mont-de-Marsan so it may be 'garrisoned and defended by men at arms, for the purpose of the war which the lord king is presently conducting against the lord Gaston, viscount of Béarn'.[22]

Edward didn't have things all his own way. From his castles on the edge of the Pyrenees, Gaston and his men launched effective guerilla attacks on the invading army, 'frequently coming and going and attacking the king's army in sudden assaults, more frequently inflicted not immoderate losses, and returning pompously with the booty they had captured'.[23]

The details of some of these '*cavalgades*' or chevauchées are contained in a surviving list of complaints against Gaston, submitted by Edward's subjects in the duchy. This alleges that Gaston's men conducted at least thirty armed raids against towns in southern Gascony, where they seized animals, plundered churches and committed other outrages. The rebellious viscomte was also said to enjoy considerable support among the lesser gentry of Béarn, and more than ninety named individuals are listed among his following.[24]

Despite these problems, and a dearth of victuals for his troops, Edward stuck to his task. On 15 December he was at Mimizan, on the coast north-west of Marsan, where he exempted the commune from military service in exchange for a sum of 200 *livres* to aid his war against Gaston.[25] He also obtained a loan of 2,000 *livres bordelais* from the bourgeois of Bayonne, again for the purposes of the war.[26] Shortly afterwards he blockaded Gaston inside one of the vicomte's mountain strongholds.[27] Gaston was forced to submit and negotiated his surrender via a papal envoy, Gerard de Roussillon, on 14 January 1274.[28] The terms of the surrender were read out at Westminster in October and took the form of an abject public apology to the king-duke:

> Gaston, vicomte of Bearn, lord of Montcada and Castellvi, gives greeting and his sincere regard to all who may look upon these present letters. The responsibility for great disorder rests upon us

> and our thoughts are filled with bitter grief when we recognise and acknowledge in manifest justice that he whom we hold and recognise to be our true lord, inasmuch as we are bound to his service by liege homage, has until this time suffered wrongdoing at our hands ...[29]

However, the weakness of Edward's position was now exposed. As soon as Gaston had agreed to surrender, he appealed to Philip III as feudal overlord of Gascony. In response the French king summoned his parlement, which ordered the suspension of hostilities. Philip then prohibited Edward from harassing Gaston and his men, and the English king-duke quickly granted a truce.[30] His vassal status as Duke of Aquitaine obliged Edward to act in compliance with Philip's orders. Since he was also King of England, this meant Edward was subordinate to a fellow monarch, a difficult and sometimes humiliating arrangement. Had Gaston been one of Edward's English subjects, the king could have dealt with the rebel as he pleased.

Events in Gascony and Limousin now started to conspire against Edward. He had no choice but to leave the matter of Gaston in the hands of his lawyers, and left the duchy in April. Instead of returning to England for his coronation, he went north to involve himself in the war between the commune of Limoges and the viscountess. This was an interesting decision, to say the least, since England was in a turbulent state and threatening to slide back into civil war. Edward was kept fully abreast of events by his regents, Robert Burnell and Walter Merton, yet he preferred to stay in France.[31]

He soon had cause to regret this decision. Edward arrived in Limoges on 10 May to find the war had resumed in spite of the recent truce. His presence did nothing to stop the soldiers of the viscountess from attacking the commune. At Pentecost (20 May) he held court in the city with local knights and barons, but otherwise stayed well clear. Instead he went off hunting in the mountains.[32] Perhaps due to his recent experience in Gascony, Edward chose to tread carefully, and dispatched envoys to Paris to ask Philip's advice before taking any action. He returned to Limoges on 5 June to find his messengers waiting for him empty-handed. They had received no word from Philip, not even a letter.[33]

The deafening silence from Paris put Edward in a difficult spot. He was still regarded as a saviour by the bourgeois of Limoges, who pressed him to lend military aid against the viscountess. He persistently refused, on the grounds he had to wait for a message from Philip. At last, on 7 June, the bourgeois confronted Edward in the abbey of St Martial, threw the keys of the city at his feet, and begged him to defend them. He was moved to tears, but again stated that he could not disobey the King of France, though he also promised not to desert those who swore fealty to him.[34]

To get out of this bind, Edward resorted to another compromise. He released the commune from the oath they had given to him, and declared he would not impede the viscountess from dispensing justice in Limoges. The following day he departed with his consort, Eleanor, but left behind a garrison to help defend the city.[35] Almost a month later his uncle William de Valence arrived at Limoges with reinforcements in the shape of a royal engineer and over 200 English men-at-arms.[36] Edward had decided to keep his oath to the commune after all, but avoided incurring Philip's wrath by taking no direct part in the war.

Along with the Seneschal of Gascony, Valence led his men and the urban militia of Limoges against Aixe. The castle was besieged and for several days bombarded with an ingenious kind of missile made of 'sulphur and bacon', fired from a siege engine constructed by the royal engineer. The garrison managed to hold out until an envoy arrived from Paris and gave the order to suspend hostilities. After laying down their arms, both sides were instructed to appear at the nearest parlement to conclude their argument legally.[37] Once again, as in Gascony, Edward's hopes had been undermined by the superior authority of the French king.

The final judgement of the Paris parlement, held at Candlemas (February) 1275, was unfavourable towards both Edward and the commune of Limoges. The King of England was to receive no more oaths from Limousin, and he was ordered not to defy the right of the viscountess to do justice, not to protect the bourgeois nor to maintain a bailiff in the city. If he disobeyed, he would be under penalty of damages and indemnities. Even as things stood, the parlement decided to fine Edward for damages to the sum of 22,613 livres. As for the people of Limoges, they were required to submit themselves entirely to the mercy of the viscountess, permit her to enter the city in triumph and hand over the keys and jurisdiction. The bourgeois continued to protest against her to the king, but Philip had made his partiality clear.[38]

For Edward, the affair of Limoges had ended in embarrassment. Even so, he dragged his feet on paying the fine and clung grimly to his rights. On 26 September 1275 Edward wrote to Philip, asking if he could delay payment until Martinmas (November) on the grounds that he needed to send word to the Seneschal of Gascony to hand over the money.[39] Whether the fine was ever paid in full is unclear.[40] With regard to his rights in Limoges, Edward had promised in June 1274 not to desert those bourgeois who wished to swear fealty to him. As we shall see, the issue would play a central role in future negotiations.

The case of Gaston de Béarn was more protracted. In the spring of 1274, shortly after Edward's arrival at Limoges, two Brothers Minor complained that Edward's men had violated the truce in Béarn; furthermore, the king-duke had allegedly issued an order prohibiting anyone in Gascony to receive Gaston's subjects, do business with them or allow them credit. Meanwhile Edward's bailiffs and officials continued to behave as if the war was still in progress. Edward agreed to make concessions and instructed his seneschal in Gascony to respect Philip's prohibition.[41]

There the matter rested until September, when Gaston appeared in the Paris parlement and issued an extraordinary set of charges against Edward. In the presence of King Philip, he denounced the Duke of Aquitaine as a 'traitor, iniquitous, and an unfair judge, to have taken and damaged his goods and things, of which he prayed that the King of England be chastised and made to suffer by the law of the land'. Gaston then tore off his gage and threw it down before Edward's representatives to issue a challenge of single combat.[42]

This outburst was not well received. A Gascon knight at the French court, Giles de Noaillon, wrote to Edward begging for the right to champion the king.[43] Edward sent five knights to the French court charged to introduce themselves as his champions. Gaston refused to fight anyone but the king, since 'the action being personal, he could not fight anyone save Edward himself'. The court then summoned the two adversaries to the next session of parlement at Candlemas.[44]

In Edward's view, Gaston's behaviour was an affront to his honour, and he looked to the French king to make things right. In January 1275 he wrote to Philip, expressing regret that the business relating to Gaston and himself had not been resolved at the last parlement, and his hopes that it would be resolved at the next.[45] Philip sat on the case for another year, when he finally tired of Gaston's presence and advised the viscount to go to London and explain his intemperate language.

One of Edward's agents in Paris, Pierre Odon, also wrote to the king to inform him of Gaston's coming. Pierre's letter provides a glimpse into the machinations of the French court, and how the affair of Gaston threatened Edward's position in Gascony:

> I learn that G. de Béarn has been sent to you in England, accompanied by Mgr Erart de Valeri and Mgr Foulques de Laon, advisers of the King of France; those who are thirsty for your honour fear that the aforementioned advisers do not work to mitigate the wrongs of the Viscount against you. I intend to say to your friends that peace to intervene will not be advantageous for you if Gaston, who sinned publicly, does not repent himself in the same way, if he does not repudiate in a full court the charges that he formulated there on your account. You know how much Gaston offended you; take guard that he dare not do more from now on; otherwise the barons of Gascony would misuse it.[46]

Edward acted upon this advice. In early 1276, when Gaston landed in England, he was made to appear before the English parliament at Westminster and publicly retract all the charges he had laid against his lord. Edward declared that Gaston's submission was the equivalent of an admission of guilt, and that only one point remained: what punishment should be inflicted on the viscount for his felony?[47]

The English king now turned his vassal status on its head. Since Philip was his overlord, it was down to the French court to deliver sentence and punishment. Meanwhile the prisoner was held at Winchester for several months.[48] Another year passed, in which Philip repeated his earlier performance and did nothing. Finally, in September 1277, Philip ordered that Gaston and his supporters should be restored to their castles and lands which they had held when he first appealed to the court of Paris, and that they be also restored to the allegiance of the King of England.[49]

If this was Philip's attempt to mollify Edward, it failed. Now embroiled in his Welsh wars, Edward wrote to Philip from Rhuddlan on 15 November 1277. Here he conveyed his feelings in the strongest terms. The king gave his account of how he had expected the Gaston affair to be handled. Then he outlined how Gaston had appeared before the French court and accused him of false judgement and denial of justice. Afterwards, when he came to England, Gaston had dropped these outrageous charges and thrown himself on Edward's mercy. Edward sent him back to the French court so Philip would do what was appropriate. Gaston was supposed to again withdraw all his charges, this time in Philip's presence, and submit to judgement. Afterwards he would return to England to hear the remainder of Edward's will in the matter.[50]

None of this had occurred. Edward accused Philip of failing to respect the English king's will or his honour. Furthermore, his seneschal had reported to him from Paris that Philip was enquiring into affairs in Gascony that did not concern him. The French king was using the situation to extend his influence into the duchy. Edward declared that it had never been his intention to submit to Philip's will in any matter, save that which arose from Gaston's verbal abuse. This was only to preserve Edward's honour by ensuring that Gaston was forced to make amends. Edward concluded by requesting two things of Philip: that he respect Edward's honour and cancel his enquiries in Gascony, and that he remove his power from Gaston's lands in Béarn.[51]

Philip's reluctance to punish Gaston was probably compelled by the trouble brewing south of the Pyrenees. The King of Navarre, Henri III, had died in 1274 with no male heir. A succession crisis blew up, and Henri's widow Blanche took refuge with her daughter in France. The neighbouring kings of Castile and Aragon took the opportunity to press their claims to the vacant throne, so the barons of Navarre asked Philip for military aid. He sent an army under Eustache de Beaumarchais, Seneschal of Toulouse, to march into Navarre and install a French garrison at the chief city of Pamplona.[52]

Matters quickly soured. The new French administration was unpopular among the Navarrese nobility, who regarded it as a foreign occupation. Some of the barons hatched a plot to assassinate Eustace, while the bourgeois chose to support the French. In the summer of 1276 these tensions exploded into violence, and Philip sent two envoys into Navarre to investigate the situation. His envoys were the prior of St Gilles and Gaston de Béarn. Thus, even as Edward repeatedly asked for Gaston to be punished, Philip was employing him as a French agent.[53]

Gaston played an important role in the campaign that followed. Once Philip had learned of the trouble in Navarre, he raised another army and sent it across the Pyrenees, under the command of Robert d'Artois and the Constable of France. They were guided across the mountains by Gaston and the Count de Foix, while the army included other Gascon nobles such as the counts of Armagnac and the Sire de Caumont.[54] This was another consequence of the Treaty of Paris, since the Gascon nobility now had two overlords in the kings of France and England, which made them liable to do military service for both.

The siege of Pamplona was notorious for an act of treachery. When the barons of Navarre were hard-pressed by the French, and on the brink of defeat, they were able to escape due to a 'coarse trick'. The traitor was named by a French chronicle as none other than Gaston de Béarn, who was a kinsman of Don Almoravist, one of the Navarrese lords. Shortly afterwards the French stormed Pamplona, but for some undisclosed reason Gaston was not punished for his crime.[55] Either the charge of treachery against him was false, or Philip deemed him too useful.

Edward was not prepared to let the matter of Gaston rest, and in February 1278 again complained bitterly to the French court. His protest was accompanied by a long list of damages committed by the viscount and his followers during the brief war of 1273–4.[56] Edward once more expressed his concern at Philip's meddling in Gascony. He also made that it clear that it was not his intention – not now, not in the past, not ever – to make the King of France the arbiter of a dispute between Gaston and himself. This would imply that Edward and Gaston were equals, which they emphatically were not.[57]

Philip seems to have realised that matters had gone too far. He prevailed upon Edward's aunt Marguerite of Provence to write to her nephew and ask him to pardon Gaston:

> To the excellent prince, our very dear nephew Edward, by the grace of God king of England, Margaret, by the same grace queen of France, greetings and sincere affection of love. Whereas lord Gaston, viscount of Bearn, our and your kinsman, has completely made himself subject with humility to your will, we ask you that you, acting, if it is pleasing, pitifully with the same man, admit him, with all rancour having been laid aside, to your grace, if it is pleasing. For we believe that he can in the future be fruitful to you, he being ready, just as he asserts, to exhibit to you a gracious and most devoted servitude. Dated at Pissiaci on Saturday after the Epiphany of the lord.[58]

Marguerite seems to have exercised considerable influence over her nephew. Almost overnight, Edward's rancour against Gaston and Philip dissolved. In March 1278 he sent a cheerful message to his officers in Gascony, Othon de Grandson and Robert Burnell, informing them that

> ... the affairs of his land of England and of the Marches are prospering by God's grace as he would wish, for even Llywelyn, Prince of Wales, appearing before the king's justices there, with good will seeks and receives justice and judgement before the justices concerning those things that he demands from others and that are demanded from him by others; and Alexander king of Scotland has offered and tendered to the king unconditionally his homage due to the king by his solemn envoys...[59]

The king also urged his representatives to take their time in Gascony, so they could do their work with the thoroughness and discretion he expected of them. He also warned them of the 'cavill' and changeable nature of the Gascons, and to set any agreement down in writing. Edward's letter makes no specific mention of Gaston de Béarn, but in context his emissaries were probably engaged in talks with the troublesome Viscount.[60]

Instead of punishing Gaston, Edward now sought to place him in debt to the king's generosity. On 28 May Gaston was formally pardoned, his lands and castles were restored, and the seneschal told to do him justice according to the *fors* and customs of Gascony. For good measure he was awarded an annual fee of 2,000 *livres tournois* from the customs of Bordeaux, while his daughter Constance was also in receipt of money.[61]

There were several reasons for this dramatic change in policy. Edward had seen that his complaints to Philip were getting nowhere, and that the dispute might drag on for years unless he came to an understanding with Gaston. There was also the danger of Philip exploiting the situation to further his influence in Gascony. The king might have been driven to this policy, but it worked. For the rest of his days Gaston was a loyal servant of the English crown, engaged on military and diplomatic missions on Edward's behalf. For these services he was rewarded with a grant of Lados, an estate on the Gironde near Bordeaux.[62]

The affair of Gaston had ended satisfactorily, but the source of all these disputes and tensions was all too obvious. If there was to be a lasting peace between England and France, then the outstanding issues of the Treaty of Paris had to be addressed. This was difficult, if not impossible, since from an English perspective the treaty was a poisoned chalice. Henry III had relegated himself and his heirs to vassal status, which meant the kings of England would be permanently inferior to the kings of France. The consequences were already manifest.

Secret Affairs

Edward I was at least able to ensure that his French dominions were governed by competent officers. These included men such as the seneschals of Anjou Jean de Grailly and Luke de Tany, Thomas of Sandwich, Seneschal of Ponthieu, and Master Bonet of St Quentin, who in 1285 was in charge of the administrative reform of the duchy. These were men of 'zeal and merit', who were not content to simply observe the status quo. The detailed reports sent to London show they continued Edward's policy of establishing a defensive line of castles on the borders of the duchy, as well as distributing liberal charters to the cities.[63]

The king's officers were also concerned to inform their master of the state of affairs in Gascony. Their secret correspondence, although dispersed and unedited, contains frequent denunciations of French encroachment on Edward's rights in Gascony. 'What to do,' wrote Luke de Tany to the chancellor, 'if the King of France, who advances towards Aquitaine, installs himself in one of the towns of our suzerain?'[64]

Three specific examples illustrate the scale of the problem. In about 1275 Luke de Tany informed Edward that certain inquisitors wanted to force him, and the bailiffs of Gascony, to lead to Toulouse certain Jews who had relapsed from the Christian faith. These Jews dwelled in Gascony and were to be taken onto French territory for judgement. When de Tany tried to explain that he was not bound to lead anyone out of Gascony, and could do justice on the Jews there, the inquisitors agreed to await King Edward's answer but threatened to remove the Jews by force afterwards. The seneschal warned his master that the business was 'extremely serious', and begged Edward to treat with the inquisitors or, if need be, with the Pope.[65]

Second, in about 1280, Jean de Grailly wrote to Edward, informing him that Ebles, son of the Viscount of Ventadour, had married the daughter of another Gascon nobleman. This was done with the approval of the suitor's friends, but against the wishes of his uncles, the Bishop of Limoges and the Count of Périgord. These two wished to disinherit Ebles and so complained to the King of France, warning the marriage would 'turn to black favours and their confusion' if it was not broken. In response Philip III ordered the bride, Galienne, to be taken under his protection. Jean begged Edward to contact Philip and request that he not disturb the marriage of a faithful vassal.[66]

In the final example, de Tany again wrote to the king on affairs in Gascony. The seneschal chose his words carefully, and mentioned that the king's subjects in Gascony were about to send a 'solemn message' to him, the nature of which is not revealed. He added that he had many things to say to the king on the state of his overseas dominions, and assured him that the situation was good, in spite of 'the annoyances of the French'. Once again, although things were generally tranquil in Gascony, the seneschal was acutely aware of French intervention.

These are just a handful of typical complaints and warnings dispatched by Edward's officers during the fragile years of peace between 1274 and 1294. The king was equally watchful, and often sent precise instructions for the remedy of each problem. For instance, in 1279 he wrote in response to another warning of French intrusion from Jean de Grailly. This time the seneschal informed Edward that the King of France had ordered a *fouage* or hearth tax inside Gascony. Edward's answer was subtle. He ordered Grailly to stop French officers collecting the tax unless they carried royal letters formally enabling them to do so. In that case, the seneschal was to answer that Edward had banned the hearth tax inside Gascony for one or two years, due to bad harvests and mortality of cattle. To enforce this claim, Edward sent forged letters to the seneschal, which he was to show to the French.[67] In reality the king had enforced no such ban, but was forced to adopt a subterfuge to prevent the French levying a tax inside his duchy.

Overall, it is clear that Edward's desire to make his rule of Gascony truly effective was compromised by the unequal feudal relationship. The Treaty of Paris had placed the king and his heirs in a bind from which it was impossible to escape.

5

THE PEACE OF AMIENS AND AFTER

In 1279 the two kings made a serious effort at resolution. Even as the controversy over Gaston and Limousin rumbled on, Edward had persistently reminded Philip of his outstanding obligations. These consisted of the resituation of Agenais and the other lands that were supposed to have been ceded to the English via the Treaty of Paris. Throughout the 1270s, every English diplomatic mission to Paris was charged by the king to serve Philip with this reminder.[1]

At last Philip gave way. On 23 May 1279, at Amiens, the kings met to discuss Edward's rights under the treaty. Edward put forward his claims, namely the transfer of the Agenais, the compensation due to him for those vassals in the dioceses of Limoges, Périgueux and Quercy whose allegiance could not be transferred to him, and the lands and rights held by Alfonse of Potiers in Quercy.[2]

The results of this new treaty were largely in Edward's favour. The Agenais was conceded along with Saintonge below the River Charente by the recognition of his lordship over the lands which Alfonse of Poitiers or his sub-vassals had held in that region. Philip also promised to arrange an enquiry into the status of Quercy, and he renounced one of the most troublesome oaths of the Treaty of Paris. This was an obligation imposed upon the Duke of Aquitaine to extract from his vassals an oath to the King of France that they would fight their duke if he failed to observe the treaty.[3] Such a promise was scarcely in the duke's interests, but Edward had done his best to enforce the oath. Even so, his vassals persistently refused to swear to it, though his seneschals had employed every method ranging from persuasion to threats and intimidation. At the Treaty of Amiens, Philip agreed to waive the oath in exchange for Edward abandoning his claims for compensation in the three dioceses. He did so, but retained the allegiance of those tenants – called the privileged or *privilegiati* – who had chosen to recognise him as their lord. Unfortunately only Raymond IV, Viscount of Turenne, Pons de Gourdon, the Abbot of Figeac and the Count of Perigord were persuaded to transfer their allegiance to the English crown. Of these, the Count of Perigord later recanted. Thus, Edward was deprived of the greater part of the dioceses; further, he did not receive the compensation owed by the treaty of 1259.[4]

The king made up for these losses elsewhere. His family had already acquired control of the county of Champagne in 1275 when his brother Edmund married Blanche, the widow of Henri III of Navarre. She held Champagne during the minority of her daughter, and so the English gained a degree of influence in one of the great French fiefdoms. Edward, however, seems to have regarded it as his brother's affair, and the acquisition was probably not part of a conscious royal policy to increase English influence in France. Champagne was lost in 1284, when Blanche's daughter came of age (at just twelve years old) and Edmund accepted compensation from the French in exchange for relinquishing the county.[5]

Edward took a more direct interest in the dual county of Ponthieu and Montreuil in northern France, on the banks of the Somme. This was gained via his consort, Eleanor of Castile. Eleanor's mother, Joan, had inherited the title and land from her mother, Marie, Countess of Ponthieu. When Joan died on 16 March 1279, Edward inherited the county in right of his wife. Within days of Joan's death he was taking steps to secure the lordship and appointed one of Eleanor's relatives as keeper or *custos* of Ponthieu. Two months later the business was concluded. On 23 May, the same day as the talks at Amiens, Edward acquired the county. This was done in a series of informal interviews with Philip, as there was no clause in the treaty that formally handed Ponthieu over to the English. No mention of such an acquisition could be made in a treaty that was merely supposed to be a sequel or amplification of the Treaty of Paris.[6]

There was a rival claimant. Eleanor of Castile's elder brother, Ferdinand, had left a son named John of Ponthieu. John arguably had a better right to Ponthieu than his aunt, though the law of descent was far from clear on this point. He was willing to argue it, and on 23 May – even as the business of Ponthieu was concluded – John turned up at Amiens and put forward his claim to the county.[7]

John did not request the title of count, but rather his share of one-fifth of Ponthieu and Montreuil, which he said his grandmother had bequeathed in her will. Edward was not prepared to divide the lordship under any circumstances, and the legal proceedings dragged on for years. At last, in 1293, John surrendered his claim in exchange for a pay-off of £14,000, the entire sum of which was paid out of the revenues of the county.[8]

Edward's determination to secure Ponthieu might seem odd. It was small, sandwiched between Normandy and Flanders, although home to prosperous agriculture and centres of cloth production. This wealth was useful, but the real value of the county lay in the influence it gave Edward in Paris: 'The English tenure of Ponthieu, moreover, was a further means whereby vigilance could be exercised over the affairs of France, and Edward I retained a permanent staff of lawyers at Paris who dealt with appeals from the *comté* to the Parliament'.[9]

On balance, the Treaty of Amiens was a success for English diplomacy. Edward had recovered some of the lands owed by the French, and made up the shortfall by acquisitions elsewhere. He had also persuaded Philip to drop a potentially harmful clause of the Paris agreement, and to enquire into Edward's rights in the inheritance of Alfonse of Poitiers. His acquisition of Ponthieu and Montreuil not only re-established an Angevin foothold in northern France, but gave the English king extra leverage at the French court.

Edward was now able to fully exploit the military resources of his lands on the Continent. In 1282 he was at war for a second time with Prince Llywelyn of Wales, and drew upon Gascony and Ponthieu for supplies and reinforcements. Over the winter of 1282–3, the king summoned contingents from Gascony to spearhead the invasion of Gwynedd. In total forty Gascon knights, 210 mounted crossbowmen and 1,313 crossbowmen on foot served against the Welsh during the winter months. These included the cream of Gascon nobility: the counts of Armagnac and of Bigorre, the lord of Bergerac, the Vicomte of Tarcazin and many others.[10] The Count of Armagnac, Girard VI, had previously done military service for the French king at Pamplona in 1276 (see above). Now he found himself fighting in the mountains of north Wales on behalf of the King of England.

The Gascons did vital service in breaking Welsh resistance:

They [the Gascons] remain with the king, receive his gifts,
In moors and mountains they clamber like lions.
They go with the English, burn down the houses,
Throw down the castles, slay the wretches;
They have passed the Marches, and entered into Snowdon.[11]

We may surmise that the *montagnards* of Béarn proved useful in the uplands of Gwynedd. Edward's new acquisition of Ponthieu, meanwhile, contributed 2,000 quarters of wheat, 2,000 quarters of oats, 300 quarters of peas and beans as well as salted meats and cheese to the king's armies.[12] Two knights of Ponthieu, Hugh of Famechon and John de Nesle, served on the Welsh campaign and received pay as bannerets.[13]

Gaston de Béarn was not part of the expedition to Wales. The viscount had initially expressed his willingness to help, but then suggested that he might do more useful service in Castile, south of the Pyrenees.[14] He had served in that region before on behalf of King Philip, though not with any great distinction as the French accused him of treachery (see above). This time Gaston offered to intervene for Edward's sake. Despite the viscount's past record, Edward agreed. On 22 December 1282, as he prepared for his final push into north Wales, the king ordered Gaston to take a hundred knights to aid Alfonso X, the King of Castile.[15] Even at this extremely difficult period, in which the majority of Edward's resources were concentrated on Wales, he remained concerned with events beyond the southern fringes of Gascony.

The conflict beyond the Pyrenees was prolonged by yet another succession crisis. After the death of his eldest son, Fernando de Cerda, in 1275, Alfonso had recognised his youngest son, Sancho, as heir apparent. This was contrary to the interests of Fernando's young sons, who were also the nephews of the King of France as his sister Blanche had married Fernando. In 1276 Philip raised an army to invade Castile and enforce the rights of his nephews, but it was forced to disband due to bad weather and lack of supplies.[16]

Edward was inevitably drawn into the tangle. Alfonso was his brother-in-law and Philip his overlord, which left him stranded in the middle. The King of Castile had attempted to recruit his aid against Philip, but Edward replied that he was constrained by his obligations towards France. Perhaps as a warning shot, Edward also reminded Alfonso of his own hereditary rights to certain unnamed lands and castles in Navarre.[17]

Otherwise Edward went to great lengths to act as mediator and broker peace between France and Castile. Indeed, he was so successful that in the autumn of 1282 his brother-in-law Alfonso of Castile publicly thanked him for his offices as a peacemaker.[18] The English king had to perform a difficult balancing act, and excused himself from doing military service for Philip on the grounds of his distractions in Wales. In any event, Edward explained, he was bound by ties of kinship and friendship to Alfonso.[19] This was all part of Edward's desire for peace on the Continent in the early part of his reign; a stark contrast to his last decade, when he found himself at war on all fronts: 'He pursued an unaggressive foreign policy himself and attempted to ensure peace on the Continent, realizing that he would inevitably be drawn into the struggles that might arise when all his energies were required for the conquest of Wales and the settlement of the Scottish succession.'[20]

Despite his best efforts, Edward could not remain entirely aloof. In 1282 civil war broke out in Castile, where his brother-in-law Alfonso had been persuaded to change policy and support the claims of his grandsons over Sancho, his son. Sancho refused to be disinherited and raised an army against his father, who immediately forged an alliance with the Moorish King of Morocco. Tit-for-tat, Sancho called in the Moorish King of Granada. The princes of Castile had thus recruited two Muslim allies to assist in a dynastic war between Christians.[21]

The Pope, Martin IV, beseeched Edward and Philip to aid Alfonso. Philip sent French troops into Navarre, from where they could strike into Castile.[22] They were joined by the knights of the King of England, led by Gaston de Béarn. Throughout January 1283 Gaston was based at Pamplona, from where he sent receipts to Edward for wages for his knights and compensation for horses lost in the king's service.[23] The campaign ended in embarrassment when the French attempted to advance from Pamplona, only to be driven back when the armies of Castile and Aragon combined against them.[24]

Perhaps mindful of Gaston's unfortunate experience, Edward would not be drawn any further into events beyond the Pyrenees. He and Philip were in any case distracted by the famous uprising of Easter Monday 1282, known as the Sicilian Vespers, whereby Charles of Anjou was driven from the island half of his kingdom of Sicily. This was another family affair, since Charles was Philip's uncle (and Edward's). His flight from Sicily encouraged the Aragonese to take it over, while at the same time renewing their claim to lands in Gascony.[25]

All of this was guaranteed to provoke the French, but war was briefly averted when Charles of Anjou came up with an alternative. He suggested that a personal combat ought to be fought between himself and his rival, Peter of Aragon, with a hundred knights on either side. The idea gained Philip's approval and, after some negotiations, a date was set for the combat on 1 June 1283. It was scheduled to take place at Bordeaux, Edward's chief city in Gascony, and the English king was invited to preside as judge.[26]

Edward would have nothing to do with it. Even before the Pope sent him a 'frenzied' appeal to stop the duel, he wrote to Charles at the end of December 1282:

> We cannot find it in our heart, nor in any manner possible, that such great cruelty should be done in our presence, nor within our power, nor in any other place where we could put a stop to it.

> And, dear cousin, it would be a very strange and grievous thing to us that we should receive you on our lands in such a manner when you did us such honour and received us so handsomely in yours when we returned from beyond the seas ... For know truly, that not even to gain two such kingdoms as Sicily and Aragon would we guard the lists where such a battle should take place.[27]

Despite Edward's disapproval, the tournament was set to go ahead anyway, with his seneschal Jean de Grailly serving as judge in the king's place. The affair descended into farce when Peter of Aragon turned up at Bordeaux in disguise, galloped round the empty lists, and then fled back to Aragon proclaiming himself the victor.[28] Furious at being tricked, Charles and Philip accused their rival of cowardice and started to plan for a new campaign.[29] In early 1284 they gained the support of Martin IV, who formally invested Charles with the kingdom of Aragon and the county of Barcelona.[30]

As usual, Edward tried to mediate. On 2 March 1284 he received a message from his agent in Paris, Mathieu de Vendome, who warned the king that 'great massacres will occur, if your wisdom do not bring a prompt remedy'.[31] Yet neither the efforts of Edward or his diplomats in Paris, or the appeal of the King of Aragon to the Pope, could do anything to halt the war. Much of the next year was taken up in preaching the crusade against Aragon, and by the spring of 1285 Philip had assembled an enormous host for the invasion.

Edward did all he could to avoid being dragged in. Peter of Aragon asked him for assistance, but got the same reply as Alfonso of Castile: the English king could not go against his homage to Philip, and would not be seen as rebelling against his lord.[32] At the start of 1285 Edward reluctantly prepared to go overseas, but then received a complaint from his subjects in Gascony and the Agenais, who argued there was no precedent for doing military service in Aragon. This gave Edward the excuse he needed to ignore the French summons. He had made no serious preparations for a campaign, and the letters of protection for the men intending to go abroad with him only lasted until Easter. This was scarcely long enough for a war in Aragon.[33]

The English king's reluctance to serve in Aragon sprang from more than a desire to avoid helping Philip. Throughout this era he did everything possible to avert wars between the rival houses of western Europe. For instance, while the Aragon crisis was brewing, members of Edward's family attempted to enforce their rights in Provence and the neighbouring county of Forcalquier. Charles of Anjou was again involved. Edward's mother, Eleanor of Provence, and her sister Marguerite were determined to claim these lands against Charles, who was equally determined to hang onto them.[34]

Tired of futile negotiations, Margaret resorted to arms and in 1281 formed a coalition of allies at Mâcon in Burgundy-Franche-Comté. They included her nephew Edmund, Edward's brother, in his capacity as Count of Champagne.[35] She also asked Edward to send troops to join the confederation. He agreed to dispatch men to join her allies in May 1282, but also begged her to act prudently. At the same time he wrote to the Pope, and to Charles of Anjou, urging settlement by arbitration.[36] To Charles's eldest son, Charles of Salerno, Edward revealed his true opinion:

> I am very reluctant in this matter. My heart is not in it, on account of the love between you and me. I pray you do not take it amiss, for I call God to witness that, if the thing affected me only, I would do nothing against your wishes.[37]

Edward clearly had no more taste for war in Provence than war in Aragon. Fortunately, he was spared the need to send troops to help his aunt by the Welsh war of 1282, which required all his attention. He wrote to his aunt, excusing himself from service on account of the crisis in Wales. She let Edward off the hook, but reminded him of his duty towards her:

> Very dear nephew, as you asked that we excuse you that you can not now come to our aid in our need in Provence, as you have always courteously promised us [you would], in your goodness, because of the problem that has occurred in Wales, know that we have excused you from this need for the present. And we beg you that you remember in the [proper] place and time that good promise that you have always made us; for as one who has been more feared and encouraged by the good will that you have for

> us and our cause we have special trust in you to advance our cause. And know that we agree to delay our cause in the matter of Spain until Our Lord has brought yours to a good point.[38]

The business of Provence came to nothing, as in 1283 the rival parties consented to abide by the judgement of Philip of France.[39] A war between Charles of Anjou and Edward's close relatives was averted, but the French crusade against Aragon duly went ahead in the spring of 1285.

Edward was wise to stay out of it. The so-called Aragonese Crusade was an utter disaster for the French. After some initial success, they were thrown back from the city of Girona and cut to bits in the mountain passes of the Pyrenees. Philip himself fell sick and had to be carried to Perpignan in a litter. There, on 5 October 1285, he died at the age of forty.[40] What was left of his army staggered back to France, disgraced and defeated: 'And I tell you that they returned in such a way that, as long as the world will last, not one will speak in France about Catalonia without remembering terrible things'.[41]

Philip was succeeded by his eldest son, another Philip. Philip IV, known as Le Bel or the Fair for his good looks, was just seventeen years old when his father died in despair at Perpignan. He inherited a disastrous legacy, with the French army in tatters and Aragonese troops ravaging his borders. His reign marked the starting point of a new era, not least in the relations between France and England.

6

THE PARD AND THE OWL

The contrast in the ambitions of Edward I and Philip IV lie at the heart of this book. It was their rivalry that compelled the war of 1294–1303 and the far-reaching consequences that lay beyond. Therefore it is appropriate to take a closer look at the personalities and contemporary reputations of these two men, before moving on to their relationship and the policies they chose to pursue.

In the mid-1280s Edward was at the height of his powers, respected at home and abroad. Since he came to the throne in 1272, he had been remarkably successful. The king had put an end to conflict in England, united the baronage and implemented a vast programme of legislative and judicial reform. He had recently completed the conquest of Wales – a feat that eluded his predecessors – and stamped his authority on the Welsh with a series of mighty castles. Overseas Edward had clawed back lands in France and did wonders for his reputation by going on crusade. His venture to the Holy Land brought little material reward, but unlike virtually all his peers he could boast of having actually set foot in Outremer. He had also risked his skin in the defence of the Christian states, and carried the scars to prove it.

Edward also enjoyed the reputation of being a skilled tournament fighter, praised by troubadours for his martial prowess. Peire Cardenal, a southern French poet, exhorted Philip III of France to follow Edward's heroic example on crusade:

> I beseech all to pray sincerely to God, Jesus Christ,
> That he may grant joy to Lord Edward over there,
> As he is the best lance in the whole world,
> And grant to King Philip the heart and desire to assist him soon.[1]

In 1274 the Pope had formally prohibited Edward from taking part in any more tournaments, but his reputation persisted in France. The French poet Sarrasin, composer of *La Roman du Hem*, an account of a tournament in France in 1278, had this to say of the king and his knights:

> Here [in England] you'll find good fighters, hard men, tough and strong.
>
> Lancelot and Gawain and the men of the Round Table, who were the best in the world. There are knights of reputation, there are many good jousters, there are brave knights … and him who is their lord and king, the valiant, generous and benevolent king Edward.[2]

Edward's reputation was also high south of the Pyrenees. Ramon Muntaner (1265–1366), a Catalan mercenary and chronicler, described Edward as 'the most acceptable king of the world, as he was one of the most upright Kings of the world and a good Christian'.[3]

A vivid physical description of Edward is supplied by Nicholas Trivet, a Dominican friar who may have actually met the king and was certainly involved with the royal court:

> He was a man of tried prudence in affairs of state. He was devoted in adolescence to the practice of arms by which he acquired a widespread reputation for chivalry – his fame excelled every prince of his time. He was elegant of form, of commanding height, exceeding an ordinary man from the leg upwards. His looks were enhanced by a beard which in adolescence turned from a silvery colour to hold, became black when he reached

> manhood, and in old age changed from grey to the whiteness of a swan. He had a broad forehead and regular features, except that the lid of the left eye was lower, recalling his father's appearance. He had a lisp but was nevertheless effectively eloquent in speech when persuasion was necessary in business. His arms were long in proportion to his agile body, and none was more able, with sinuous dexterity, to wield a sword. His stomach protruded, and his long thighs made it impossible for him to be unseated by the galloping or jumping of the most spirited horse. When he had finished with fighting, he indulged in hunting and hawking. He especially hunted the stag, which he pursued on the courser and when he had caught one, he struck it with his sword instead of using a hunting spear.[4]

This paints an image of a man of action, with some notable physical oddities: Edward's drooping eyelid, apparently inherited from his father, and his speech impediment. To judge from this, the king's popular nickname of 'Longshanks' – referring to his height and long limbs – was well deserved.

A less glowing picture of Edward is found in the *Song of Lewes*, a tract written by a Montfortian cleric during the civil wars in England in the 1260s. The song accuses Edward of treachery and achieving his aims via crooked means:

> He is a lion by his pride and ferocity; by his inconstantly and changeableness he is a pard, not holding steadily his word or his promise, and excusing himself with fair words. When he is in a difficulty, he promises just what you will; as soon as he has escaped the danger, he forgets his promise … the treachery or falseness by which he gains his ends he calls prudence; the way by which he arrives at his object, be it ever so crooked, is reputed to be straight; when wrong serves his purpose, it is called right; he calls lawful whatever he wills, and thinks himself absolved from the law, as though he were greater than a king.[5]

Modern assessments of Edward tend to vary, though it is not difficult to find echoes of the *Song of Lewes*, particularly among Welsh and Scottish historians.[6] A balanced and perceptive judgement was supplied by the late R. R. Davies:

> Edward has divided historiographical opinion in the British Isles from his own day to ours as no other British ruler was to do until the time of Oliver Cromwell. He was soon hailed as Edward the Great, the Conqueror, and such compliments are still not unknown in historical writing; but he was also denigrated in his own day as '*le roy covetous*', although mere covetousness appears in the eyes of some Scottish and Welsh historians as one of the lesser of his moral flaws ... As to his power and status within Britain we need not assume that his attitude was unchanging, cynical, or conspiratorial. Like most men of power he was the servant of circumstances and, where he could be, the master of opportunities.[7]

Eloquent contemporary descriptions of Edward's rival, Philip IV, are thin on the ground. A hostile French bishop, Bernard Saisset, once famously compared the French king to an owl: '... the handsomest of birds which is worth absolutely nothing ... such is our king of France, who is the handsomest man in the world and can do nothing except to stare at men'.[8]

Saisset acknowledges that Philip is handsome (hence his nickname, Philip the Fair), but otherwise implies the king is both worthless and inscrutable. One of Philip's modern biographers has pointed out the enigmatic nature of his character: 'Philip the Fair is a hard man to get to know. His contemporaries were puzzled by him, and later historians have found him no easier to understand. Very formal, very conscious of his royal dignity, he seems always screened off from the world by his chief ministers and bureaucrats.'[9]

One interpretation is that Philip's inscrutable nature, the sheer impossibility of gauging his thoughts, enabled him to deceive political opponents such as Edward.[10] Another is that it concealed his lack of any real influence or control of events. Most French writers of the day believed that Philip was dominated by evil counsellors who ruled in his name.[11] This was also the view of foreign chroniclers such as the Italian Villani and the Fleming Giles de Mussis, who regarded Philip as a mere figurehead. Another Italian chronicler, Dino Compagni, thought Philip was responsible for French policy towards the Church.[12]

Pope Boniface VIII, when listing Philip's offences against the papacy, accused the king's counsellors of feathering their own nests. However, Boniface also added that Philip bore full responsibility for promoting such men in the first place. At the same time he was convinced of the evil influence of Philip's counsellors. In a remarkably tactless letter to Edward in 1301, Boniface admonished the king not to blame Philip for his misconduct; he was merely guilty of youthful fervour and led astray by the seduction of evil counsellors and the malice of flatterers. Edward, who was more mature, more circumspect and more moderate, should content the younger man until God brought forth more helpful fruits.[13]

To these should be added Philip's own assessment. On his deathbed in 1314, Philip is reported to have said that if he had erred by following bad counsel, he himself was the cause of that counsel.[14] Whether or not Philip was overly influenced by his counsellors in the matter of the Anglo-French war, or drove events himself, is a theme that shall be explored later.

At first relations between Edward and Philip were amicable, though there were hints of tension. On 5 June 1286 the English king knelt before his kinsman in Paris and swore homage and fealty for Gascony. Edward's chancellor, Robert Burnell, expressed in his opening speech the doubts among members of the king's council. He told the French court that Edward had been advised to dispute the terms of homage, because the 1259 treaty had still not been fulfilled and because certain assaults had been committed by the French in his lands. The king was not yet prepared to take action on that advice, being content to wait upon restitution from Philip. Yet a warning note had been sounded.[15]

As a result of the advice of his counsellors, Edward swore a strictly conditional oath to Philip. Just as he had done in 1273, he swore to become Philip's man for the lands which he held over the water 'according to the form of the peace made between our ancestors'.[16] The young French king might have taken this as provocation, but he let it pass. He was still struggling to restore order to his kingdom after the disastrous Aragonese war, and (for now) had no wish to enter into a conflict with England.[17]

He also showed himself amenable in the negotiations that followed. Edward's advisors placed several key issues in front of Philip, relating to problems in Gascony and the execution of the Treaty of Paris. Philip dealt with them in a conciliatory fashion. In July 1286 he made a remarkable grant whereby it was conceded that when an appellant in Gascony defaulted or was convicted of an unjustified appeal, neither the English king or his representatives were to be disturbed by the French. In addition, appeals for false judgement were to be returned to Edward and his officials for three months to allow them to make amends and do justice. Only after this time had elapsed could an appellant take his case to the Paris parlement.[18]

The jurisdiction over appeals was a thorny issue, and one that cropped up time and again. Put simply, any of Edward's subjects in Gascony who rejected his justice could appeal over his head to the French court, since the King of France was his overlord. There are many such recorded cases. For example, in 1281 one Bernard de Ravignan, a knight of the Agenais, contested the right of Edward's seneschal to build a house in a place over which Bernard claimed jurisdiction. His response was to claim denial of justice and appeal directly to Paris, bypassing the ducal court. Parlement decided that the case should be referred back, but a few years later Bernard tried his luck again. In 1289 he was charged by John de Havering, lieutenant of the Seneschal of Aquitaine, of misdeeds and assaults upon the Benedictine monks of St-Sever and the prior of Buzet. These charges included dragging the prior from his deathbed and seizing his finances. Bernard again claimed denial of justice and appealed to the parlement, which set up an enquiry into his actions. He eventually appeared as a wronged party in Philip's summons to Edward in 1293, just prior to the outbreak of war: a classic example of how the French crown took up and exploited the cases of Gascon appellants.[19]

In 1286 these issues had yet to come to a head. Apart from granting Edward the concession over appeals, Philip also admitted the English right to the lands of Alfonse of Poitiers in lower Saintonge. These had already been granted via the Treaty of Amiens in 1279, but a contrary decision had been issued by the parlement in 1281. Philip chose to reverse that decision and, in addition, confirm Edward's rights to the homage of the *privilegiati* of the three dioceses of Limoges, Périgueux and Cahors.[20] Edward in turn abandoned his claim to Quercy, another part of the inheritance of Alfonse of Poitiers, in exchange for compensation of 3,000 *livres tournois* in annual rents.[21]

At this point, therefore, all was give and take between the two kings and (reasonably) good fellowship. They also showed a willingness to work together to guard against potential threats. In 1286 Edward and Philip combined against our old friend Gaston de Béarn, who had finally overreached himself.

After his service for Edward in Navarre in 1282, Gaston was quiet for some years. His daughter Constance briefly earned Edward's displeasure by attempting to extend her family's interests in Bigorre, a much-contested province of southern Gascony. In 1284 she deemed it necessary to travel to Caernarfon in north Wales, where Edward was attending to the government of Crown lands, to make her peace with him.[22] The king's displeasure extended to withholding payments of Gaston's annuity, but in June 1285 he ordered his seneschal to pay the arrears upon getting security from the viscomte. When his temper had cooled further, Edward changed his mind again and ordered the payments to be made without the condition of security. This was a reflection of the king's conscience – *de nostra conscienca*.[23]

Gaston chose to push matters further. He had no son, so in 1286 he vested Béarn in his second daughter, Margaret, who had married the Count of Foix. This arrangement was sanctioned by Edward, but he and Philip may have been alarmed at the prospect of the union. It threatened to advance the territorial ambitions of the house of Foix, whose absorption of the vicomté of Bearn would make them the single most powerful dynasty in the south-west. Their own family chronicle described the counts of Foix as ruling 'by the grace of God', and in the following years they successfully carved out a semi-autonomous empire stretching along the Pyrenean frontier.[24]

None of this was in the interests of the kings of England and France, whose authority was challenged by the rise of a combined Foix-Béarn. Yet neither Edward or Philip had any technical reason to block the marriage of Gaston's daughter to Count Roger-Bernard, and the wedding went ahead. Both kings, however, seem to have decided it was high time to put an end to Gaston de Béarn. In the summer of 1286 they ordered him to go to the Holy Land, never to return unless recalled by Edward. In his absence Edward would keep Gaston's lands for the debts owed to him, and Gaston's castles would be destroyed except those retained in the hands of the king-duke.[25]

This ploy was collusive, but had Edward's fingerprints all over it; it was precisely the same 'offer' he had made to Dafydd ap Gruffudd, the rebellious Welsh prince, in 1282. Dafydd had refused, but Gaston agreed to take the cross. With two kings breathing down his neck, he had little choice. He was spared the journey, however, since the confiscation of his lands was part of a joint crusade that Edward and Philip never undertook. Gaston was permitted to remain in Béarn until his death in 1290, and in his last will and testament he provided that five knights of Béarn should go to the Holy Land to redeem his vow.[26] His son-in-law, Count Roger-Bernard, was destined to play an important role in the war that erupted a few years later.

That war would take Edward completely by surprise. He had little cause to suspect Philip of any ill will, and at this stage there was nothing to suggest that England and France would plunge into direct conflict. It was essentially a family quarrel, an extension of the cycle of wars and disputes between the interrelated dynasties of western Europe. The potential roots of the war shall now be explored.

7

THE LOVE BETWEEN YOU AND ME

While Edward negotiated his own interests with the new King of France, he also continued to play the role of mediator. After much effort, he finally managed to persuade France and Aragon to agree to a truce. On 26 July 1286 they consented to cease hostilities until March 1287, and Edward wrote to the Pope, asking him to approve the truce. This he did, as did Peter of Aragon's brother James, King of Majorca.[1]

There remained another difficulty, which Edward went to great lengths to resolve. His cousin Charles of Salerno, son and heir of Charles of Anjou, had been captured at sea during the disastrous Aragonese Crusade. His captor, Alfonso III, who succeeded his father Peter in 1286, would not give up his valuable prisoner lightly. Edward took it upon himself to secure Charles's release, and went from Paris to Gascony to begin an intense round of negotiations with Alfonso. The talks went smoothly, bar one embarrassing incident when Edward's pet lion escaped and killed a horse.[2]

He was also engaged in attempting to arrange the release of another political prisoner. This was Henry 'the Senator' of Castile, younger brother of the late Alfonso X and hence Edward's brother-in-law. The king knew him quite well, since Henry had spent several years in England during Edward's youth. The Castilian prince had been captured at the Battle of Tagliacozzo in 1268, fighting Charles of Anjou. Charles had his prisoner exhibited in a cage at Apulia in Sicily, loaded down with iron fetters.[3]

Edward and his consort, Eleanor of Castile (Henry's sister), first attempted to secure his release in 1273, but to no avail. Charles of Anjou died in 1285. This meant that Edward was now trying to arrange the release of the late King of Sicily's son, Charles of Salerno, and his enemy Henry of Castile!

Castilian troubadours urged Edward to redouble his efforts to free Henry. One of them, Austorc de Segret, warned the king that if he failed, he would forfeit the respect of the French:

> Now Edward will need valour and courage if he wants to avenge Henry, who was unparalleled in wisdom and knowledge, and he was the very best of his kin. But if he now stays shamed in this matter, the French over here will leave him neither root nor branch nor well-armed forces, if his worth is stripped of merit.[4]

Another troubadour, Cerverí de Girona, called upon Edward to avenge Henry's imprisonment:

> If Edward immediately and without delay divides his name into three, it will make it impossible for anyone anywhere to despoil him of what is his, since by having ships to sea and by bestowing generous gifts he will outdo the richest, and by employing stratagems and striking hard, he will avenge Don Enrique [Henry] on land.[5]

Thus the Castilians urged the King of England to be wary of the French in his dealings, and even to make war on them on Henry's behalf. Such pleas were in vain, since Edward had shown time and again that he would not fight France on any account. He preferred diplomacy, and to that end continued to lobby on Henry's behalf. For that to happen, he first had to arrange the release of Charles of Salerno, now the uncrowned King of Sicily since his father's death in 1285.

Despite Edward's best efforts, it was impossible to avoid offending the French. His efforts to free Charles and find a settlement to the Angevin–Aragonese conflict reversed the previous roles of the English and French monarchies in diplomatic arbitration.[6] The treaty that was finally agreed upon, at Oloron-Sainte-Marie, was not to the advantage of the French. Philip IV threw every obstacle he could in the way, alarmed at a clause whereby he stood to lose Provence to the Aragonese if a final peace was not agreed within three years.[7]

The French had other vested interests. Philip's brother Charles of Valois had been invested with the kingdom of Aragon by the papacy in 1283. He was just thirteen at the time, and it has been said of him that 'he had been addressed as a king during his teens, and had never quite recovered from the experience'.[8] His father, Philip III, had conducted the Aragonese Crusade in his name. He had good reason to resent Edward's handling of arbitration in the Charles of Salerno affair, since the outcome effectively deprived him of his title. He was afterwards dubbed 'Carlo senza Terra' – Charles the Landless – by mocking Italian chroniclers, even though he was granted considerable lands in France by his brother. Yet, thanks to the French defeat in Aragon and Edward's meddling (as Charles might have seen it), he did not wear a crown. He clung to his empty title until 1295, a year after the outbreak of the Anglo-French war.[9]

In his desire to secure Charles of Salerno's release, Edward seems to have been blind to all of these dangers. There is no reason to suppose he acted out of anything other than concern for his kinsman. Their correspondence was affectionate – he had previously referred to 'the love between you and me' – and Charles was an attractive, chivalric figure.[10] Edward was also ready to agree to the most outrageous demands made by Alfonso of Aragon, who exploited the value of his prisoner to the hilt. In exchange for releasing Charles, Alfonso obtained a payment of 30,000 marks from Edward, as well as seventy-six English and Gascon hostages as security. These included some of Edward's most important followers, such as John de Vescy, Othon Grandson, John de St John and even the old troublemaker Gaston de Béarn. The terms of their captivity were not harsh, but the king's willingness to hand over such high-ranking individuals, all for the sake of his kinsman, is extraordinary.[11]

Edward's hopes of a lasting peace were soon disappointed. Shortly after his release, Charles went to Paris to talk with Philip IV, who again refuted the treaty. The Pope, Nicholas IV, absolved Charles from the terms, and granted him the use of a crusading tenth to persuade Charles to continue the war with Aragon. Nor did Edward receive any financial compensation. Charles was supposed to repay the 30,000 marks Edward had handed over to Aragon for his release, but there is no evidence of it being paid over.[12]

The king did at least obtain one concession. In 1291, after decades of futile pleas, Edward persuaded Charles to release Henry of Castile. Charles had already relaxed the terms of Henry's brutal imprisonment, and in September 1298 permitted him to ride out on a mule once a week. At Edward's request, he finally let the old man go free in July 1291. Henry would later serve as regent of Castile and play a role in the Anglo-French war. His son, James, was raised in Edward's household during Henry's long captivity. Known as Master Jacobus de Ispania, king's clerk, he rose to become a canon of Exeter Cathedral and one of the founders of Oriel College, Oxford .[13]

Edward's strenuous diplomatic efforts in Europe were not simply intended to secure peace for the sake of it. His concern was to enable another crusade, which could not take place if the Christian kingdoms were at war.[14] There was no attempt to hide this policy. In his later futile negotiations with the French, Edward's brother Edmund explicitly stated that English policy was driven by 'the peace of Christendom, and the furtherance of the Crusade'.[15]

The king's desire to organise another crusade came to nothing. He was constantly impeded by quarrels with the papacy over the use of crusading tithes, and twice required to take an oath to lead the expedition in person. This proved impossible, as he was distracted by wars in Wales and the crisis of the Sicilian Vespers.[16] Meanwhile the military situation continued to deteriorate in the East, despite Edward's willingness to send money and small numbers of troops to bolster the defence of the crusader states.[17] At one point he offered to send Edmund to lead the crusader army in his stead, but this was rejected by the papacy.[18]

The fall of Acre, the last major Christian stronghold in the Holy Land, in 1291 briefly jolted Edward's peers into action. Or at least, they discussed what action might be taken. While Edward continued with his own plans for another crusade, the English and French clergy discussed the need for a leader to organise the expedition. Edward cannot have been flattered when his own clergy, led by Archbishop

Peckham, emphasised the need for an immediate imperial election in Germany, so the new emperor could impose peace in Europe. The French clergy also highlighted the need for a powerful leader, but no names were put forward.[19]

Edward's cousin of France, Philip IV, showed rather less enthusiasm. In September 1287 he greeted Rabban Sauma, an envoy from the Mongols, in Paris and pledged to participate in an expedition to the Holy Land. Two years later he received another envoy from the Mongol il-khan, Arghun, who reminded Philip of his pledge. Arghun gave the French king an appointment to be at Damascus in the spring of 1291. If the Franco-Mongolian alliance was victorious, Jerusalem was to be awarded to the French. The envoy, a Genoese named Buscarello de'Ghisolfi, then went to England to treat with Edward.[20]

Despite his promises, Philip showed little practical interest in the crusade until Edward's death in 1307. To the end of his days Edward was regarded by contemporaries as a '*rex crucesignatus*', the only king in Christendom who might deliver the Holy Land and took a genuine interest in its salvation. As late as 1306 Pierre Dubois, a French chronicler, dedicated the longer and more grandiose part of his book, *The Recovery of the Holy Land*, to Edward. The second and lesser part was dedicated to Philip.[21] After the passing of his rival, Philip would pick up the torch and present himself as the leader of the next crusade. This was all part of his campaign against the Templars in France, whereby Philip placed their arrest and persecution in the context of his nation's mission to rescue the Holy Land.[22] Philip would not take the cross until 1313, and died in a hunting accident the next year before he could fulfil his vow.[23]

The distractions of the crusade meant more to Edward than to Philip. After the fall of Acre in 1291, the English king pressed ahead with his plans for the Holy Land, but his cousin had other priorities. Within a few years these became painfully evident.

8

CASUS BELLI

Apart from Edward's diplomatic involvements, there was always the issue of Gascony. Since he came to the throne in 1272, Edward had sought to strengthen and reorganise the administration. This ran contrary to French interests, since the Capetian kings wished to extend their influence into every corner of their kingdom. It may be that Philip IV and his counsellors came to see Edward as a serious threat. His negotiations with Aragon, however well intentioned, were to the detriment of France. His recovery of lands on the Continent threatened to restore the influence of his dynasty, which the Capets had worked to undo since the days of Louis VII. To cap it all, Edward's success in overhauling Gascony was perhaps viewed with alarm at the French court.

For all that, Edward cannot be accused of consciously provoking the French. As we have seen, he refused several requests for military aid from Aragon and Castile, on the grounds that he could not be seen as rebelling against his overlord. Even under duress, such as Philip III's efforts to use the Gaston de Béarn affair to meddle in Gascony, Edward did not resort to force. His personal rule of Gascony in these years, leading up to war, was carefully designed to avoid handing the French a *casus belli* or motive for conflict.

The king's chief concern in Gascony was to extend his seigneurial influence and make the duchy profitable. On his first visit as king, in 1273, he conducted a general enquiry into the rights and feudal duties that were owed to him, which resulted in a massive set of returns known as the *Recognitiones Feudorum*.[1] A major element of his policy was the creation of over fifty new towns, called *bastides*. These were mostly constructed around a rigid grid-iron pattern, with a central marketplace, and intended as a source of profit. These towns were typically founded by an act of *paréage*, a form of partnership agreement with local lords.[2] They would provide the site, and in return the king gave the new town his protection and a charter of liberties. Profits were then shared by all.[3]

This may sound as though Edward was deliberately constructing a new chain of fortified sites in Gascony, to guard against French invasion. However, two-thirds of the bastides had no defences and were sited on land suited to commerce rather than military engagement.[4] One exception to this trend was the castle of Sauveterre-la-Lémance, the only proper castle Edward built outside of Wales. Work on Sauveterre began in the late 1280s, at a time when Anglo-French tensions were starting to escalate, and it was situated on the eastern frontier of the Agenais.[5] This was the very edge of Edward's dominions in France. The castle may have been intended to guard from within as much as without, for he had only acquired the Agenais via the Treaty of Amiens in 1279. As the outbreak of war in 1294 would prove, the inhabitants were by no means English loyalists.

The major bone of contention, as always, was the issue of Gascon appeals. During his stay in the duchy, Edward oversaw the creation of a set of ordinances, designed to increase the efficiency of the administrative and judicial system. They were also meant to limit the number of discontented litigants taking their appeals to Paris. The creation of a new judicial system in Gascony, which bypassed the Paris parlement and the court of the French Seneschal of Périgord, threatened the prestige and authority of the French crown.[6]

Philip exploited the issue to enforce his sovereignty. Between 1291 and 1293 a glut of appellants appeared before his parlement, all of them claiming denial of justice by the king-duke and his officials in Gascony. Among these were Bernard de Ravignan, the knight who had assaulted the dying prior of Buzet, and other lords such as Gombaud de Tiran, lord of St-Médard-en-Jalle in the Bordelais region.[7] These men had already caused Edward considerable embarrassment. Gombaud had been at loggerheads with the English administration since 1272, and over the years he had complained of unjust persecution by the king-duke's officers. This 'persecution' was done with good reason, since Gombaud and his men had broken into houses in Blanquefort and ransacked them. They were afterwards banished from the duchy and sought justice in Paris. As Edward's proctors rightly pointed out, nobody under sentence of banishment could claim protection of the crown of France. Yet Gombaud did so anyway, and in 1291 Edward and his seneschal were condemned to pay a fine of 2,000 *livres tournois* for disobedience to the French crown.[8]

While Philip used Gascon appellants to heap pressure on Edward, he also exploited his position to muscle in on English territorial rights. In 1292 he confiscated the county of Bigorre, a Pyrenean lordship adjacent to Béarn in southern Gascony. The county was claimed by Constance, one of the daughters of Edward's old foe Gaston de Béarn. She had been married to Henry of Almaine, the king's first cousin, in 1269, but widowed thanks to his brutal murder in Italy in 1271. In 1284 she claimed that Edward's Seneschal of Gascony, Jean de Grailly, had attempted to forcibly remove her from Bigorre, a charge that led to Grailly's dismissal. After the marriage of Constance's sister Margaret to Count Roger-Bernard of Foix in 1290, he too laid claim to Bigorre. The renewed squabble gave the French an opportunity to intervene. Edward's argument that Bigorre was held freely from the English crown, so the King of France had no sovereign authority there, was dismissed by Philip's lawyers.[9]

Philip and his officers were determined to seize Bigorre. Edward found himself ranged against not only the Count of Foix but another rival claimant in the bishop and chapter of Le Puy in Velay. The canons of Le Puy claimed to have bought the homage of Bigorre from Henry III in 1253, and in 1290 the Paris parlement upheld this claim in the teeth of Edward's protests. Philip's seneschal used the Le Puy claim as a means of extending direct control over the county. In October 1292 the deputy seneschal of Toulouse arrived at the castle of Vic-de-Bigorre with the dean of Le Puy and ejected the Count of Foix. According to Roger-Bernard's own testimony, he was seized by the clothing and physically thrown out. The banners of the King of France and the church of Le Puy were then flown over the barbican.[10]

These issues, though damaging to Edward, may not of themselves have led to war. After all, he had weathered similar disputes with his kinsman's predecessor, Philip III. Yet they were a sign of escalating tension at the worst possible time. The immediate cause of conflict had little to do with either king, though they were quickly drawn into it.

The true *casus belli* is found in a private feud at sea between the Normans on the one hand and the English and the Bayonnais on the other. Bayonne, a sea-port in south-west Gascony, was a wealthy community and of vital importance to English commercial and maritime interests. The Bayonnais were skilled and active privateers – 'the Genoese of the northern seas' – and among the most loyal of Edward's Gascon subjects. In the war to come, they would provide Edward with men, money and ships.[11]

Their maritime rivals, the Normans, were of equal importance to the French crown. As well as taxes, they supplied large military forces to the Capets. Between 1284 and 1293 Philip constructed a major shipyard, the Clos des Galées, at the Norman capital of Rouen to provide the Crown with its own galleys for operations in the Channel and in the Atlantic. When Philip and Edward went to war, Norman ports would supply over half the ships in the French fleet.[12]

The Normans and the Bayonnais had been at feud since at least 1282. In that year the two sides agreed to a peace treaty, after the Normans had led a raid against the English and Bayonnais up the Charente River.[13] As might be expected, this was very much a conflict over maritime trade and trading rights. For instance, in the 1290s Bayonnais merchants secured rights from the Duke of Brittany to 'drying' areas in Brittany north of St Mathieu, used for the catching and drying of fish. These areas were frequently attacked by Norman pirates, though the Bayonnais clung on and still had a mercantile community there in 1296.[14]

The bitter, long-running feud came to a head in 1292–3. Unfortunately, due to the biased reportage of English and French accounts, it is difficult to untangle the precise sequence of events. Much of the detail comes from a series of complaints laid before King Edward by the men of the Cinque Ports: that is, the ports of Sandwich, Rye, Deal, Hastings and Winchelsea on England's southern coast. The Portsmen gave an inevitably one-sided report of the war at sea, which may be compared with differing versions found in chronicle accounts.[15]

The Portsmen's account runs as follows.[16] During Lent in 1292, some Norman and Bayonnais mariners got into a fight over who was to draw water first from a freshwater source on an island off the coast of Brittany. One of the Bayonnais was killed, and this triggered a series of attacks by Norman sailors on Anglo-Gascon ships. A number of Bayonnais vessels were plundered and their crews slaughtered. These actions caused the Constable of Bordeaux to gather together all the English, Bayonnais, Irish, Norman and Breton sailors in that town and make them swear to keep the peace. When the English and Bayonnais left Bordeaux in groups of five or six vessels, they were pursued by a fleet of eighty Norman ships. Further attacks followed, all through the spring and summer of 1292, as the Normans plundered English, Bayonnais and Irish ships up and down the coast of Normandy. There were many atrocities, including the mutilation and beheading of forty sailors and pilgrims aboard ships from Winchelsea and Hastings.

The following year, in 1293, the Portsmen claimed to have been attacked off the coast of Brittany by a Norman fleet. Seventy ships were plundered and all the crews and merchants killed. Further atrocities occurred at St Malo, where two Bayonnais ships were attacked by the Normans, and seventy mariners either flayed or hanged in their skins like dogs.

Finally, the English gathered together a great fleet of merchant ships – the greater number for protection – and on 24 April set sail to trade in Gascony. Due to contrary winds, they were becalmed for a long time off the coast of St Mathieu in Brittany. The Norman wine fleet then came sailing up from the south, armed for war, and a pitched battle took place. After a hard fight the English were victorious and the Normans fled after suffering the loss of 200 ships.

The Portsmen's report finishes on a threatening note, in which Edward and his council are warned that the mariners of the Cinque Ports will desert and turn to piracy unless they receive justice: 'And let the King's council be well assured that if wrong or grievance be done to them in any way against justice, they will forthwith forsake their wives and children and all they possess, and go to make their profit upon the sea wheresoever they think they will be able to acquire it.'[17]

The Portsmen obviously wished to pose as victims, and the report contains no mention of their own misdeeds. These included the sack of La Rochelle in May 1293, apparently in reprisal for earlier Norman attacks.[18] This was important, since La Rochelle and Poitou had been part of royal French territory since 1271. The sack of the town was thus a direct attack upon the French Crown.[19]

There was indeed a major battle off St Mathieu, where the English and their allies were victorious. The Portsmen claimed to have been ambushed by the Normans, but other accounts describe the English as seeking revenge:

> A great dissension arose between the English and the Normans, for the natives of the sea-coast of Normandy, in the violence of their rage or ignorance, slew some of the English by different kinds of death, and hung others in the yards of the masts of the ship, together with some dogs, at which the barons of the Cinque Ports were indignant, and speedily equipped their ships with all necessary naval appointments, to avenge the injury done to the English. And passing over the swelling back of the sea with a numerous fleet, they slew with the sword their enemies who came to encounter them, and threw their carcasses into the sea, without respect to their rank, and did not let one single survivor escape, and brought back their vessels, and baggage, and wines, and other necessaries to their own homes, and all the contents of their ships, dividing the ships and their spoils among themselves.[20]

The author of the *Flores* also claimed that Edward refused to take any share of the plunder, because he had not sanctioned the assault on the Normans.[21] Several other English chroniclers lay emphasis on the role of Charles of Valois, Philip IV's brother, and claim he deliberately encouraged the Normans to attack the English.[22]

Unsurprisingly, French chroniclers give a different version of events. Guillaume de Nangis, chronicler of the Abbey of St Dénis, claimed the war at sea was caused by Edward I's evil intentions. The treacherous English king assembled a fleet, particularly from Bayonne, under the pretence of going on crusade. He then secretly ordered his mariners to attack the Normans. Nangis's account was echoed by Guillaume Guiart, a French soldier-poet, who repeats the theme of Edward's pretence of going on crusade. Another French source, the *Chronica Sancta Bertini*, states that the war had its origin in a brawl between sailors rather than the evil will of kings. Yet another source, the *Chronographia Regum Francorum*, directly implicates Edward and (uniquely) has Flemings rather than Normans as the original targets of English aggression.[23]

Chronicles aside, there is little to suggest that Edward was in any way responsible for the war, even if he was pleased by the English victory. After the naval battle at St Mathieu, he ordered his mariners to cease hostilities. The initial writ noted that 'God has given them victory over the malice of their enemies'; this was perhaps considered unwise, as when the order was repeated the triumphant phrase had been scrubbed out.[24]

Both kings attempted to halt the war at sea. Edward forbade his mariners from attacking the French at sea on at least four occasions, while Philip prohibited his mariners from attacking English subjects.[25] One of Edward's orders to the Portsmen, from 1293, runs as follows:

> Warning to the men of the Cinque Ports not to molest those of Normandy.
>
> The King to all his faithful and liege men of the commonalty of the Cinque Ports, and of Bayonne, Yarmouth, Ireland, and elsewhere in his realms, to whom [these presents shall come]. Greetings. Whereas we have now understood that you are now in readiness to go, in the way of trade, to Gascony and Poitou; and whereas we have already forbidden you, on pain of heavy penalty, to harm or molest those of the realm of the King of France; We now command you, at the risk of your persons and property and all that you can forfeit to us, and straitly charge you, that in this voyage, from henceforth, you make no attack either upon the Normans or any others of the realm of the said King of France; and that you neither harm, molest, nor in any way damage, any of them; and that in all ways you bear yourselves so wisely or discreetly, as well in your merchandising as in landing anywhere, that no ill or harm happen to you.

> We also command you, that you cause this to be proclaimed and enforced through the whole fleet, and wherever else you shall find seafaring people of our realm.[26]

Despite Edward's threat of heavy penalties, he and his rival failed to stop the mariners from attacking each other. This would imply that, far from being instigators of the war at sea, the English and French courts were powerless to prevent it.

English diplomats moved quickly to patch up the situation. In May 1294, the same month as the naval battle of St Mathieu, a delegation arrived in Paris led by Edward's brother Edmund and Henry de Lacy, Earl of Lincoln. Another embassy with greater legal expertise followed in July. Various solutions were suggested. One was that Edward would do justice to any Frenchman who had suffered at the hands of English mariners. If that was insufficient, a commission of two Englishmen and two Frenchmen might be set up, while a third option was to place the dispute in the hands of the papacy.[27]

Philip took a hard line. He rejected all these proposals on the grounds that the matter was too serious. As sovereign lord of Gascony he would exercise his ordinary authority, and commanded the mayor, jurats and a hundred leading citizens of Bayonne to be delivered to him for imprisonment at Périgueux. This was 'on account of the damage done to Normans on the coast of Brittany', probably a reference to the fight at St Mathieu. The Gascons appealed to their own customs with regard to disputes; this included the law of Oléron (maritime law relating to Gascony) to settle any disputes arising at sea.[28]

Edward's diplomats were on a hiding to nothing, since the build-up to war had already started. In July, even as his lawyers pleaded with Philip in Paris, a Norman fleet sailed up the River Charente and raided the town of Saintes in southern Saintonge. This had been Edward's territory since 1279 and was governed by his seneschal, Rostand de Soler, a former mayor of Bordeaux. Rostand later submitted a full report to Edward of the raid, which took place from Easter to Ascension (21 May). It comprises a list of horrific atrocities. The Normans were hunting for Englishmen and Bayonnais in particular, and chopped up three Navarrese merchants misidentified as the latter. One of the pirates spiked the entrails of his victim on the end of his spear, and then rode about the town shouting: 'Who wants to buy entrails from Bayonne? I am selling!'

Another Norman pirate, Gaufridus Gossa, stole the Holy Eucharist from the church of St Nazaire and chewed it; one of his comrades ripped off the ear of a local merchant and ate it. These violent acts were not random or done for mere pleasure. Rather, the Normans were showing dominance by staging mock executions and enforcing private justice upon their enemies, presumably as payback for St Mathieu.[29]

There was other sinister business afoot. In July 1293 – the same month as the talks in Paris and the raid on Saintonge – Philip began to send troops into Gascony and Poitou. The garrison of La Rochelle received an extra fifty crossbowmen, dispatched from Paris on 4 July, and another seventy troops were fetched by Pierre de Bailleul, Seneschal of northern Saintonge, 'on account of the assault made upon the town by the Bayonnais'.[30] This was a reference to the recent sack of La Rochelle in May by the Bayonnais. The French could argue they were justified in fortifying the town, but the military build-up didn't end there.

One of Philip's key advisors, Pierre Flote, was present in Saintonge at this time to oversee the reinforcement and restocking of castles. In the autumn he arrived at Blaye, one of the Plantagenet strongholds guarding the northern reaches of Gascony, and gained entry to the town. On 21 September, while Flote was busy in the south-west, the French king's vassals in the Languedoc were summoned for a campaign in Gascony. This did not proceed without difficulty. In October the inhabitants of Narbonne pleaded for a delay so they could complete the grape harvest.[31] Still the French continued to prepare. In December the garrison at Blaye was reinforced by eighty French sergeants, while the castle of Fronsac in Bergerac received thirty.[32]

A more personal glimpse into these events can be found in the later petition of one Thomas de Lancastre, an English soldier. Thomas claimed that 'before the beginning of the war, when the Vicomte of Fronsac surrendered Fronsac to the King of France, he loaded a small boat with herring at Bordeaux, to travel to Libourne, and it was robbed in the Dordogne opposite Fronsac, by malefactors who were then in the castle on behalf of the King of France. Then, when the land was in the hand of the King of France, Thomas was exiled by the French, and had to abandon his wife and children, who then died.'[33]

The dating of the petition is vague, though clearly it is from shortly before the outbreak of war. This would fit with the arrival of thirty French sergeants to garrison the castle at Fronsac, after the vicomte had delivered it to Philip.

It is impossible to know for certain if Philip was responsible for the Norman attack on Saintes. Despite the coincidence of timing, this might well have simply been a continuation of the private war at sea. On the other hand, Philip must have approved the dispatch of French troops into Gascony and Poitou, which in turn implies he negotiated with the English in bad faith. This much is bluntly stated by an English chronicler, Pierre Langtoft:

> At Paris, his city, he [Philip] goes and holds parliament,
> With his brother Charles, the count of Artois agrees
> To a great act of treachery by design.[34]

This is a pro-English source, of course, and we have already seen how the chroniclers on both sides accused each other of treachery. In light of Philip's actions in 1293, however, it is difficult not to conclude that he was resolved on conquest. The negotiations with the English were essentially a bluff, designed to cover his real intentions for as long as possible.

On 27 October 1293, after months of futile peace talks, Philip issued his citation against Edward. This was an even more severe version of his earlier demand in July. The king ordered Edward, as immediate lord of the Bayonnais, to reply to a list of grave charges. He insisted that hostages would be taken from Bayonne and imprisoned at Périgueux, and that Bordeaux, the Agenais and 'all that other land which your men hold in your name within the limits our sénéchaussée of Périgord and in the three dioceses of Périgueux, Cahors and Limoges' were to be taken into French custody. Furthermore, twenty hostages were to be taken from among Edward's officers in Gascony who, it was claimed, had insulted the crown of France and attacked its agents.[35]

For good measure, Philip issued specific charges against certain of Edward's Gascon subjects. Among other things they were alleged to have killed several Normans who had lived at Bourg and Bordeaux for ten or more years, simply because they spoke the French language. The corpses of the victims had been dismembered and thrown into the river. A royal sergeant had had his hand cut off and four royal customs collectors had been beheaded; on the latter occasion the killers cried, 'We're doing this to spite the King of France and his brother Charles.' And so on.[36]

Unsurprisingly, Philip's commands were disobeyed. They were seen as not only excessive, but in flagrant violation of the normal means of resolving disputes. In response, Philip ordered Edward to appear before the Paris parlement soon after Christmas 1294, to explain the conduct of his subjects.[37]

Meanwhile Philip's minister, Pierre Flote, continued to busy himself in Gascony. On 1 December 1293, at Agen, he and other Capetian officers proclaimed their king's citation against Edward. Twelve days later they were at Libourne, where the citizens denied them entry to the town. This was the first sign of Gascon resentment against Philip's actions. After summoning the mayor and jurats to meet them outside, the French read Philip's citation aloud and ordered the townsmen to accept a copy. They refused, so it was nailed to one of the town gates.[38]

Flote and his companions received an even colder welcome at St Emilion. Here the citation was again proclaimed outside the town, after the French took up a position of safety under an elm tree. When a clerk tried to nail the document to the gates, he was prevented by the captain of the town garrison, Eble de Puyguilhelm. Eble then gathered a force of sergeants armed with crossbows, shields and lances just inside the town gate adjoining the Dominican priory. The town bell was rung, the citizens gathered, and the French delegation hurriedly departed.[39] Eble would serve as a member of Edward I's household and fight for him during the war of 1294–1303.[40]

Elsewhere the Anglo-Gascons had already started to take action. According to Jean d'Arrablaye, Seneschal of Périgord and one of Flote's companions, six ships manned by Englishmen and Bayonnais set out from Libourne to prevent all French-speaking subjects of Philip from sailing on the Dordogne towards Bordeaux or elsewhere. They attempted to attack the nearby castles of Blaye and Fronsac, but were repulsed.[41]

Edward's officers in Gascony, John de St John and John de Havering, were certainly not idle. In January 1294 a force of nobles and their companies was raised in the Agenais, supposedly 'to guard the roads and highways against robbers and malefactors'. Their true purpose was to guard against the presence and intervention of Capetian officers in the duchy. More Gascon nobles were retained for military service '*cum equis et armis*' – with horses and arms – at Bellegarde, Puyguilhem, Castelnau-de-Riviere, Lectoure and Mauléon.[42]

At this point, with the situation in Gascony on a knife edge, Edward and his brother made one last effort to avert war. Edmund was sent on another diplomatic mission to Paris, with instructions from the king to find a peaceful solution. His mission would end in disaster.

9

TAKE SPEAR IN THY FIST

On the face of it, Edmund was a perfect choice to pour oil on troubled waters. He had close links to the inner circle of the French royal family, and in this respect was better qualified to conduct the talks than Edward himself. As we have noted, he had married into the French aristocracy in 1275 by taking Blanche of Artois, Countess of Champagne, for his second wife. Blanche's daughter by her first husband, Henri I of Navarre, had become the wife of Philip IV. This made Edmund not only second cousin to the King of France, but also stepfather to the queen.[1]

Early in the new year of 1294, Edmund devised a new set of proposals with the help of his stepdaughter and Mary of Brabant (Philip III's widow and stepmother of Philip IV). The result was a secret treaty concluded in February, the original French version of which is still held at the Archives Nationales. It was never sealed, though it has holes for sealing cords, and there is no clause of attestation. It bears the words, written in a later hand: 'Certain conventions which the King of England's men requested before the war, but the lord king Philip refused to consent to them.'[2]

The content of the secret treaty reveals Edward I's desire to loosen (since he could not sever them entirely) the links of the feudal chain that bound him to France. His brother proposed that peace would be settled by the marriage of Edward to Philip's sister, Margaret of France. The duchy of Gascony would be held by the children of this union, rather than Edward's heirs by his deceased first wife, Eleanor of Castile. This meant that Gascony would be one step removed, as it were, from the main English line of succession. It would also spare future kings of England from having to perform the humiliating rite of homage and fealty in Paris to the kings of France.[3]

The treaty also attempted to put an end, once and for all, to the stormy issue of Gascon appeals. Edmund proposed that Gascon appellants would no longer be granted exemptions from ducal justice. This in turn meant that the French royal *pennonceaux*, symbolic of Capetian power and protection, would no longer fly over the castles, houses or *maison-fortes* (fortified manors) of Gascon appellants. Should an appeal against the king-duke or his heirs succeed, they would not be punished with dispossession of Gascony. If the impending marriage between Edward and Blanche proved childless, then all these concessions would apply after the king's death to his current heir, Edward of Caernarfon.[4]

Edward and his brother were asking for major concessions, and may have gambled on exploiting Philip's desire to avoid war. This seems inexplicable, since the French king had refused to accept the terms of previous diplomatic missions. Nor had he made any effort to prevent the build-up of French military forces in Gascony and Poitou; indeed, to judge from the presence of Pierre Flote in those regions, Philip was actively encouraging it. How much Edward and Edmund knew of the infiltration of French agents and garrisons is unclear. Their own agents on the ground, John de St John and John de Havering, were certainly taking steps to prepare for invasion over the winter months of 1293–4.

The main terms of the treaty were essentially a face-saving compromise. Acting in his brother's name, Edmund of Lancaster agreed to deliver to the King of France several towns in Agenais and Saintonge as well as a number of hostages. Once these gestures had been made, the summons of 27 October 1293 against Edward would be repealed. The towns were to be returned and the hostages released. A safe-conduct would then be granted to Edward, so he could meet Philip at Amiens. It was also agreed that the marriage of Edward to Margaret, Philip's sister, would go ahead.[5]

As a further guarantee, Philip gave Edmund a verbal assurance that the treaty would be honoured. At this point Edmund might have done well to suspect his kinsman's intentions, since Philip insisted the terms should be kept secret. This, he claimed, was because some of his counsellors would be opposed to them. Indeed, to save his honour and placate his council, Philip argued he had to give the impression of dealing harshly with Edward. To that end he issued letters patent ordering the whole of the duchy of Gascony to be seized. This was done with Edmund's consent, on the understanding the order would not be carried out.[6]

It was carried out, albeit in farcical circumstances. On 20 February 1294 a French delegation arrived at St-Macaire bearing orders for the surrender of the duchy. The seneschal, John de St John, at first refused to admit them. Eventually two clerks were smuggled into the castle, where they presented a letter from the Constable of France. After much wrangling, John's clerk pointed out that the letter bore a seal that he did not recognise. The French had no answer to this and were obliged to depart: as one historian has remarked, without a proper seal the letter had no more validity than a photocopy of a legal document would have today.[7]

St John had seen off Philip's officers, but he could not defy a direct order from his master. Shortly before 3 March he had received Edward's order, via Edmund of Lancaster, requiring him and other ducal officers to surrender the duchy and their hostages.[8] Bordeaux, the chief city and centre of the wine trade, had already been surrendered on 22 February. When Edmund protested to Philip IV that this total seizure was against the terms of their secret treaty, Philip again gave assurances that he would abide by their agreement. He told Edmund that a royal letter would be sent to the Constable of France, ordering him to restore what had been taken contrary to the treaty. When the constable was approached, he refused to give back anything since he had received no such letter.[9]

Edward was perfectly aware of the treaty. Throughout the negotiations he stayed in touch with his brother in Paris, and kept the talks a secret from his own magnates. They appear to have suspected something was amiss: while the king toured East Anglia over the winter months, the magnates stayed away from court. His chancellor,

John Langton, shared St John's misgivings and advised Edward against the secret deal. The king ignored him.[10] Edward appears to have been so confident in his diplomacy, and so trusting in Philip's promises, that he kept no counsel but his own.

All the while, French troops poured into Gascony to tighten their hold on the towns and castles Edmund had meekly surrendered without any security except Philip's sworn word. According to the English chronicler Walter of Guisborough, Philip sent first a few men, then many, then an army.[11] Edmund, who must have been desperate by this point, appealed yet again to the French king. Philip replied, through his secretary and in the presence of Joan of Navarre, that no attention should be paid to the harsh answer which was to be given in council. As soon as the counsellors who opposed him in the matter had left, Philip would honour the secret treaty.[12]

When the harsh reply came, Edward was told that Gascony would remain in French hands. He made several more attempts to gain satisfaction, only to be informed by the bishops of Orléans and Tournai, two of Philip's counsellors, that the king's decision was final. There was no point attempting to pursue the matter any further. On 21 April 1294, the previous citation against Edward of 27 October 1293 was published once more. Philip refused to allow Edward a safe-conduct, making it impossible for him to obey the summons and appear before the Paris parlement.[13]

The diplomatic failure of the English in 1293 and 1294 has been condemned as 'among the most dismal episodes of English foreign policy', on a par with the appeasement policies of the Second World War.[14] This severe assessment has been challenged as a misunderstanding of the situation in which the English found themselves. The war that ensued was not of Edward's choosing, and he had instructed Edmund to treat for peace. Edmund agreed to a temporary surrender of the duchy as the price for peace in Christendom and the furtherance of a crusade to recover Acre. This, after all, had been the general thrust of Edward's foreign policy since he came to the throne. Furthermore, the papacy was vacant from April 1292 to July 1294, which meant there was no hope of papal mediation between the two parties.[15]

A more straightforward interpretation is that the French were bent on war, and that nothing the English did could have prevented it.[16] This much is implied by the account of Pope Boniface VIII, when he later asked French envoys if their master intended to drive the English from their last holdings on the Continent. The reply, from the lips of Pierre Flote, was, 'Certainly, sir, what you say is true.'[17]

Philip also grasped the opportunity to take control of Ponthieu, which he achieved by another piece of devious legal footwork. We have seen how Edward acquired the county in right of his wife, Eleanor of Castile. There was a rival claimant in the shape of John, Count of Aumale and son of Eleanor's older brother Ferdinand. After years of litigation, John had surrendered his claim to Ponthieu in exchange for a pay-off from Edward. In 1294, however, John re-submitted his claim to the Court of Appeals in Paris, which took the county into French custody while the issue was discussed by Philip's lawyers. In the meantime his administrators moved in and collected the revenues.[18] The timing is distinctly suspicious, and the likelihood is that John submitted his claim at Philip's behest.

In context, the policy of Philip and his counsellors was clear, deliberate and clinical. First they deprived Edward of Bigorre, then Gascony and Ponthieu. The remnant of his lands and rights, including those in the much-disputed dioceses of Limoges, Cahors and Périgueux, were also taken into custody. In the space of just two years, from 1292 to 1294, Philip had taken all the English land holdings on the Continent. This bloodless victory was achieved via the exploitation of feudal custom and process, a task made easier by Edward's subordinate status to the French crown. Finally, the dream of Philip Augustus had been fulfilled.

It was done at the cost of Philip IV's historical reputation. Assessments of his behaviour have not been kind. At best the king made promises to Edmund he could not fulfil, having underrated the power and influence of his council.[19] This is to assume that Philip's policy was dictated by his advisers, something the king himself refuted on his deathbed in 1314. A more likely – and damning – assessment is that Philip had deliberately deceived Edmund from start to finish.[20] Whatever the influence of men such as Pierre Flote or Charles of

Valois, the policy ultimately came from Philip, and he must shoulder the blame:

> Edmund's lame apology to his brother on his return to England that he had been 'as a fool or as one seduced' is no doubt true, but it is hard to credit Philip with any more noble quality than crass and faithless opportunism.[21]

French historians also tend to frown upon Philip's conduct. To Robert Fawtier it was 'inexplicable'.[22] Trabut-Cussac remarked that Philip had exploited the naivety of Edmund of Lancaster, and that it was very difficult to doubt the sincerity of Edward's desire for peace.[23] Charles Victor Langlois, after weighing up the opinions of English and French historians, concluded that Philip was indeed guilty of outrageous duplicity.[24] A rare dissenting voice was Edgard Boutaric, writing in 1870, who declared that Philip took appropriately energetic measures against the perfidious English.[25]

The real question, aside from Philip's duplicity, is why Edward fell for the ruse. The English king was an experienced politician, and until this point had scarcely put a foot wrong. He was just as capable of duplicity and stooping to low methods to gain his ends, particularly in Scotland. Indeed, Edward's experience was paradoxical, since he treated the Scots in the same way as he was treated by the French. It has long been established that the king's claim to the overlordship of Scotland was unjust, and rested on his manipulation of the Scottish succession crisis after the untimely death of Alexander III in 1286.[26] Once John Balliol was installed as King of Scots, Edward bullied and cajoled his vassal just as the French did to him and his officers in Aquitaine.[27]

The apparent gullibility of Edward and his brother is best explained by their connections with the French court. Edward had quarrelled at times with Philip's father, Philip III, but their disputes never seriously threatened to end in war. Since the Treaty of Paris in 1259, relations between the English and French royal families had generally been amicable, and the two were closely related in blood and marriage ties.[28] When he first came to the throne in 1285, Philip IV had pursued this conciliatory line. His attitude hardened after 1290, when he started to use the issue of Gascon appellants as a weapon against the English. Perhaps Edward perceived this as all in the way of business, and had no inkling of the enormity of Philip's plans.

It could be argued that the real fool was Philip. He succeeded in deceiving Edmund of Lancaster, but – as the king's biographer has queried – why was it necessary to deceive him?[29] The terms of the secret treaty show that Edmund and his brother recognised the sovereignty of the King of France, and were willing to allow a token occupation force into Gascony as a symbol of Capetian supremacy. They were also willing to surrender hostages into French custody, as well as key towns and castles. At this point Edward had clearly demonstrated that he did not want a war, and that Philip did not need one.[30]

The result was war, as Philip should have realised. Edward was never going to surrender his inheritance without a fight: his prestige would have taken a fatal blow, and the king's honour and reputation were at stake, as well as the politico-economic importance of English links with Gascony.[31]

Before he could seek revenge on Philip, Edward had to face criticism at home. On 20 April the former Seneschal of Gascony, John de St John, arrived in England to inform the king of what had transpired. The news came as a dreadful shock. Usually so composed in public (if not always in private), for once Edward let his mask slip. The king was observed to turn red in the face, said one chronicler, 'and became very afraid, because he had acted less than wisely'.[32]

When the loss of Gascony was announced in the English parliament in May 1294, there were angry scenes. Edward was forced to apologise and asked for counsel over what should be done. He even had to endure the embarrassment of assuring his council that he had not acted out of lust for Margaret, Philip's sister. Instead his motive was peace with France, for without it he could not fulfil his oath to go on crusade.[33]

Once this act of contrition was made, Edward's counsellors rallied round the king. Antony Bek, the fighting Bishop of Durham, advised war:

> Since thou hast done it,
> No one ought to fail thee in thy need.

If thou wilt recover thy land of Gascony,
And take good care that Philip dissimulate with thee no longer,
Arise and bestir thyself, sleep not like a monk;
Put on the hauberks, trample down the carrion,
Mount the steeds, and take spear in thy fist.[34]

Perhaps encouraged by Bek, Edward declared that 'had he no other following than one boy and a horse he would pursue his right to the death'. His barons in turn professed themselves 'ready to follow him in life and death against Philip for the recovery of Gascony'.[35]

The die was cast. Shortly afterwards Edward formally renounced his homage and declared war against Philip, one crowned head against another.

10

THE FORCES WITHIN OUR POWER

To begin with, Philip held most of the advantages. He had possession of Gascony, and the English were faced with enormous logistical and financial difficulties. At best, the voyage from London to Bordeaux took about ten days. The sea-journey from Plymouth has been estimated at two weeks, providing the winds were favourable and the seas calm. Even then, the journey might be full of delays.[1] Certainly, English diplomats were in the habit of travelling to Gascony from Paris, as the journey was safer and quicker.

The remoteness of the Gascon command from England meant delays in communication, as well as problems in ferrying troops and supplies to the duchy. It was vital to keep the sea-lanes open, and both sides appreciated the role of sea-power in the conflict. Here, at least, the English began with a slight advantage thanks to the victory of the Portsmen and their allies over the Normans at St Mathieu in 1293. This helped to secure early control of the sea-lanes and the Channel, though the French would soon challenge this supremacy.[2] Since December 1292 Philip had been building a fleet of galleys in his new shipyard at Rouen in Normandy. He had claimed that these ships were meant to convey an army of crusaders to Sicily. In retrospect, it was obvious they were meant to fight the English.[3]

From the start, Edward realised the scale of the challenge that faced him. A war against France was an entirely different prospect to Wales, where he had destroyed the native princes and imposed a permanent conquest. Unlike the Welsh and the Scots, the French had equal, if not greater, resources than the English. Thanks to Edward's botched diplomacy, French garrisons occupied all the major towns and castles in Gascony. Dislodging them would be impossible unless the English found a way of widening the conflict.

The king's strategy was to construct an elaborate system of alliances in the Low Countries, Germany and Franche-Comté in eastern Burgundy, meant to encircle the French and stretch their forces to breaking point. His grandfather King John had adopted a very similar strategy against Philip Augustus in 1214, which may have provided the template for Edward's plan in 1297.[4]

According to Langtoft, the idea of resurrecting this strategy came from Anthony Bek, at the tumultuous May parliament of May 1294:

> Seek for thyself friends with power of money,
> The king of Allemaigne [Germany], the bishop of Cologne,
> The king of the Aragonese, that he keep not aloof from thee,
> The count of Savoy, the count of Burgundy,
> And then deal with Philip, without further difficulty.[5]

The plan was ambitious, and bound to be expensive, but there was plenty of scope for enlisting allies. Philip had adopted an aggressive policy towards other realms on the borders of France, principally the Holy Roman Empire and Flanders. This alienated the rulers of those lands, who were not powerful enough to challenge the French by themselves. Edward and his advisers spotted an opportunity to buy their support and work in tandem to defeat Philip.

A key member of the coalition was Adolf of Nassau, King of Germany and titular King of the Romans. Adolf had been elected in 1292, and rendered virtually powerless by territorial and financial concessions he was forced to make to the Electors.[6] His position was further compromised by the general weakness of the German monarchy after the Interregnum (1250–73), during which the imperial throne was vacant. This lack of centralised authority had enabled princes of the empire to become more independent, and encouraged the kings of France to extend their power into German territory.[7]

Philip's method of encroaching on German lands was to deal with each prince individually. He put pressure on Henri III, ruler of the county of Bar, a principality of the Holy Roman Empire encompassing the *pays de Barrois* and centred on the city of Bar-le-Duc, making it an immediate neighbour to France. Henri had a dispute with the abbey of Beaulieu, which lay inside French territory, but Philip had pardoned him in a royal letter of March 1291. In late 1293, at the same time as he summoned Edward I to Paris, Philip reopened the Beaulieu case and sentenced Henri to pay the abbey a fine of 10,000 marks.[8]

It is possible that Philip was nervous of Henri's marriage alliance with Edward. Henri had contracted to marry one of Edward's daughters, Eleanor, in the summer of 1293, and the wedding duly went ahead in September 1294. The dower provided by the count to his bride consisted of castles and estates in Bar, which meant the Plantagenet dynasty would eventually gain possession of a large chunk of the county. This would give them a foothold on the borders of north-east France.[9] In this context, Philip's policy was as much defensive as aggressive, but it only strengthened Henri's alliance with England. Sensing the coming storm, Henri was among the first to join Edward's coalition.

Another of Philip's aims was to detach the county of Burgundy from the empire. To this end he attempted to secure the homage of Count Otto IV of Burgundy, a move bitterly opposed by King Adolf and a league of nobles of Franche-Comté in the east of the county. Otto himself see-sawed between the rival factions until he surrendered all his domains to Philip in exchange for a one-off sum of 100,000 *livres*, and 10,000 *livres* in annual rents.[10] This prompted the Burgundian league, led by Jean de Chalon-Arlay, to declare they would never swear homage to King Philip, or surrender their rights to him or his heirs.[11] Already at war with France, they made ideal recruits for the English alliance.

Adolf tired of French aggression. On 10 August 1294 the Anglo-German treaty was drawn up, whereby the kings of England and Germany promised to aid each other against the French. They were to conclude no separate peace or truce with France, and agreed to join forces on a certain day to be decided by Edward and the German ambassadors.[12] Adolf ratified the treaty on 21 August, and ten days later sent his formal message of defiance to Philip:

> Adolf, by the grace of God king of the Romans, forever august, to the noble sovereign lord Philip, king of France.
> Since the goods, possessions, laws and administration of justice, and territories of our empire have been held by your ancestors and yourself for so long as a result of unlawful occupation, having been appropriated without cause, the evidence of which being manifest in many and various places, we, being unable henceforth to ignore the truth of these matters under the guise of forbearance, inform you by these present letters that we intend to pursue the redress of such great injustices and to bring the forces within our power against you.
>
> Given at Nuremberg, on the 31st day of August in the year of our Lord 1294 and the third year of our reign.[13]

Adolf quickly secured the services of other German princes on Edward's behalf. Across late October and early November he induced the Archbishop of Cologne and the Count of Katzenellenbogen to join the alliance, for which the latter received a subsidy of £250. A fee of the same amount was promised to the count when (and if) Edward arrived in Germany to join forces with Adolf.[14]

Apart from recruiting the enemies of France, Edward also sought to exploit Philip's aggressive policy towards his vassals. One of these was Guy of Dampierre, Count of Flanders. Prior to 1294, Guy had for several years been engaged in a struggle to ward off French influence. His conflict with Philip had its roots in a long-running dispute between himself and the aldermen of Ghent. In a bid to extend French royal influence, Philip took the side of the aldermen and installed his officials in Ghent, to act as a barrier between them and Guy. The French king also prohibited trade between Flanders and England, with an inevitably disastrous effect on the Flemish economy, and constantly outmanoeuvred Guy in various financial and territorial disputes.[15]

In 1293 the exasperated count looked to support from England and started negotiations for the marriage of his daughter Philippa to Edward I's heir. The engagement was confirmed on 31 August 1294, along with a promised subsidy of 200,000 *livres tournois* from Edward to Guy.[16] England had been at war with France since May, which meant Guy had concluded a marriage alliance with the enemy of his lord, Philip. The French king summoned Guy to Paris, where he and Philippa were held captive for a time. Guy was eventually released on condition he abandon the English alliance, but his daughter spent the rest of her days in custody at the Louvre.[17] For the time being, this severed the prospect of an Anglo-Flemish alliance.

Other allies Edward enlisted at this stage included the Duke of Brabant, John II, and Count Floris V of Holland. As with the Count of Bar, Edward used his children to cement relations with these foreign powers. John had married Princess Margaret in 1290, while Floris had affianced his daughter to Edward's son Alfonso in 1281. The wedding was prevented by the boy's early death, so a decade later an alternative was arranged with Floris's son and heir, John, affianced to Edward's daughter Elizabeth.[18]

The financial cost of purchasing these allies was immense. Adolf was promised that he would receive £40,000 by Christmas 1294, and a further £20,000 when Edward arrived in Flanders. The Duke of Brabant was offered 200,000 *livres tournois* (£50,000) and another £4,000 out of customs duty. Edward's allies in Franche-Comté were owed 60,000 *livres tournois* for the first year of the alliance, with 30,000 for each subsequent year. Count Floris V of Holland was owed 80,000 *livres tournois*. The Count of Bar was owed 30,000 marks in return for service with 1,000 cavalry. Yet another subsidy of 10,000 marks was paid out to the Archbishop of Cologne, with an extra £2,000 as a gift, while smaller sums were paid out to lesser German allies.[19]

The enthusiasm of some of these men may be doubted. Shortly before his death at a tournament in April 1294, the Duke of Brabant's father disclosed to a friend that he meant to remain neutral in the coming war, while selling his services to the highest of the two bidders.[20]

Personal animosities also threatened this rickety coalition, held together as it was by English money and mutual self-interest. There was no love lost between Count Guy of Flanders and Count Floris of Holland, who had already clashed over their competing rights to the Zeeland islands. In 1290 Guy took Floris hostage for a time, to compel him to agree to amicable terms. Floris in turn sought to undermine his Flemish rival by securing the support of the Avesnes family of Hainault, Guy's arch-rivals. The feud continued to simmer, even after both joined Edward's alliance against the French.[21]

Above: Edward's forebear King John, whose uncharacteristic success at Mirebeau in 1202 Edward perhaps sought to emulate. (Courtesy of the British Library, Royal 16 G VI)

Below: Built by Richard I overlooking the Seine, the loss of Chateau Gaillard in 1204 epitomised the failure of English policy in France. (Courtesy of Zairon under Creative Commons)

Above: The castle at Mauléon. Controlling the pass to the Iberian peninsula, it proved to be instrumental in the outbreak of the Gascon conflict. (Courtesy of Pauline Afflatet under Creative Commons)

Left: King Edward I.

Philip IV, Edward's dogged enemy in the Gascon conflict. (Courtesy of the British Library, Add MS 10341)

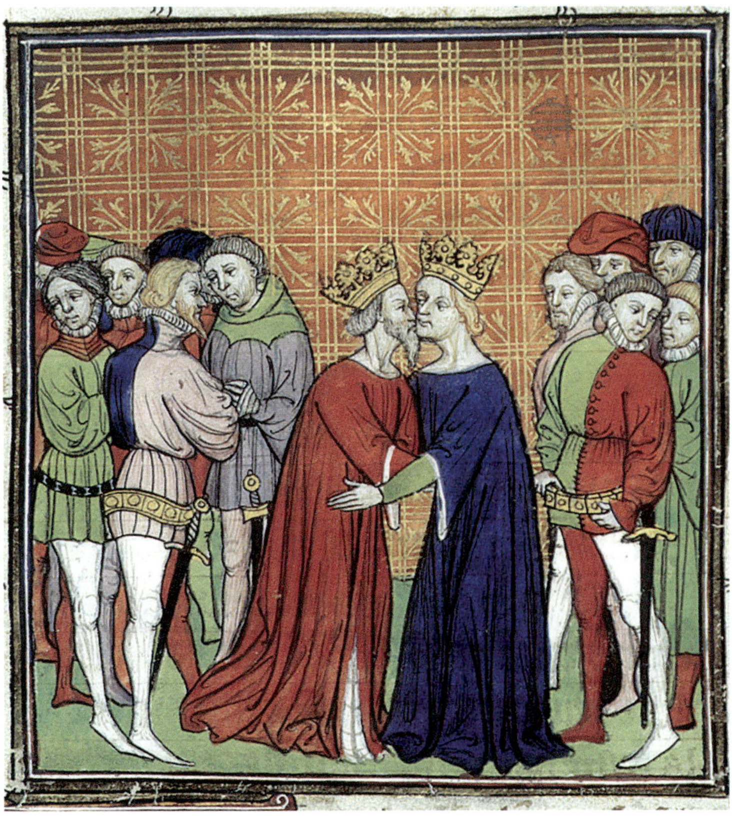

Edward pays homage to Philip IV. This symbolic act became a key sticking point in the war. (Courtesy of the British Library, Royal 20 C VI)

Bordeaux, jewel in the Gascon crown, as it appeared in the thirteenth century. (Sketched by Leo Drouyn)

An image of the town square at Monpazier, founded by Edward I in 1284. This is a classic example of the so-called 'bastide' towns founded by Edward and his father, Henry III, to encourage new growth and trade inside Gascony. (Author's collection)

One of the surviving town gates at Monpazier, preserved as it would have looked after the foundation in 1284. Edward briefly visited the town in November 1286 to inspect the works. (Author's collection)

The Hotel d'Edouard I, a hotel in Monpazier named after the founder of the town. (Author's collection)

Left: An internal view of the streets of Monpazier, showing the regular grid pattern of bastide towns and the arms of local medieval gentry families. (Author's collection)

Below: The castle of Sauveterre-le-Lémance on the eastern border of Périgord, built in 1289 to guard the frontier of Edward's expanded duchy after the Treaty of Amiens a decade earlier. This is the only proper stone castle Edward built outside Wales. (Author's collection)

The House of the Black Prince at Monflanquin, another of Edward I's bastide towns. His great-grandson Edward of Woodstock, the Black Prince, stayed here on several occasions during the Hundred Years War. (Author's collection)

Madog ap Llywelyn, leader of the Welsh revolt of 1294. His incursions diverted Edward away from a potentially decisive attack on France. (Courtesy of Llywelyn2000 under Creative Commons)

Left: King Philip's brother Charles of Valois, who brought the French field army into Gascony in 1295. (Courtesy of Acoma)

Below: Robert II, Count of Artois, another of Philip's commanders, depicted in battle. (Courtesy of the British Library, Royal 20 C VII)

A contract from 1286, whereby the formidable and troublesome Gaston de Béarn agreed to go to the Holy Land under pressure from Edward I and Philip IV. (Courtesy of The National Archives)

A military contract from March 1298, sealed at Aardenburg, whereby Edward renewed his military contract with Jean de Arlay and the barons of Burgundy, who had refused to accept the ceding of the county to Philip IV. (Courtesy of The National Archives)

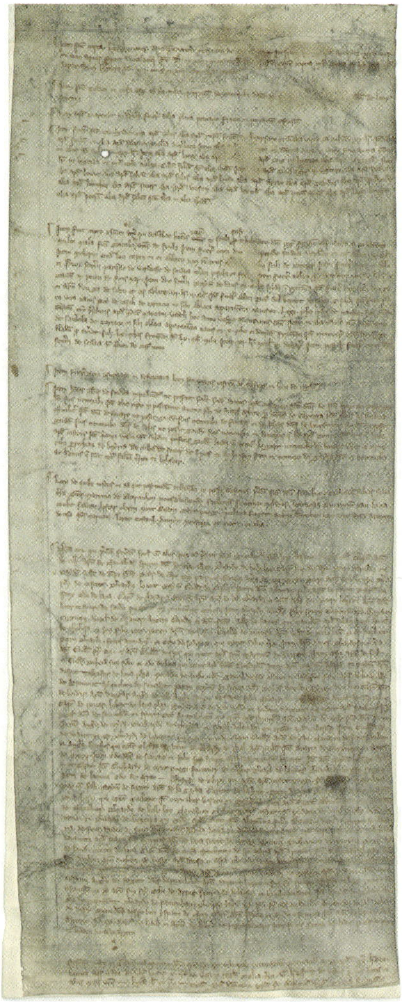

Left: A surviving membrane from 1274, listing complaints against Gaston de Béarn, after his short-lived revolt against Edward. The documents lists damages and raids committed by Gaston and his men in southern Gascony. (Courtesy of The National Archives)

Below: The first membrane of a lengthy roll of Gascon exiles, when they embarked at Portsmouth in March 1303 to recapture Bordeaux, the capital city, after nine years of French occupation. (Courtesy of The National Archives)

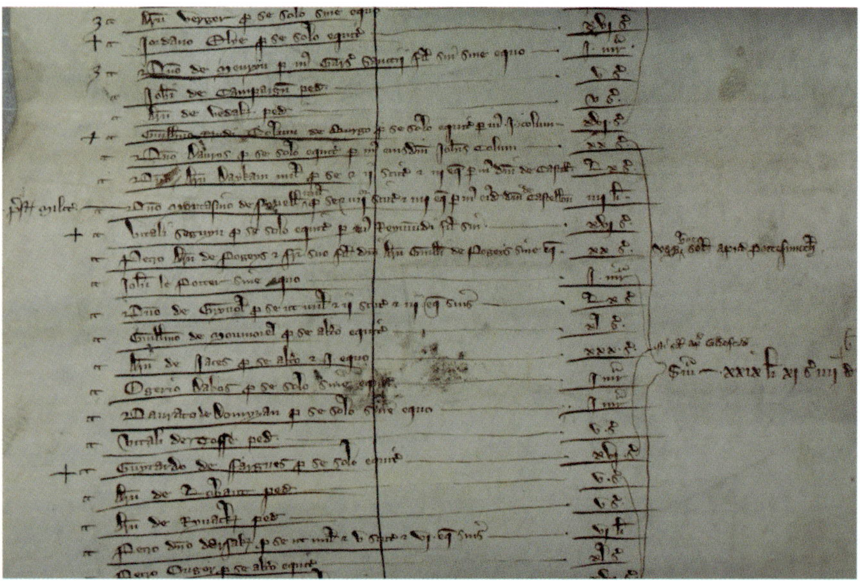

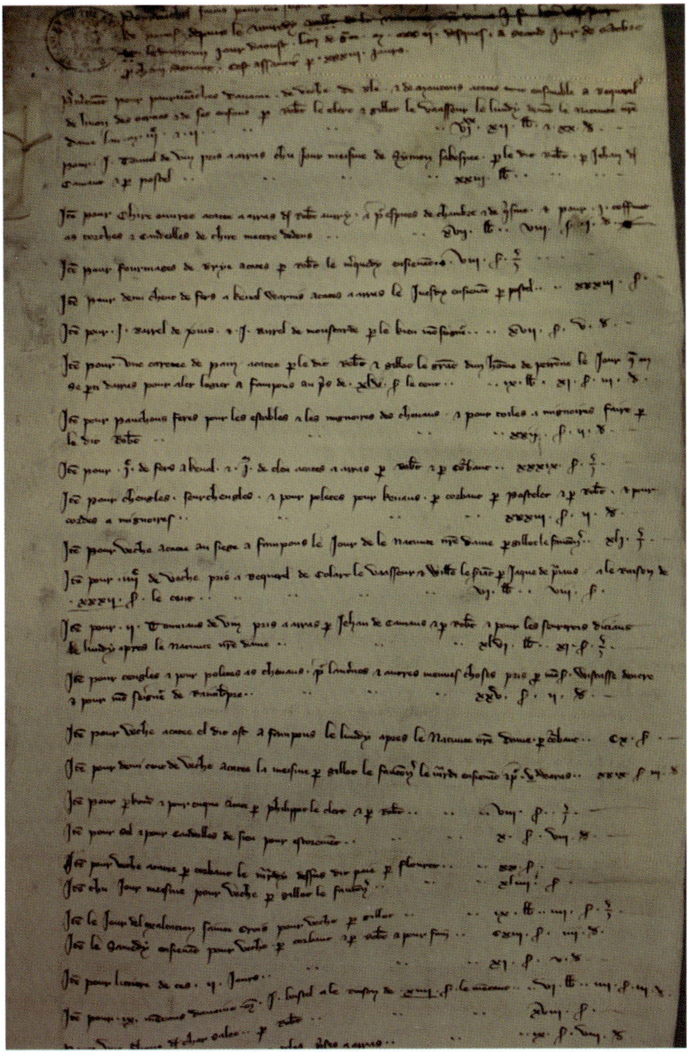

The muster roll for a baron of Ponthieu doing military service for Edward in 1302–3. (Courtesy of Michael Prestwitch)

A letter from Edward I to Philip III, c.1274, in which the former explains he cannot send military aid to the King of France, on account of wars in Wales and Ireland. (Courtesy of The National Archives)

Left: Othon de Grandson, one of Edward's foremost officers in Gascony. (Courtesy of AJ Marshall under Creative Commons)

Below: John de St John, another of Edward's stalwarts, sails away from Bordeaux having failed to take the city. They would soon move upriver and besiege Rions. (Courtesy of the British Library, Royal 20 C VII)

The ruins of the Château des Rudel at Blaye, a reliable stronghold for Edward's forces. (Courtesy of Pinpin under Creative Commons)

St-Sever, which suffered greatly during the conflict and was subjected to a thirteen-week siege. (Courtesy of Gilles Guillamot under Creative Commons)

In the lead-up to the conflict in Gascony and then throughout, various popes were called upon to mediate. From top to bottom: Martin IV (1281–1285), Nicholas IV (1288–1292) and Boniface VIII (1294–1303). (Courtesy of the British Library, Harley MS 1340)

Above: John de St John is captured at Bellegarde by Robert d'Artois. (Courtesy of the British Library, Royal 20 C VII)

Below: The Battle of the Golden Spurs at Courtrai in 1302 saw an army of Flemish commoners inflict a massive defeat on the French, with d'Artois among the slain. (Courtesy of the British Library, Royal 20 C VII)

Above: John Balliol, king of Scotland, pays tribute to Edward I. (Courtesy of the British Library, Royal 20 C VII)

Left: With the war over, Philip IV was struggling for funds. Eventually, he made his infamous decision to turn on the Templars, ostensibly to appropriate their silver. Manuscript illuminations depict their arrest and execution by burning. (Courtesy of the British Library, Royal 20 C VII)

11

THE FIRST EXPEDITION, 1294–1295

While his allies (hopefully) attacked the French, Edward planned to embark on a tripartite expedition to reconquer Gascony. The details are contained in a letter dated 1 July 1294 addressed to his Gascon subjects. The first expeditionary force, under John de St John and John of Brittany, would sail from Portsmouth on 17 August. The second, under Edmund of Lancaster and the Earl of Lincoln, would sail on 8 September. The third and largest, led by the king in person, would set off on 30 September.[1] If all had gone ahead as planned, the English would have hit the French in Gascony with three successive waves of attack in the space of a mere nine weeks. The cumulative weight of this assault combined with the efforts of his allies to the north (though without Guy, detained at the Louvre) may well have proved decisive.

Unfortunately for Edward, he was obliged to divert most of his army to crush the revolt of Madog ap Llywelyn in Wales. Yet the first expedition under St John and Brittany had already sailed and could not be recalled. The success of this force in Gascony, given they were only supposed to be the vanguard, hints at what might have been achieved.

The first fleet sailed from Portsmouth on 17 August. It was led by John of Brittany as King's Lieutenant, John de St John as Seneschal of Gascony and 'that most gallant soldier, William Latimer'. They were armed with letters from Edward, apologising to the Gascons for having surrendered the duchy without consulting them, promising early help and calling on them to rally for the defence of his rights. They almost immediately encountered storms and were driven into Plymouth harbour, not to set off again until the second week of October.[2]

The size of Brittany and St John's army is difficult to determine. Guisborough gives a figure of 500 cavalry and 20,000 infantry, which is scarcely credible for just one division of the army.[3] One account shows a total of 1,537 horses assembled at Portsmouth, waiting for shipment to Gascony.[4] Unfortunately complete payroll accounts do not survive for the expedition, though the number of men-at-arms has been calculated from existing protection lists. These reveal a total of 301 bannerets and troopers accompanied the first expedition. This figure may be compared with English chronicles, which record variously 500 or 7,000 men-at-arms.[5] The number of infantry is unknown, though they included a group of Bayonnais mariners led by Pascal de Viele.[6]

Information for the French military preparations is equally sketchy. In March 1294 the inhabitants of Narbonne, who had previously asked for a delay in military service, refused to pay for the campaign in Gascony. Otherwise Philip recruited nobles to fight against Edward's allies in the north. These included Philippe de Vienne, lord of Penguy in Burgundy, who promised to serve in August 1294 with forty men-at-arms. Robert II, Count of Artois, had placed the castle and garrison in a state of defence between August and December 1293. Apart from the normal wages of the garrison, there were additional costs for saltfish, shield, lances, helmets, crossbow bolts and other items of equipment.[7]

The English fleet finally got underway again from Plymouth about 10 October. On the way down the French coast they ravaged the islands of 'Huys' (possibly L'Isle Dieu) and Rhé near La Rochelle, burning several villages.[8] Afterwards they recovered possession of Oléron, a large island off the north-east coast of Gascony. According to Guisborough, they were received 'with much rejoicing' by the lord of the Chateau d'Oléron, who yielded himself up to them and the King of England.[9] Another chronicle, however, says the English were only able to recover the island with difficulty.[10]

Brittany and St John entered the mouth of the River Gironde by the end of the month. Over the next few weeks they were able to move at relative speed, thanks to their exploitation of navigable rivers and waterways.[11] This in turn enabled them to outmanoeuvre the French, who never knew where the fleet might appear next. Their aim was to recapture, in turn, every strategically important fortified town which controlled the northern approaches to the duchy: 'The Gironde provided a natural waterway into the heart of Guienne [Gascony] via the Dordogne into Périgord, or up the Garonne into the Agenais, Quercy and Bazadais. It was therefore the obvious invasion route.'[12]

The prime objective was the recapture of Bordeaux, the 'metropolis of the duchy, the military key to victory, the political and administrative capital whose possession gave also an overwhelming prestige to its possessor'.[13] These were the dominant themes of English strategy for the remainder of the war.

Brittany and St John benefited from the general support of the populace, who resented the French occupation. They quickly retook the castle and town of Macau, surrendered to them by the citizens on the Vigil of All Saints (31 October).[14]

On the following day the English appeared before the walls of Bourg-sur-Mer, one of the main Plantagenet outposts in northern Gascony. The town was held against them by a garrison of Picards. When the citizens attempted to surrender the town, these men sallied out and slew a great number of them. The citizens sent word to the English, pleading for aid, and the Picards were driven back into the castle. This enabled the English to take possession of the town.

When morning came, the Picards asked for a truce and permission to send word to the French at Bordeaux. If no help came they offered to surrender. The Constable of Bordeaux and the Marshal of France replied they could send no immediate help, but ordered the Picards to defend themselves boldly. They promptly surrendered and were allowed to march away in peace.[15]

The English remained at Bourg for eight days before moving on to the twin town of Blaye, two leagues away. There the garrison again sought and obtained a truce, and were permitted to depart when no help arrived. Doubtless the English celebrated their success with some of the ample supplies discovered in the town, including 2,500 casks of wine. Roger Mortimer and Richard Boys were left in charge of the twin towns along with many 'people of the land' – native Gascons – while the fleet sailed on to attack Bordeaux.[16]

If the English had recaptured Bordeaux, the French occupation of Gascony might have unravelled in short order. Unfortunately the English didn't have the numbers or the siege engines to attempt a direct assault, and unlike elsewhere the citizens didn't rise in their support. This was probably because Philip had taken hostage 153 of the most anglophile inhabitants in March.[17] Twenty-nine of them died in prison, which can have done little to endear the Gascons to the French regime.[18]

After a desultory exchange of missiles, the English gave up and sailed further upriver to Rions. Here the lord of the place surrendered the town and castle to them, and they were able to take their horses ashore after seventeen weeks at sea.[19] The castles of Podensac and Villeneuve surrendered at about the same time.[20] When the army had rested, it was split into two parts. John of Brittany and William Latimer stayed at Rions to secure their position, while John de St John went south to try and recover Bayonne.[21]

The situation at Bayonne was complex. Prior to the war it had been a faction-ridden city, similar to the feud between the Colom and Soler at Bordeaux. When the French occupied Gascony the aristocratic party in Bayonne, led by the de Manx family, forged an alliance with the invaders. This forced their rivals, the leaders of the 'popular' party made up of shipmasters, craftsmen and mariners, to flee into exile in England. These men, led by Pascal de Viele, had been implicated in the attack on La Rochelle in May 1293. After months of exile, they accompanied St John in his effort to recover Bayonne.[22]

When the Anglo-Gascons approached Bayonne, the citizens immediately rose against their occupiers and shut them up in the castle, 'for they hated them, because they abused the power which had been wrongly committed to them'. They also had fond memories of St John from his time as Seneschal of Gascony.[23] On 1 January 1295 the citizens yielded up the city and told St John not to trouble himself further, since they would take care of the French.[24] English and Bayonnais ships succeeded in blockading the estuary and captured two large French galleys, which were immediately requisitioned.[25]

After holding out for a few days, the French and their partisans surrendered. As at Macau and Bourg, the garrison was permitted to leave unharmed.[26] Most of the leaders of the aristocratic party of Bayonne fled the town, and those who remained suffered loss of property and imprisonment for their support of the French. The 'popular' party led by Pascal de Vielle had triumphed, and were soon rewarded by King Edward. Pascal was made mayor, provost and castellan of Bayonne for the duration of the war, and he and others involved in the attack on La Rochelle promised protection from French lawsuits in relation to this.[27]

The recapture of Bayonne was the single most important English achievement of the war. After the loss of Bordeaux, they now had an alternative capital, and a reserve operational base from which to launch attacks on French-held territory. It was the one major ducal bastion Philip's armies were never able to threaten again, and so thwarted his ambitions to conquer the entire duchy.[28]

The campaign was not quite over. From Bayonne St John advanced further south, to the edge of the Pyrenees, and retook a town given as St Jean de Sordes (possibly St Jean de Luiz in the Basses Pyrenees). A number of other towns and villages surrendered to the English, and a multitude of Gascon gentry rallied to St John's banner.[29] There his progress was halted. The Viscountess of Béarn, Constance, widow of Henry of Almaine and daughter of Gaston de Béarn, was willing to receive the English, but the people of Béarn refused to admit them.[30] This was probably due to the influence of her brother-in-law, Roger-Bernard, Count of Foix, who had gone over to the French.[31]

Despite the setbacks at Bordeaux and Béarn, the expedition had achieved remarkable success. Brittany and St John managed to recover the port of Bayonne and the Chalosse hinterland, as well as Bourg and Blaye in the north and most of the towns along the upper Gironde.[32] The French seem to have been caught ill prepared, and were unable to cope with English exploitation of the waterways.

Edward took the opportunity to secure these gains. In early 1295 he granted the castles of Louvigny, Montgaillard, St Loubouer and Hagetmau to Fortaner de Lescun, a Gascon nobleman. These castles had been surrendered to the French when they overran the duchy, but were now back in English hands. The grant to Fortaner was made at the expense of his brother-in-law, Arnaud-Guillaume de Marsan. In the absence of his father, taken hostage by the French, Arnaud-Guillaume was the acting head of the Gaveston family.[33] His younger brother was a certain Piers, who would achieve notoriety as the favourite of Edward II.

If Edward had sailed for Gascony in the early months of 1295, before the French could organise a counter-attack, there is every reason to suppose he would have quickly recovered his inheritance. This was the great missed opportunity of the war. If Brittany and St John could do so much with a small force, what might the entire feudal host of England led by the king in person have achieved? Edward had planned to bring his full military power against the scattered French garrisons in the duchy: 'An impressive galaxy of English, Irish and Scottish earls and barons marshalled in a flexible host of some two thousand cavalry comprising the flower of the knights and squires or men-at-arms (*armigeri*) who had lands in their shires of the annual value of £20 or more.'[34]

Unfortunately for him, and English prospects in Gascony, the king was still mired in Wales. The revolt of Madog ap Llywelyn had proved far more serious than expected, and Edward was obliged to spend the winter months at Conwy in north Wales, patiently building up troops and supplies for an offensive in the spring. He was even besieged there for a time by the Welsh, until reinforcements were able to get over the swollen River Conwy and break the siege lines.[35] Until Madog and his allies were defeated, there could be no question of diverting resources to Gascony.

Nor was there much hope of assistance from Edward's allies in northern Europe. Two of them, Count Guy of Flanders and Count Floris of Holland, had gone to war after Floris invaded the Flemish territory of Zeeland in early 1295. Edward hurriedly persuaded the rivals to make peace, and sweetened Guy with a repayment of money owed by the Count of Guelders. The English king used harsher methods to retain the support of the Flemish towns. He prohibited the sale of English wool to the bourgeois, crippling their industry and forcing them to take his part. This was a repeat of the successful strategy he had used against the Countess of Flanders over twenty years previously.[36]

While all these wars raged in Gascony, Wales and Flanders, yet another was brewing in the Holy Roman Empire. Adolf of Nassau, King of the Germans and another of Edward's allies, wished to expand his power base. He had only been elected king because he was territorially weak, and thus posed no threat to the princes of the empire. He was further weakened by the exorbitant demands of the Electors, who demanded lands and money from Adolf as the price of his election. In 1293 he added to his debts by purchasing Thuringia, in east-central Germany, from the Margrave Albert the Entarteter (the Degenerate).[37]

The margrave's disinherited sons, Frederick and Diezmann, rose in arms to defend their rights. This prompted Adolf to launch an invasion of Thuringia and adjoining lands. Prior to the invasion, he was so chronically short of funds he had to pledge land in lieu of his debts: for instance, Adolf pledged the imperial cities of Mühlhausen and Nordhausen to compensate Albrecht 4,000 marks owed as part of the purchase of Thuringia.[38]

The invasion of Thuringia began in the second half of October 1294. While his campaign was in progress, Adolf received the first two of three subsidy payments from the English. Between 22 July and 10 October the Exchequer was instructed to pay Robert de Segre, the English representative at Dordrecht, the sum of £20,000, promised to the German king as a subsidy to fight the French. Another £20,000 was paid over shortly before Christmas.[39]

Contemporary German chroniclers believed that Adolf used these enormous sums of money for wrongful purposes. Ellenhard, the commissioner of a historical codex of the Holy Roman Empire and Strasbourg, accused Adolf of keeping the money to himself instead of distributing it among his nobles; hence they refused to help him support the English. A slightly later chronicler, Mattias of Nuremburg (b. 1295), complained that Adolf did not use the money to purchase armaments but to buy Meissen.[40] The view that Adolf misused English money for his own ends is echoed in more recent German historiography.[41]

Adolf's actions after the campaign only reinforce this impression. He somehow found the money to attract additional partisans. For example, Count Johann von Sponheim was paid a thousand pounds (*pfund heller* in German currency) for his 'welcome services'. Lord Albrecht von

Barby was paid 300 marks.[42] This was all distributed from the largesse of a king who, prior to the receipt of English money, had been forced to borrow 100 marks from local Jews to pay one of his allies.[43]

The German king was certainly not shy of admitting what he had done. On 24 January 1295 he wrote to Edward, announcing the successful conclusion of his campaign:

> Adolf, by the grace of God king of the Romans, forever august, offers greeting and the continuing increase of our alliance and friendship to his most dear friend, the renowned lord Edward, august king of England.
>
> Since an account of our good fortune may please you well, see now how we may bring joy to you, because, in entire fulfilment of our vows, and by the strength of the victorious army which we recently created, with the Lord of Hosts our helper, we have added the provinces of Thuringia, Osterland and Meissen to our dominion and empire; the prince-electors, barons, nobles, citizens and commoners have come under our command, and, both in those lands and also in Saxony, we have ourself caused a general peace to be sworn. Now, however, with all things favourably concluded, we have returned rejoicing to the Rhineland.[44]

Adolf went on to inform Edward that he had summoned a parliament at Frankfurt to discuss matters 'regarding your and our work in building an army to go against the king of France'. Hence Edward was requested to send envoys to the parliament to discuss this business. What Adolf's 'most dear friend' made of the use of his money for a war in Germany is unknown.

The alliance against Philip IV had so far proved a complete misfire. Thanks to the revolt in Wales, Edward was unable to sail to Gascony as initially planned. His allies in northern Europe were either fighting each other or using his money for their own ends. Meanwhile his men in the south-west were left isolated against the inevitable French counter-attack.

Edward's captains in the duchy had only a short time to brace themselves. In early spring 1295, Charles of Valois brought the French field army into Gascony.

12

IN BATTLE ARRAY WITH LANCES

Charles and his constable, Ralph de Nesle, arrived in the duchy in March. Their task was to reconquer Gascony and erase the English gains of the previous summer and autumn. The size of Charles's army is again largely a matter of conjecture. The Lanercost chronicle claims he brought '6000 horse and innumerable foot', which reads like guesswork.[1] It is known that Toulouse, in south-east France adjoining Gascony, received supplies of 2,000 crossbows, 300 gorgets and 3,000 bascinets, probably for foot soldiers, at about this time. This equipment was intended for the French naval forces gathering in the Norman ports as well as Charles's expedition to Gascony.[2] Guisborough, rather unhelpfully states that the French brought 'many thousand horse and a large army'.[3]

To fund the expedition, Philip chose to debase the French currency. This was the first of a series of debasements to which he was forced to resort since France did not have the same tradition of direct and indirect taxation as other kingdoms. As his military expenditure increased, debasement became a key source of income for Philip. This led to a short-term flow of funds, but in the long term his policy devalued French coin at an unprecedented rate. Within a few years (as we shall see) the effect would have a severe impact on Philip's capacity to wage war.[4]

Whatever the precise size of the French host, it was too large for the Anglo-Gascons to challenge in the field. Instead they focused on defending the towns along the upper Gironde. Charles concentrated his efforts on the reduction of Rions and Podensac, 25 miles south-east of Bordeaux and on either side of the river. What followed was a truly shameful episode in English military history.

The castle of Podensac was defended by John Giffard. When Ralph de Nesle came up to Podensac with part of the French army, Giffard offered to surrender if he and his English troops were allowed to depart. In exchange the French might do as they pleased with the Gascons. This was agreed, and Giffard abandoned his post. De Nesle took sixty Gascon prisoners back to Charles at La Réole, where they were hanged on a gallows on Easter Thursday.[5]

After taking Podensac, the French crossed the river to attack Rions. They appeared before the gates on Palm Sunday, 'not in procession with branches of palm but in battle array with lances'.[6] The English attempted a sortie, but were driven back by the larger French force 'like sheep into a sheepfold'.[7] This futile attempt was apparently made on the advice of a mysterious old man.[8] After a siege of eleven days, the English captains decided they could not hold out and it was best to abandon the town. Under cover of night, they would retreat by boat and sail along the riverbank to the safety of Bourg and Blaye.[9]

Disaster struck on the eve of their departure. Following his craven surrender of Podensac, John Giffard had fled to Rions and been placed in custody. This was done to calm the Gascons, who wanted revenge on him for their hanged comrades. The marshal of the army, Ralph Gorges, proposed to put Giffard on trial. His decisions only inflamed the English soldiers, who had drunk too much wine and were in a bellicose mood. They warned Ralph that they would not allow justice to be done on Giffard. A fight broke out, one soldier was killed, and a full-scale riot was in progress when the French suddenly attacked.[10]

Panic swept through the ranks. The English horsemen fled to the boats, only to be blocked by the infantry, who realised they were being deserted. Many English knights were forced to take refuge in the castle. John of Brittany managed to get away, but his foot soldiers were slaughtered. Those knights inside the castle were soon forced to surrender, and twelve taken prisoner along with a number of men-at-arms.[11] One English knight, Adam de Creting, was killed.[12]

These disasters were partially redeemed by the actions of John de St John and Hugh de Vere in the south. In early April they advanced from Bayonne and attacked St-Sever, a fortified town some 60 miles to the north-east. The town fell to them on the 7th, after the citizens surrendered and the French garrison was allowed to leave on terms.[13] By an odd coincidence, this was the same day as the fall of Rions.

After his triumphs at Rions and Podensac, Charles of Valois marched south to reclaim St-Sever. It was defended by Hugh de Vere with 200 men-at-arms and a number of foot. His commander, St John, had withdrawn to Bayonne.[14] De Vere put up a much sterner fight than his colleagues in the north. The ensuing siege lasted thirteen hellish weeks, in which the French died in droves: 'The Frenchmen died by thousands, like pigs, on account of the use of arms and the excessive heat. Charles had them buried in a new cemetery which he made on the field and caused to be consecrated by some bishops who were in his company.'[15]

Guisborough's excitable account of French casualties is tempered somewhat by other sources, though it is clear Charles's men suffered heavily.[16] One English man-at-arms, Stephen FitzWalter, is recorded to have died in the siege.[17]

At last, with supplies running out, de Vere offered to surrender if the French promised not to harm the town or its inhabitants. This was agreed, and he marched away to Bayonne. After installing a strong garrison inside St-Sever, Charles took the shattered remnant of his army back to France. Once he was gone, the citizens drove out his men and invited the English back in. Within a few days of its surrender in late July, the Angevin banner once again flew from the battlements. All of Charles's efforts – and the loss of so many soldiers – were in vain.[18] The treacherous inhabitants, raged the French chronicler, had failed in their allegiance to the King of France.[19] This was perhaps not an opinion that many Gascons would have shared.

The siege of St-Sever was the last action of the summer campaign in Gascony. At the end of it, the English still held Bourg and Blaye in the north, and Bayonne and St-Sever in the south. Lesser strongholds in English hands included St Jean de Sordes, St-Quiterie, Bellegarde, Peyrehorade, Sault and Rochefort.[20] Much of the rest of the duchy was in French hands. Charles had achieved a partial success, but until the English enclaves were overcome his conquest of Gascony was incomplete.

Another man who distinguished himself at St-Sever was Arnaud-Guillaume de Marsan, eldest brother of Piers Gaveston. King Edward sent him a fulsome letter of praise:

> The King to his well-beloved and loyal servant, the noble Arnaud, squire of William de Marciano, with sincere affection, greetings. As a result of the excellent service which your father, the noble lord Arnaud de Gaveston, and you have thus far provided us and continue unceasingly so to do, we can feel nothing but praise for the loyalty and love which you have borne and still bear towards us. You should know then that it is with pleasure that we have received your letter, from which we understood what was very clearly known to us before; to wit, how you, when your aforesaid father was seized and held, did firmly hold to us and devoted yourself passionately to our service; indeed, in defence of our right, you marched to Saint Sever with an honourable company of men-at-arms, defended that place boldly, and, manfully opposing our enemies, endured many perils, losses and costs in your continuing allegiance to us.[21]

Arnaud had probably sent a letter to the king as a reminder of his family's good service and subsequent lack of reward. Perhaps it was also meant to highlight Edward's questionable judgement. In early 1295 he chose to disregard Arnaud's claim to the castles of Louvigny, Montgaillard, St-Loubouer and Hagetmau, and instead grant them to his brother-in-law, Fortaner de Lescun. These were all in the region of St-Sever, and when Charles of Valois took the town in July he also came into possession of the castles. He granted them to Roger-Bernard, Count of Foix, who in turn regranted them to Fortaner.[22]

It appears that Fortaner had repaid Edward's generosity by defecting to the French. Arnaud was compensated by being made custos (keeper) of the castles of Sault and Rochefort, which he held with five men-at-arms and fifty foot.[23] Edward took further steps to ensure his loyalty by paying Arnaud one-half the annual value of his lost castles, 200 *livres chipotois* (£40 sterling).[24]

The defection of Fortaner de Lescun opens up the wider question of conflicting loyalties. One of Edward's first acts was to secure the support of the Gascon nobility. On 29 June 1294 he addressed a circular letter to the lords of Gascony, calling upon their loyalty in the recovery and defence of the duchy, snatched from him by the French. A list of about 100 nobles was drawn up, bound by homage and fealty to serve Edward against Philip IV.[25]

By the autumn of 1295, at least twenty of these nobles had defected to the French, thanks to the effect of the occupation and the associated bribery and coercion. Most of these defections were concentrated in the Agenais, which may be significant. Edward had only acquired this region in 1279, via the Treaty of Amiens, and the inhabitants might have felt their true loyalties lay with Philip. On 19 October Edward wrote to those who had deserted him. He appealed to the honour of the recipients and reminded them he was their 'natural lord', to no obvious effect.[26]

Of major concern to Edward was the wavering loyalty of the counts of Armagnac and Foix. These were two of the most powerful families in southern Gascony. At the start of the war Bernard VI, Count of Armagnac was an English partisan: in January 1294, for example, he received £200 from Bordeaux's seneschal as a wage payment. In October, however, he was one of the recipients of Edward's desperate plea for loyalty. The others included Roger-Bernard, Count of Foix and Constance, the aged Viscountess of Marsan and daughter of Gaston de Béarn.[27]

Edward's aggressive policy towards these families now came back to haunt him. At first Constance supported the English, but she changed her mind and allowed the French to occupy her town of Mont-de-Marsan. In return she was given a furred gown and hood by Robert d'Artois.[28] Evidently old resentments died hard, and she had not forgotten Edward's treatment of her father or her diseissin of Bigorre. Her brother-in-law, the Count of Foix, defected early to the French and may have prevented the Béarnais from supporting the English in 1294. His willingness to break with Edward was not shared by some of his followers. One of his men, Bernard d'Ortes, informed the king that he and his twelve companions had been exiled from Béarn by the count for fighting against Charles of Valois at St-Sever.[29]

To counter these defections in the south, Edward promoted rival dynasties. He particularly favoured the house of Albret, one of the oldest families of Plantagenet Aquitaine. From poor origins, they had steadily built up significant territories in the north and south of Gascony. Their lands in the south bordered those of Foix-Béarn, held by the French partisan, Count Roger-Bernard. The head of the Albret, Amanieu VII, was a frequent beneficiary of grants from Edward, and he and his affinity served the king loyally in Gascony and Scotland. He was mentioned in *The Song of Caerlaverock*, a praise poem composed by a royal herald for Edward's Scottish campaign in 1300.[30]

Edward's decision to favour Amanieu was vindicated, and helped to remedy his mistakes elsewhere. The house of Albret enjoyed wide influence. Their list of vassals included the Sescas family of Bayonne, and Barrau de Sescas was reported to be the 'man' of Amanieu VII in letters to Edward I.[31] In 1295 Edward and John of Brittany appointed Barrau as 'captain and admiral' of the combined maritime resources of England and Aquitaine, described as one of their wisest acts.[32] Albret influence also helped to cement the uncertain loyalty of the house of Armagnac. Count Bernard of Armagnac had taken Isabelle d'Albret for his first wife, and Amanieu's eldest son married the count's daughter.

Whatever pressures were applied on them by the kings of France and England, the great houses of the south put their own interests first. This is especially true of Roger-Bernard, the Count of Foix. In 1295 he chose to accept the lieutenancy offered to him by King Philip, not out of any great love for the French but rather a desire to dominate the south-west below Bordeaux. He exploited his new position to the hilt and in 1297 claimed he was owed over 50,000 *livres tournois* in unpaid wages by the French crown. The French in return were suspicious of his greed and ambition. In 1300 Philip's proctors, headed by the ubiquitous Pierre Flote, accused the count of intriguing with the anti-Capetian Bishop of Pamiers. The bishop, it was alleged, had offered to make Roger-Bernard lord of Toulouse, so 'his power would be feared from Bordeaux to the Pyrenees'. These charges were denied, but their mere existence implies Philip distrusted his expensive ally.[33]

Much depended on the loyalties of the Gascon nobility. They in turn were perfectly aware of this, especially the great houses, and could sell their services to the highest bidder. Other Gascons who served on the French side included Jordram Bertram, the lord of Aspremont, Bernard de Durfort, Jordan de Lisle, Dieudit de Montlaur, Raymond de Villeneuve, Sicard de Lordat, Pierre-Raymond de de Rabastens, Otho de Monthaut, Izarn de La Graulet and Arnold-Raymond, Count of Tartas, the Count of Périgord and Bérenger de Thezan.[34]

Against these can be ranged those Gascon nobles who supported the English cause. At least eighteen nobles of the south – the Landes, Chalosse, Marsan, Béarn, Sault and Labourd – mustered for the king-duke at Hagetmau and Roquefort in December 1294. Between March 1297 and March 1298, no fewer than ninety Gascon nobles received wages from Edward's clerks.[35] The number of Gascons who chose exile in England eventually swelled to more than 500. In July 1297, men of the towns of St-Sever, Oléron, St Jean de Sordes, Sauveterre, Bourg, St-Quiterie, Bordeaux and Blaye were noted as resident in London.[36]

Thus, with some notable exceptions, the majority of the Gascon nobility chose to support the Plantagenet regime. There were several motives for their loyalty. Edward I and his father, Henry III, had made considerable concessions to the lesser and middling gentry. Between 1254 and 1307 they deliberately alienated most of their assets in the duchy, with the exception of twenty castles and the profits of the wine trade at Bordeaux. The rest, encompassing more than a hundred castles and towns, were granted to the gentry. This was the price of securing their allegiance.[37] The cost was high, but the policy of alienation proved its worth when most of these men held true to the English claim. This loyalty endured across the generations: a list of supporters of the English regime in the mid-fourteenth century, decades later, contains the names of many families loyal to Edward I.[38]

Pope Boniface VIII, when he met with Pierre Flote and other French envoys in 1299, had this to say of Gascony:

> We will tell you another thing. The Gascons would not wish at all to be under the sovereignty of the king of France without the mesne lordship of the king of England. It could well be, perchance, that some through some singular disposition might wish it, but I am speaking to you of the people generally. For such is the way of subjects; they wish to have several lords, so they cannot be greatly oppressed by one.[39]

Boniface evidently took a somewhat cynical view, claiming the Gascons preferred to live under two kings so neither could oppress them. Therefore Philip IV's preferred style of direct overlordship was not to their taste. The Gascon nobility certainly had a multitude of tenurial obligations, and the most powerful, such as the Count of Foix, were virtually ungovernable.[40]

Edward was well aware of the unpredictable nature of the Gascons. In 1278 he had described them as changeable and full of 'cavill', i.e. trivial or uncertain. To retain a hold upon their allegiance, against French bribery and coercion, was no easy task. In 1297 Piers Gaveston's father, Arnaud, told the king that if he wished to persuade any of Arnaud's friends and relatives back to English service (they had evidently defected to the French), he would have to offer them material reward. Edward replied they would be paid wages and rewards according to their status. Arnaud's advice proved sound, as the men in question re-entered English service on 6 May.[41]

The material incentives Edward offered to the Gascons have been defined under six main headings: wages for military service; *restaur* (compensation) for horses lost during that service; pensions and fees; prests (advance wages) for military equipment; plunder and booty; and compensation for the loss of lands, lordships and goods.[42] During these years the Exchequer at Westminster frequently paid out prests, wages and *restaur* to Gascon nobles, who thus had an additional incentive to serve Edward in Scotland.[43] Although payment was often fitful and dilatory, thanks to the parlous state of his finances, the king did his best to see the Gascons got their due. On 16 October 1297 he wrote from Ghent in Flanders of his debts to the men of Bayonne, informing the treasurer and barons of the Exchequer: 'We wish that you should always have such concern for the needs of Gascony that our men who are there shall be relieved and aided as far as possible in the best manner ... For our honour or dishonour lies in this business, and that of all those who love us, and especially those responsible for our affairs in the places where you are at present.'[44]

Many of the Gascons served Edward because they had nothing left to lose. They lost their lands and goods as a result of the French occupation, which left the king with the task of compensating them. This was an added burden to his already strained finances, but from 1299 a series of grants were made based on a valuation of lost lands and tenements.[45] Others were taken into the king's household and enjoyed the additional income of a fee or pension.[46]

Finally there is Edward's personal reputation to consider, and his relationship with the Gascon gentry. More than any other king of his dynasty, Edward paid close attention to the duchy: 'Edward I, both as prince and king, was responsible for the shape of English rule in Gascony. For the first time since Richard the Lionheart a century before, Aquitaine had as duke an English king who knew Gascony well and spent sufficient time there to understand the people and customs of that turbulent land. Edward has often been called the English Justinian, but until recently both French and English historians tended to overlook his remarkable organizational work in the duchy.'[47]

The king knew this 'turbulent land' well. As we have seen, he gained his first experience in war and politics in Gascony at the age of fifteen. He spent three consecutive years of his reign (1286–89) in the duchy, sharpening and reorganising the administration. The Gascons in turn knew Edward well, and may have been impressed by his chivalric reputation. At times they benefited from his liberality. On Easter Day 1287, for instance, Edward knighted Auger, son of the lord Meilhan, at Bordeaux. Auger would later serve the king as sub-seneschal of the Agenais and household knight. In the same year Edward gave two pieces of cloth of gold for the funeral of Guitard de Bourg, an ex-mayor of Bordeaux who had served the king in Wales. There were other, smaller instances of generosity, such as the 8 shillings he paid to the minstrel of Arnaud-Sanche, lord of Tardets.[48]

Edward also showed pity to those Gascons who fled to England. One such was Bernard de Panissau, a knight who had previously served as bailiff of Monpazier and Molières.[49] Described by Bémont as a 'minor and rather pathetic figure', Bernard claimed to have mustered 4,000 sergeants in Edward's service at Roquepine, Molières, Lalinde and Monpazier. After being taken prisoner by the French, he escaped with his family and brought them to England. In May 1297 he begged the king-duke to grant a position to one of his sons, an unbeneficed clerk. Edward declared himself 'well content' with Bernard's service over the past thirty years, and waived the need for proof of his claims. He was provided with compensation for his losses and eventually regranted the bailiwick of Molières until he could recover his lands. Even then, the war had left Bernard so impoverished he would have sunk into destitution without an extra royal grant of 50 *livres tournois*. This sorely tried individual vanished from the record in 1308.[50]

Edward's success in retaining the allegiance of most of the Gascon nobility was crucial to the survival of the Plantagenet regime. Without them, the defence and recovery of the duchy was impossible. This is shown by the wages bill for Gascon knights, men-at-arms and sergeants, which exceeded that of the English by over £100,000.[51]

Yet the war could not be won in Gascony. For Edward, the war in the south-west was a holding operation while he assembled his grand coalition in the north. For Philip, the conquest of Gascony was merely one part of his expansionist vision of a greater France. As military operations in the duchy ground into stalemate, both parties looked to widen the conflict.

13

LINGUAM ANGLICANAM

In mid-1295 it seemed the time had come for Edward's great offensive in northern Europe. The revolt in Wales was quelled, his men in Gascony had clung on against Charles of Valois, and King Adolf of Germany had apparently completed his conquest of Thuringia and was now released from internal commitments to link up with Edward against the French.

Edward had carried on making preparations even while the Welsh revolt was in progress. To compensate for the loss of Flanders as an ally, he focused on building alliances with other princes of the Netherlands. On 6 April, at Conwy, he received Count Rainald of Guelders and purchased his military services against the French, on the same six-month commitment as other allies.[1] Later, on 28 April, Edward met his son-in-law John II, Duke of Brabant, at Llanfaes on Anglesey and secured his services as well. This would have long-term consequences for the coalition, since Edward agreed to switch part of the English wool trade from Holland to Brabant. His decision was at the expense of Count Floris of Holland, who had hoped to make his town of Dordrecht the centre of the trade. A large consignment of English wool was sent there, but in August 1295 Edward ordered English merchants to forsake Dordrecht for Malines in Brabant, and then Antwerp. It is probably no coincidence that Floris started to consider forsaking the English alliance at about the same time.[2]

Philip had no intention of allowing his enemies to seize the advantage. In the summer he opened talks with the Scots, who objected to Edward's aggressive enforcement of his lordship in Scotland. In 1294 he had summoned John Balliol and eighteen Scottish magnates to perform feudal service against the French, but the Welsh rebellion meant the muster never took place. Edward's demand was very different from previous military service the Scots had done for him in Wales, which had been for the lands they held in England. After the coronation of Balliol in 1292, as Edward's vassal, the king tried to enforce direct control over Scotland in a way that the magnates found unacceptable.[3]

The Scots were an ideal weapon to use against Edward to prevent the threat of an Anglo-German union. On 5 July an embassy left Scotland to treat with Philip in Paris. Long before the Franco-Scots treaty was ratified on 23 October, Edward was made aware of the danger and took steps to counter it. He welcomed the offer of mediation from Pope Boniface VIII, who wished to avert war in the west to enlist French co-operation in the ongoing struggle to restore Sicily to Angevin rule. On 14 August Edward agreed to a truce to last until 1 November. This was done without consulting Adolf, but on the same day Edward sent envoys to Germany to explain to his ally what had been done. To avoid isolation, Adolf had little choice but to agree to the truce.[4]

Edward's plans to launch his campaign in Europe were delayed a second time. He dared not go overseas while his northern borders were at risk, and there was an extra threat in the shape of King Eric II of Norway. The Franco-Scots alliance was in fact a three-way treaty between France, Scotland and Norway, in which John Balliol was described as a third party after Philip and Eric.[5] Under the terms, Eric agreed to supply the French with 200 helmets and 100 great ships as well as 50,000 fighting men, as long as the war should last against England and Germany. In exchange Philip would pay him £50,000 sterling. The French king, then, was buying allies in exactly the manner as his rival in England.[6] It would appear he was also attempting to copy Edward's strategy of encirclement: 'The French encircling alliance with Norway and Scotland seems an obvious counterpart of Edward I's encircling alliances with Germany, Spain and the Low Countries.'[7]

In the event the Norwegians fulfilled none of their promises, since Philip only sent 6,000 marks of the promised fee. It is likely that Edward later bribed the Norwegians into neutrality, and doubts have been cast upon Eric's capacity to raise such an enormous number of troops.[8]

In the midst of his difficulties, Edward received some welcome support from Castile. His brother-in-law Henry of Castile had not forgotten the English king's efforts to rescue him from an Angevin prison. When he returned home after his long captivity, Henry became regent during the minority of his grandnephew Ferdinand IV. As such he was in a position to help Edward, and in August 1295 offered to send Castilian knights across the Pyrenees to attack the French in Gascony. Edward's response was suitably grateful:

> To Henry son of the late king of Castile, the king's brother-in-law. His letters have reached the king, to his great joy. The king specially thanks him for the great and powerful aid offered by him, to wit to send five hundred, a thousand, or two thousand knights of the realm of Castile to Gascony to the king's aid at his pleasure, as contained in the said letters. The king assures himself that his brother-in-law, mindful of bond of relationship and of ancient gratitude, will always do with promptitude the things that concern the increase of the king's honour and convenience.[9]

As the letter implies, the actual number of knights sent to aid the English is uncertain. A later account of outstanding wages for soldiers in the Anglo-French war refers to knights of Spain, Aragon, Catalonia and Navarre in English service. It is impossible to judge how many armed horsemen came from which region, but the total payment of over £137,000 suggests a considerable number of barons and knights of Spain fought in Gascony on Edward's behalf.[10]

Philip now unleashed the fleet he had been patiently constructing in Normandy since 1292. In August the French landed at Dover, set the town on fire, raided the priory and killed several monks. The raid ended in disaster for the French, as most of their sailors were caught and beheaded by local militia.[11] Even so, it raised fears of a full-scale invasion. At the same time the fleet of Yarmouth was ravaging the coast of Normandy, and sacked the town and abbey of Cherbourg.[12]

Fresh from his reconquest of Wales, Edward had to rush down to the south coast and oversee preparations for defence. He ordered the removal of all foreign clerks from the seacoast and from access to navigable waterways near the coast.[13] On 28 August he appointed keepers of the seacoasts, telling them to be active, to be strong, and to exercise caution in guarding their areas from the danger hanging over them.[14] The keeper of Hampshire was Adam Gurdon, an elderly knight who had fought a personal duel with Edward in their youth. Now the king looked to his old foe to guard the coastline of Hampshire against the French.[15]

So much for the truce, which was supposed to hold from 14 August to 1 November. The day after Edward started to organise his defences, another French fleet threatened Winchelsea. It was intercepted by the Yarmouth fleet, on its return journey from plundering Cherbourg, and driven away. Meanwhile a French galley ran aground near Hythe. The crew was slaughtered by the coastguard, 'like sheep in a fold', and their headless bodies thrown into the sea.[16]

The French raids had proved ineffective, but the English stepped up their defensive plans. In an atmosphere similar to the Nazi invasion scare of August 1940, troops were placed on high alert from Hampshire to East Anglia. Edward had already ordered the building of thirty galleys, each with 120 oars, and taken merchant ships into his service. Each section of the coast was guarded by a separate squadron of ships, while elaborate plans were laid for the recruitment and organisation of forces on land. Local militia were raised to act as a first line of defence, with a second line of knights and men-at-arms. The Isle of Wight was garrisoned by seventy-six cavalrymen.[17]

Fear of invasion and occupation played on English minds, and caused the war to take on the aspect of a national struggle. Edward encouraged this impression. On 30 September, from Wingham in Kent, the king issued his clarion call:

> You no doubt know, and it is already spread abroad all through the world, we believe, how the king of France fraudulently and deceitfully tricked us out of our land of Gascony, and wickedly

> detains it from us. Now, not content with the aforesaid deceit and wickedness, he has got together for an attack upon our realm a great fleet and a host of warriors, with which he has already invaded our land and its inhabitants, and proposes, if his force corresponds with the detestable project of iniquity he has conceived, which God forbid, to remove the English tongue from the face of the earth.[18]

Edward's statement that the English language itself was under threat seems a deliberate ploy to bind his subjects in a common cause. To that end the language received a sudden boost in 'national' esteem: in 1295, just two years previously, the prior of St Neots had expelled all those who used the English tongue – *linguam Anglicanam* – from his service.[19] Now, thanks to the king's necessity, English was something to be treasured and protected.

Not all Englishmen rallied around the flag. Thomas Turberville was one of the English knights captured at the fall of Rions in the spring. He agreed to turn traitor and in September went back to England, claiming to have escaped from a French prison. Thomas was kindly received by Edward, but soon afterwards wrote a treasonable letter to the Provost of Paris, to whom he had assigned the custody of his two sons.[20] In his letter, Thomas reported on the weak points of England's defences and the king's dealings with Germany:

> And know that there is little watch kept on the sea-coast towards the South; and know that the Isle of Wycht [*sic*] is without garrison; and know that the King is sending into Almaine two earls, two bishops, and two barons, to speak to, and counsel with, the King of Almaine as to this war...[21]

Turberville also reported he had made contact with one 'Morgan' in Wales, and that the Welsh and Scots were ready to rise against Edward when the French invaded England.[22] Morgan was probably Morgan ap Maredudd, the only Welsh nobleman at this time with the power to raise his countrymen. It may be that Morgan was playing a double game in order to draw Thomas out: he certainly acted as a spy for Edward against the Earl of Hereford in 1297.[23] Thomas was also being watched by William Wither, a royal agent, paid £1 to spy on the traitor in Gloucestershire on 23 September.[24]

In late September Thomas was captured, tried and executed for treason. His betrayal must have shaken Edward, for Thomas had been a member of the *familia regis*, the king's own household, privy to his innermost thoughts.[25] The personal nature of Thomas's crime might explain the gruesome display of his execution. He was laid down on a bull's hide, dragged at the tails of six horses through the streets of London, then beaten and reproached by four masked executioners bearing clubs. After this punishment, he was hanged on a gibbet and left there to rot, so passers-by might say, 'Is this Thomas Turberville?'[26]

Thomas had no sympathy in England. Shortly after his death, an English versifier composed an epitaph for the traitor:

The cruel Thomas Turbeville
Disturbed our peace with wicked will;
He was a spark; but now the king
Has made him ashes, a vile thing.
He joined himself to Satan's crew,
This happy country to undo;
Till stretched upon an ox'es hide,
He found the end of all his pride.
To vex the country he delighted,
Which now his treason has requited.
By justice fair he was overborne,
And righteously by horses torn.
So David's foe, Achitophel,
Perished, and met his meed in hell:
And Thomas, who for bribes did sell
Fair England, is undone as well.[27]

The treason of Thomas Turberville was one of the great scandals of the age. It exposed the fragility of Edward's position, betrayed by one of his own household knights even as England was under threat of invasion. Everywhere he looked, his problems were mounting. The campaign in Wales had drained his coffers, and there was no hope of taking an army to the Continent. After waiting in vain for Edward to arrive, King Adolf led a second campaign into Thuringia. Yet more of Edward's subsidy money was spent on private wars in Germany. This only dissipated resources meant for the French war, and increased Adolf's unpopularity among his countrymen.[28]

Edward adopted a new strategy. Instead of taking a single army to Germany, he planned to lead a campaign against the Scots while sending reinforcements to Gascony, led by Edmund of Lancaster and Henry de Lacy. Some troops had already been sent in July, but in August these plans stalled when a group of magnates, headed by the Earl of Arundel, refused to serve in Gascony. Edward reacted furiously. He ordered the collection of all the debts these men owed to the Crown, and that they be persecuted in every conceivable way. Cowed into obedience, the dissidents agreed to join the expedition.[29]

At the end of 1295, the strain of war was starting to tell. Edward's cash surplus, built up at the start of the decade, had largely been spent on the Welsh revolt and subsidies to his allies.[30] From this point he would have to rely on heavy taxation. His enemy Philip was in a slightly better position, but only due to the short-term benefit of debasing the French currency. This flow of revenue would not be sustained for much longer.

Neither king showed much concern for depleted resources. As 1296 dawned, they prepared to renew the struggle.

14

FAILING MONEY AND SPIRIT

The year got off to a dreadful start for Edward. On 6 January the Count of Holland, Floris V, abandoned the English alliance and joined the French. This was partially out of resentment over the favour Edward had shown to the Duke of Brabant, and partially because of the promise of a fee of 4,000 *livres* for life, together with a lump sum of 25,000 livres.[1] This was yet another diplomatic success for Philip, after his alliance with the Scots and severing of the Anglo-Flemish alliance.

Edward's prospects looked bleak, but he carried on with his plans for a dual campaign in Scotland and Gascony. The situation in Gascony was so urgent he was prepared to send an expedition overseas in the depth of winter, long after the campaigning season was over. It may be that Edward feared the inability of his troops in the duchy to hold on until the spring, or the onset of an early French offensive that would wipe out his scattered garrisons.[2] This was not the first time Edward had risked a winter campaign: he had done so in Wales in 1282–3, when the gamble paid off.

The expedition, led by Edmund of Lancaster and Henry de Lacy, sailed from Plymouth at the start of January. As with the first expeditionary force in 1294, it is possible to reconstruct the size of their force from surviving letters of protection, letters of attorney, quittance of debts and so on. These reveal that 227 men-at-arms accompanied Edmund to Gascony, a significant reduction from the 301 who had accompanied John of Brittany and John de St John. This was also a reduction of almost 50 per cent of the 417 men-at-arms that were supposed to sail with Edmund and Lacy as part of Edward's tripartite expedition in 1294. Due to the strain of military commitments in Wales and Scotland, the planned English involvement in Gascony was almost halved.[3] The number of infantry is unknown, but some Welsh troops were included: on the journey down to Gascony, the Welsh plundered the town of St Mathieu in Brittany.[4]

Edmund followed the same strategy as Brittany and St John. Like them, he focused his efforts on the capture of Bordeaux and re-establishing the northern borders of the duchy. This would cut French communications and reinforcements to the south of the River Gironde. Bourg and Blaye, the twin ducal strongholds in the north, would act as a bridgehead for his campaign. Bayonne and St-Sever, the main bastions in the south, acted as a reserve base where ducal forces could retreat in extremity.

The fleet landed at Blaye in mid-Lent and disembarked their horses at Castillon. They were joined by loyal Gascons, who came flocking to the ducal standard, and elements of the first expedition under Brittany and St John.[5] The first and second expeditions had now melded into a single field army.

Their first move was to cross the river in force and take the castle of Lesparre (22 March) and other castles in Medoc, north-west of Blaye on the left bank of the Gironde.[6] Edmund's capture of Lesparre was significant, since it was among the most important seigneurial fortresses of the region. The keep was possibly damaged when his forces stormed the place, since it was rebuilt by Guillaume-Ayquem, lord of Lesparre, after the war.[7] According to the Westminster chronicler, the town was only surrendered after the defenders were worn out by a siege.[8]

The Anglo-Gascon army then swung south to attack Bordeaux. On 27 March the combined Anglo-Gascon army camped at Bégles, about 2 miles south of the city. The French, supported by loyal Bordelais militia, sallied out to meet them: 'They were in sight of each other, and thirsting for battle. However, our men [the English] waited, and partly retreated, feigning flight, till they were separated by a considerable distance from the city. Then, turning round, they forced them to retreat, killed about 2000 and pursued the others right to the city gates.'[9]

Guisborough's claim of 'about 2000' French casualties is probably an exaggeration, though the feigned retreat is an interesting detail. The initial English success went awry when some of Edmund's knights pursued the enemy through the city gates, which were shut behind them. These men – two English and three Gascons – preferred to die fighting than surrender.[10] Both sides then fired the suburbs, but Edmund's lack of artillery forced him to abandon the siege.[11] Once again the English had failed in their main objective of securing Bordeaux.

Edmund and Lacy marched downriver to attack Langon, where the lord surrendered the town and the French garrison fled at their approach. They remained there three days and sent to St-Macaire, 2 miles to the east, to demand its surrender. The men of the town sought and obtained a three-day truce, during which they sent a message to Bordeaux asking for help. When told no relief force would be sent, they surrendered the town. The French garrison of the castle, commanded by Thibaut de Cheppoix, refused to submit and held out against repeated assaults for three weeks.

King Philip reacted decisively to the arrival of the English. He dispatched his foremost general, Robert d'Artois, with 'a great French army' to raise the siege of St-Macaire and sweep his enemies out of Gascony altogether. Artois was tasked with destroying the English in revenge for their countless outrages.[12] When Artois and his relief force hove into view, Edmund broke off the siege and withdrew.[13] He lost the town soon afterwards thanks to the poor discipline of his troops, who robbed the citizens and ransacked their property. As a consequence the French experienced no difficulty in retaking the place.[14]

While at St-Macaire, Edmund was offered a chance of redemption. Five loyalist burgesses of Bordeaux came to him and promised to surrender the city at dawn two days hence. In return Edmund had to pay them £5,000 of silver and guarantee his troops would spare all who bore the sign of St George. The English rushed back to Bordeaux, only to find the gates closed against them. In the meantime the plot had been discovered, and the five conspirators arrested and hanged.

After the failure of his attempt, and with his men starting to desert for lack of pay, Edmund gave up and retreated to Bayonne.[15]

These setbacks had a shattering effect on Edmund's morale. He was already in poor health. In December 1295, shortly before the expedition set out, he had been temporarily replaced in command by Henry de Lacy. This was on account of sickness, and Edward informed his men in Gascony that his brother was impatient to be well again so that he could join them.[16] Edmund apparently recovered in time to resume command in January, but his fitness is questionable. After the mixed fortunes of his campaign – which was not a complete disaster – he seems to have fallen prey to remorse: 'But when Edmund had collected many paid soldiers, and used much treasure, as a kindly and generous man, since he could not retain so large a host, because he had no wages for it, his face fell and he sickened about Whitsuntide…'[17]

As Lawton points out, it is unlikely that a physically and mentally fit man would have fallen into a state of delusional self-recrimination.[18] On 5 June, haunted by remorse, Edmund 'went the way of all flesh' at Bayonne. He ordered his men to carry his bones with them and never lay him to rest until his debts were paid – an interesting parallel to the tale of his brother, King Edward, ordering his bones to be carried at the head of the English army in Scotland. Edmund's final instruction was disobeyed, and he was conveyed back to England for honourable burial at Westminster.[19]

Edward was deeply affected by his brother's death. He enjoined his churchmen to pray for 'our dearest and only brother, who was always devoted and faithful to us, and to the affairs of our realm, and in whom valour and many gifts of grace shone forth'.[20] Perhaps the king's sorrow was tinged with guilt. He had, after all, sent Edmund to Gascony in spite of his ill health.

There was at least one piece of good news from the duchy. On 14 May 1296, Edward declared the community of Bayonne had been united indissolubly to the English Crown. Strikingly, this had been done at the request of the community. The timing of this request, when things looked bleak for the English in Gascony, was no coincidence: 'The indissoluble and irrevocable unification of Bayonne and the English Crown was more, however, than just a heartening show of Bayonnais loyalty at a moment of disillusion and reversal. It was, from the community's point of view, a calculated quest for a positive insurance against any second cession of the duchy under the pressure of adversity. Against that, the men of Bayonne were giving notice that they would fight to the bitter end. They and the King-duke were thus of one determination.'[21]

At the same time Edward took drastic steps to bring Holland back into his coalition. His first response to the defection of Count Floris had been to impose a trade embargo on Holland. In the spring he entered into a conspiracy with certain Dutch noblemen. Floris was unpopular with many of his own nobles, principally Gijsbrecht van Amstel, Hermann van Woerden and Gerard van Velzen. The Duke of Brabant, Floris's rival for the profits of the English wool trade, was also involved. Van Velzen had some personal grudge against Floris, and within a few years rumours circulated that Floris had raped his wife. It is not possible, on the basis of currently available source evidence, to establish the truth of this accusation. However, the story was mentioned as rumour in Lodewijk van Velthem's continuation of *Maerlants Spiegel historiael* (*circa* 1315), and manuscript A of a Dutch rhyming chronicle, *van de Rijmkroniek* (*circa* 1330–40).[22]

The conspiracy against Floris was organised by Jan de Cuyck, an important envoy and diplomat in English service. The plan was to kidnap Floris and smuggle him over to England, where he would be forced to break the alliance with Philip or resign his title to his anglophile son, John.[23] In June 1296 Floris was captured by the conspirators while out hunting and imprisoned at Muiden Castle, near Amsterdam. News quickly spread of the incident. On 27 June, when they tried to move their captive to a safer place, the conspirators were confronted by an angry mob. They panicked, stabbed Floris multiple times and left him to die in a ditch.[24]

Edward's involvement in the kidnapping is scarcely in doubt. The organiser, Jan de Cuyck, was in receipt of a payment of 200 *livres tournois* per year from the king, and Edward stood to profit from Floris's removal.[25] The murder appears to have been a mistake, done on the spur of the moment, but it served Edward's purpose just as well. He had the dead man's only legitimate son, John, in his custody, and within a few months would use him to renew the Dutch alliance.

While these events were in motion, Edward concentrated his military resources on Scotland. At the end of March 1296 he led an army about 25,000 strong across the border. After the sack of Berwick-upon-Tweed and defeat of the Scottish feudal host at Dunbar, most of the major towns and cities fell into Edward's hands. The only significant resistance was at Edinburgh, which surrendered after a five-day bombardment. In July the defeated King of Scots, John Balliol, was captured and ritually humiliated by having his coat of arms publicly stripped from his tabard. He was then sent south to custody in the Tower of London, along with the Scottish regalia and the enthronement stone from Scone.[26]

Edward's success in Scotland is unsurprising. He had a large, well-equipped army, hardened by the experience of the Welsh wars. By contrast, the Scots had fought no major wars for decades, and were both outnumbered and out-resourced. The success of his first Scottish campaign inspired a number of popular songs in England, intended for knightly and common audiences. One of them has been loosely rendered into modern English:

For those Scots,
I rate 'em as sots,
What a sorry shower!
Whose utter lack
In the attack
Lost 'em at Dunbar.[27]

Edward himself shared the contempt of his subjects for the Scots. After his victory, he is said to have remarked to Earl Warenne that a man did good business when he rid himself of shit.[28] The king's hostile attitude may have sprung from frustration. Whatever his designs on Scotland, it should be borne in mind that Edward did not want to be campaigning there in the spring and summer of 1296. By this stage he was two years over schedule for his planned campaign on the Continent. Once again his allies simply had to wait for him to settle his affairs in the British Isles. As for his beleaguered men in Gascony, they were on their own.

Command of the army in Gascony had passed to Edmund's lieutenant, Henry de Lacy, Earl of Lincoln. He was a popular choice with the troops, appointed with their consent.[29] Lacy was unable to move for six weeks after his appointment, since he needed that time to rebuild the ducal army. The debts Edmund left behind had exhausted the military coffers, and at first Lacy struggled to find enough money and men. He only managed to hire one recorded soldier, Sir Montasivus de Noaillan, who received £40 sterling to continue on the king's wages after completing his feudal service.[30]

While the English laboured to raise a new army at Bayonne, the French under Robert d'Artois took full advantage. They launched two simultaneous attacks, one on Bourg in the north and the other on Bellegarde in the south-east, the edge of ducal territory. If Bourg was taken, the twin town of Blaye would soon follow and the English would no longer have a foothold in northern Gascony. The capture of Bellegarde would breach their southern defences and open the way for an advance on Bayonne and St-Sever.

The siege of Bourg was conducted by the lord de Sulliaco, dispatched by Artois to take the town.[31] Stones were purchased from local stonecutters for the siege engines, while French ships attempted to halt the flow of supplies from England by blockading the Gironde. Despite costing over 23,000 *livres*, the naval operation seems to have failed, as the garrison continued to receive corn, hay, beans, bacon and other victuals.[32] After several weeks of siege, the garrison followed the usual custom and asked for a truce so they could send to Blaye for relief. Their request was granted, and for once the call was answered. A knight of the Blaye garrison, the 'vigorous and intrepid' Simon Montague, sailed a supply ship down the Gironde and smashed through the middle of the French blockade.[33] Montague's exploit appears to have coincided with the arrival of Lacy at the head of a relief force from Bayonne.[34] The French were obliged to raise the siege and withdraw, leaving the twin outposts on the Gironde in English hands.[35]

There was more drama at Bellegarde in the south-east, where the town was attacked by the Count of Eu and his lieutenant, the provost of Toulouse. After sallying out to meet the French, the garrison staged a feigned retreat into the town: Edmund of Lancaster had made use of a feigned retreat at Bordeaux, suggesting it was a favoured English tactic. When Eu and his men gave chase, the gates were slammed shut behind them and English soldiers sprung an ambush. One of them impaled the count with a lance, though he survived. The overexcited provost then leaped over the ditch on his charger and slashed a cable with his sword. Alas, he failed to realise it was attached to some baskets full of large stones on the battlements. The baskets overturned and tipped the stones onto his head, crushing him to death. After witnessing these unfortunate events, the French army took to flight.[36]

The combined French offensive had ended in disaster. Perhaps encouraged, Lacy laid siege to Dax, some 25 miles north-east from Bayonne. The capture of Dax would give the English a third operational base in the south, along with Bayonne and St-Sever. Lacy pressed the siege with great determination. It lasted seven weeks, from about 24 June to 12 August, and he used workmen as well as men-at-arms to blockade the town by land and river. The effort failed due to several factors. There was a shortage of food, and the threat of a French army raised at nearby Mont-de-Marsan.[37]

There was also the issue of conflicted loyalties. Unlike many towns in Gascony, the citizens of Dax seem to have favoured the French. In 1278, long before the war, Edward I had issued a charter of pardon to the citizens for their 'disobedience' to him, and restored their communal rights and privileges. During the occupation of 1294–1303, Dax remained solidly in French hands, and repelled Lacy's attempt to recover it for the king-duke. According to Guisborough, the young men of the town, 'trusting in their valour and their youth', often sallied out to attack the English.[38] In December 1295 King Philip ratified Edward's charter of 1278, which suggests he appreciated their loyalty. After the failure of Lacy's siege, Robert d'Artois granted a privileged exemption of tolls to the city on 25 August.[39] The situation at Dax was the reverse of St-Sever, where the citizens had ejected a French garrison and invited the English back. Some Gascons at least chose their own fate, and the success or otherwise of military operations depended on their allegiance.

As the campaign season drew to a close, neither side had much to celebrate. The English expedition, which had started with such zest, spluttered out after three months and ended with the death of Edmund of Lancaster. Lacy had failed to regain the initiative. As for Robert d'Artois, he had scarcely fulfilled his mission of driving the

English out of Gascony. Despite holding every advantage, he failed to take Bourg and Bellegarde or bring the Anglo-Gascon field army to battle. Perhaps mindful of Philip's anger, Artois resorted to a desperate strategy. On 16 October 1296 he granted the citizens of Bayonne an identical charter to the one he had granted Dax in August. This was presumably supposed to lure the Bayonnais to the French cause. It had no effect, and the town remained a key English stronghold.[40]

Lacy and his lieutenant, John de St John, made an effort to end the season on a high note. After the failure at Dax, they mounted a large-scale raid or 'chevauchée' into the Toulousain in south-east France. It lasted from late summer into the autumn, and was perhaps intended as a morale-booster for their troops after a bleak year. The Anglo-Gascons burnt many towns and villages and returned to their strongholds laden with plunder.[41] This was an extra embarrassment for Artois: not only had he failed to destroy the English presence in Gascony, but he was even unable to prevent them ravaging French territory.

Both sides were exhausted. Apart from Edmund's incremental gains in the spring, neither had made or lost any ground. For the second year in a row, the war had ended in stalemate. The only other recorded operations are the return of demobilised and invalided soldiers to England in October. These included eighty-five infantry, archers and crossbowmen sent back to England under Thomas de la Panetria, *vintenarius* (an officer of twenty foot). This was one of two companies who came to King Edward in person and complained they had not received their wages. They were only able to obtain enough money to pay for their voyage home.[42] Another troop consisted of wounded, sick and infirm English infantry who returned home with William de Vescy, himself in poor health.[43]

While his men had made little headway in Gascony, the year ended for Edward in diplomatic success. On Christmas Day 1296 a group of his allies convened at Grammont in Franche-Comté. Apart from Edward's ambassadors, there was Adolf of Nassau, the Count of Bar, the Duke of Brabant, the Count of Guelders, the young Count of Holland, the Count of Juliers and the envoy of Count Guy, Geoffroy de Ranzières. This meeting was a reaction to Philip's efforts to attract the Duke of Lorraine, the Count of Hainault and the Dauphin de Vienne to his cause. Along with Count Othon of Burgundy, these men formed a counter-alliance to the confederation Edward had built up on the eastern borders of France.[44]

The cynicism and self-interest underlying these alliances was expressed by the Duke of Brabant, in an undated meeting with Jan de Cuyck. Lodewijk van Velthem, who was also present and describes the conversation, gave the following account:

> The duke John (of Brabant) was at a summit where the insubordinate behaviour of the count [of Flanders] was being handled, but he didn't want to take the situation in hand, because he preferred war to break out. At this time, I myself heard him talking one day, face to face, with the *sires* of Valkenburg and Cuyk. They said, '*Seigneur*, is there someone who can, better than you, keep the peace by reconciling the king and the count?' and I heard John of Brabant reply: 'Let things get confused, may I see the king go to war against the count! I would take care not to find a remedy for it. Because I say to you in truth, if I already had a foot in heaven, I would leave to come to the great uproar at the place of battle.' And as the *sires* of Valkenburg and Cuyk were asking what he meant by that, he replied: '*Messeigneurs*, I will begin operations, but keep my troops in the background, and when they are on the point of coming to blows, I will take up my position between them, and in any case I will harm anyone who does not do what I want. And that day I will perhaps earn more in summit talks than my country produces in a year's income. So I let the conflict begin, and do not wish to take sides before seeing the end of things.'[45]

In early January 1297 Edward was able to cement renewed alliances with Holland and Flanders. The murder of Count Floris of Holland, while unintended, had the desired effect of severing the Dutch alliance with France. His heir, Count John, was already in custody in England. On 8 January 1297, John's marriage to Elizabeth of Rhuddlan, Edward's daughter, went ahead at Ipswich.[46] On the previous day Count Guy of Flanders had agreed to renew his alliance with Edward against the French, and on the 9th he formally broke with Philip.[47] This provided Edward with a convenient landing place in Flanders for his campaign. As he later explained to Adolf of Nassau, to land further north, in Holland, would require the use of inferior and unfamiliar ports, and a much longer march south.[48]

The French king's treatment of Guy, after luring him away from the English alliance, was remarkably short-sighted. He had continued to undermine Guy's authority in Flanders, repeatedly summoning him to answer charges at the parlement in Paris. At first Philip had tempted Guy by permitting him to receive a fiftieth of all his subjects' possessions in tax. The count was persuaded to use heavy-handed methods to levy the tax on Flemish towns, which resulted in the citizens of Bruges, Lille, Douai and Ypres offering the money to Philip instead. Naturally, he was only too happy to take it.[49] These heavy-handed tactics – which echoed Edward's oppressive treatment of John Balliol – only served to drive Guy back into the English camp.

Another conference of Edward's allies followed on 8 February, at Koblenz, where Adolf assembled the nobles of Burgundy. After having promised to take back as direct fiefs of the empire lands they previously held from the Count of Burgundy, they carved up the lands of those Burgundians who had joined the King of France. Adolf gave the Count of Bar the fiefs that Guyot de Jonvelle had held of the Count of Burgundy and those confiscated from Jean de Bourgogne as far as Conflans in the *châtellenie* of Vesoul. Philip had already seized Bar's townhouse in Paris. He responded to the Koblenz assembly by confiscating the land of Toucy and all that the count possessed in the provostry of Paris, to give to Charles of Valois.[50]

At Koblenz the Burgundians also obtained Adolf's promise of support against the French. In return they pledged to lay their castles open to him and act as his vassals. Adolf vowed to bring his troops to Franche-Comté before 22 July. In the meantime he granted them subsidies in advance, as well as leave to enter King Edward's service on the same terms that they served him.[51]

In early 1297, after three years of delays and frustration, Edward was almost ready to embark for the Continent. His grand alliance was restored. He had the extra resources of Scotland to draw upon. Finally, the moment had arrived to recover his inheritance and wreak vengeance on Philip le Bel.

As ever, it wasn't that straightforward.

15

AS THE PHILISTINES EXULTED OVER SAMPSON

The war had continued to rumble on in Gascony. In late January 1297 Henry de Lacy took a supply column to relieve the ducal fortress of Bellegarde, which had repelled a French assault the previous summer. Bellegarde, along with the other strongholds of St-Quiterie and St-Sever, was badly in need of victuals. Threatened on all sides by the French, their only hope was the arrival of fresh supplies from Bayonne.[1]

They must have been in desperate straits for Lacy to take such a risk. There was only one ducal field army in Gascony, and a single defeat might destroy it. He and his predecessor, Edmund of Lancaster, took pains to avoid battle. When the French field army had advanced to raise the sieges of St-Macaire and Dax, ducal forces chose to withdraw rather than risk an engagement.

The Count of Artois was in the north besieging La Réole (another ducal stronghold) when his spies reached him with news of Lacy's advance. Their information must have been precise, for Artois gave orders for twin observation posts to be set up at Tilth and Estibeaux, either side of the English line of march. French garrisons of 150 men each were quickly set up at these posts.[2]

On 30 January Lacy's column was approaching a wood on the final stretch to Bellegarde. It was late in the afternoon. His men were weary after a long march and eager to reach their destination before nightfall. The vanguard descended into a narrow dip or pass inside the wood, which they would have to ascend before emerging onto level ground beyond. Between them and Bellegarde lay a tributary of the Luy de Béarn river, swollen by the heavy rains of winter.[3]

Lacy took all due precautions. He had divided his army into three columns, advancing by squadrons with supplies of corn and other victuals conveyed between them. The vanguard was led by John de St John, the second division by John of Brittany, the rearguard by Lacy himself.[4] What happened next seems to have been the result of faulty intelligence, rather than any negligence on the part of the English commanders.

The French were lying in wait beyond the steep rise of the valley. They were also arrayed in three (some accounts say four) divisions or lines. The first was led by Thibaut de Cheppoix, the French captain who had successfully defended St-Macaire for several weeks against Edmund of Lancaster. The second was commanded by the Count of Foix and the Count of Périgord, while the third was divided between Artois, the Count of 'Sanceurre' and the Count of Boulogne. A slightly different order of command is given by the *Anciennes Chroniques de Flandre*, which adds the detail that Foix had only arrived that morning with 'a fine company'.[5]

According to Langtoft, the English blundered into an ambush due to the treachery or incompetence of a spy:

> They were passing through a narrow pass, led by their spy,
> Who tells them for truth that in the company
> Of the French at that time in the country were no more
> Than five hundred men-at-arms, having lied by a thousand or more.[6]

As soon as the vanguard emerged from the wood, they spotted the French. The English commander, John de St John, immediately clapped in his spurs and charged the French first division:

> Places himself in the vanguard, and displays his banner.
> When the pass was formed, he found in ambush
> Fifteen hundred men-at-arms, and battle formed
> In four great squadrons; and the baron raises the cry upon them,
> Discomfits the first, and engages the rest.[7]

Langtoft depicts St John charging the entire French army with his division, overcoming the first French line and ploughing into the second. He then more or less accuses Lacy of cowardice, or at least taking dishonourable advice. While St John was left to fight the French all by himself, the rest of the English army hurriedly withdrew:

> The earl of Lincoln, Henry de Lacy
> Returned by advice, the rearguard agrees to it,
> The provision is lost, and the money plundered.
> Sir James de Beauchamp has abandoned the battle,
> With many of our English of his cowardice.[8]

French accounts of the battle are far more generous towards Lacy. Guiart, the contemporary French soldier-poet, describes Lacy rallying 600 of his men and leading a counter-attack against Artois. This almost succeeded, since most of Artois's knights had rode away in pursuit and he was guarded by just 100 men-at-arms. The outcome hung in the balance for about half an hour until Lacy's men were finally routed.[9]

The defeated Anglo-Gascons fled into the woods. But for nightfall, states one French chronicler, their entire army would have been wiped out.[10] Some English and Gascon knights were captured: a composite list, drawn up from English sources, names these as John de St John, William de Mortimer, William le Suleya, John de Ross, Adam de Huddlestone, John de la Garde, Reginald de Nowers, Thomas de Mose, William de Pontons, Henry de Schadewrche, Gerard de Leseyn and William de Birmingham. Philip de Matersdon was killed in the fight, and James de Beauchamp, Alan de 'Tuycham', his son and their squires 'shamefully' drowned in the river when they tried to flee. The recorded number of infantry slain varies wildly from 700 to 3,700.[11]

Bellegarde was a major reverse for the English. The outcome Lacy had wished to avoid – defeat in battle – had come to pass, and the urgent supplies for Bellegarde left abandoned on the battlefield. Those English knights taken prisoner suffered the indignity of being paraded as trophies of war through the streets of Paris, '*in pompam truimphi*'.[12] The capture of St John in particular gave the French great joy; they exulted over him 'as formerly the Philistines exulted over Sampson'.[13]

The defeat was not quite so disastrous as it seemed. When some fugitives from the battle reached the town, they were refused entry. Word of the defeat had already reached Bellegarde, and the citizens were disgusted by the men who had deserted their comrades. The fugitives were obliged to move on to the refuge of St-Sever, where they were received. When a second group of survivors reached Bellegarde, they were admitted and told the citizens where the battle had taken place. Acting on this information, some of the citizens sallied out at dawn and salvaged much corn and 'booty' left on the battlefield.[14]

There was more relief for the ducal cause when Lacy turned up at the gates of Peyrehorade, safe and sound, after wandering alone in the woods for most of the night. It seems he had been cut off from his men during the confusion of battle and the ensuing rout. He returned to Bayonne, where the remainder of his army trickled in over the following days. The victorious Artois, meanwhile, had gone to Orthez to celebrate his victory.[15]

As a consequence of the defeat, Lacy abandoned any hope of reconquering those parts of Gascony under French control and resorted to defending the towns and fortresses still in English hands.[16] Artois, meanwhile, sought to press his advantage. In the weeks after the battle he cut off ducal supply lines in a bid to starve the remaining fortresses into surrender. At the start of the year several of these had appealed to Lacy at Bayonne for help, if they were not to capitulate through starvation. Repeated references to the poverty of the beleaguered strongholds – '*qe sount en mult povre estat*' – are made in bonds given in money and supplies for their relief. The towns of Bellegarde, St-Sever and St-Quiterie are explicitly named as being at dire risk.[17]

All now depended on Edward. Only his arrival on the Continent, at the head of a fresh army, could stop the French throttling his last garrisons into surrender.

16

YOU WILL GO OR YOU WILL HANG

Edward was well aware of the danger. He planned a two-pronged attack on the French, whereby the earls of Norfolk and Hereford would take one army to Gascony while he took another to Flanders. The strategy foundered at the Salisbury parliament in February. Here the Earl of Norfolk, Earl Marshal of the army, flatly refused to serve overseas except under Edward's personal command. According to Guisborough, the king repeated his request and asked the earl to go:

> 'Willingly, O king,' he said, 'I will go with you, and march before your face in line of battle, as is my duty by hereditary right.'
> The king answered, 'You will go without me, with the rest.'
> 'I am neither bound nor am I willing, O king, to set forth without you.'
> The king in a rage burst out, 'By God, sir earl, you shall either go or hang.'
> 'By that same oath,' replied the earl, 'I will neither go nor hang.'[1]

Edward's attempt to browbeat his nobles into obedience had failed, and he was forced to abandon his strategy. There would be no twin-pronged campaign. All he could do was send more supplies to Gascony and prepare to sail for Flanders. In early April a consignment of corn was sent, carried by a ship called the *Hulk of St John of Sandwich*, to be carried to Bourg 'as soon as God shall grant time for a ship to sail there, under the king's standard'. More transports were sent to Bourg on 12 and 16 April, taking corn and Aberdeen stockfish to feed the garrison. Finally, at the end of April, a great fleet of ships from Looe, Southampton, Fowey, Shoreham, Dartmouth, Weymouth, Winchelsea and other places was assembled to take supplies and munitions to Bourg.

Edward's personal concern for his garrisons is shown when he paid for all these supplies at his own expense. Henry de Lacy was told not to burden himself with victualling, but take counsel as necessary to prevent a surprise attack by the French on Bourg and Bayonne.[2] Another forty ships loaded with money and supplies were dispatched to Gascony at the end of May.[3]

It was in the context of the desperate situation in Gascony that Edward decided to go to Flanders, after three years of delay. He was warned by his baronage not to go in light of the unrest in Scotland and Wales.[4] Edward would not be dissuaded, but he had great difficulty raising an adequate force to take overseas. There was little enthusiasm for the campaign in England, and his efforts to raise money and supplies met with considerable opposition from the English clergy and laity. As a result of the crisis, Edward made no efforts to recruit infantry in England, though he did manage to raise up to 822 cavalry.[5] In addition, a few Scottish knights captured at the Battle of Dunbar the previous year agreed to serve in exchange for their freedom.[6]

Most of the infantry were raised in Wales, a risky decision given that much of the principality had been in revolt in 1294–5. Perhaps mindful of recent events, Edward couched his summons to the Welsh in the form of a request. His officers in north Wales, Glamorgan, parts of south Wales and Powys were instructed to assemble the most 'powerful and fencible' Welshmen before them. These men were to be informed that the king had undertaken the war in Flanders for the 'common profit and salvation' of the entire realm. The Welsh should be asked, in the most 'loving and courteous manner', to provide military service for the king overseas. If they were to grant this service, 'in good manner and will', they were to assemble at certain places prior to embarkation.[7]

With the exception of Powys, which was controlled by the loyal dynasty of de la Pole, most of these areas of Wales had been in revolt against Edward three years earlier. The exception in Gwynedd was the commote of Penllyn in Meirionnydd, which provided Edward with several hundred infantry.[8] In Glamorgan the Welsh claimed to be in revolt against their lord Gilbert de Clare, Earl of Gloucester, rather than the king. A public reconciliation was staged in June 1295, when Edward met Morgan ap Maredudd, the leader of the Glamorgan rebels – in the teeth of angry protests from Clare – and pardoned him along with 700 of his followers.[9]

The king's efforts at persuasion bore fruit. On 2 August 1297 John de Havering, the justice of north Wales, wrote to the king that the north Welsh were coming into the muster 'of good will'.[10] This positive response was repeated elsewhere. By the time of embarkation on 22 August, the numbers of Welsh foot consisted of the following:

Glamorgan	898
West Wales	1,789
Barons' lands	640
North Wales	1963
Welsh March and England	923
Total	**6,213**[11]

The total number of infantry to serve in Flanders, including reinforcements shipped over in September and October, was 7,630. Of these, 2,278 came from England and the Marches, 151 from Ireland, and the rest were Welsh.[12] Most of the Welsh infantry are described as archers with the exception of the men of Snowdon and Caernarfon under Gruffudd ap Rhys, who are simply described as infantry. One small company of twenty-one crossbowmen was raised in west Wales.[13]

Edward went to great pains to ensure adequate supplies and equipment for his army in Flanders. His officials of the royal household were responsible for gathering provisions, as well as transportation to storehouses at Bruges and Ghent. The logistics were daunting, but Edward's officers worked efficiently. Some food and wine was bought in Flanders and Brabant but the bulk came from England. The total cost for all provisions was £11,741, 17 shillings and 4.5 pence.[14] The army was also equipped with a number of springalds and bolts for crossbows, indicating Edward was aware of the need for siege equipment.[15]

Hostilities began shortly before 4 June, when Count Henri of Bar invaded the county of Champagne, held by Joan, Queen of Navarre and queen consort to Philip IV. Henri split his forces in two, with the other led by his vassal, the Sire de Blâmont. The count attacked the abbey of Beaulieu, where his forces plundered and burnt the abbey, the treasury and the archives, as well as the nearby village. Meanwhile his lieutenant ravaged Champagne, destroyed villages and stormed the castles of Andelot and Wassy. Philip's seneschal, Gauchier de Castillon, counter-attacked and ravaged the frontiers of Bar. This forced Count Henri and his lieutenant to return to defend their lands.[16] They had wreaked considerable havoc in Champagne: Philip's officials were later obliged to impose a special subsidy on the county to pay for the war, at a total assessment of 94,562 *livres*.[17]

Guiart gives a vivid account of the French counter-invasion of Bar:

> When the king heard news of this, he sent Gauchier de Chasteillon towards Bar, at which we wondered little. He turned to attacking it, burning villages and seizing livestock – anything that mooed or whinnied – and despoiling trees and vines of timber, of leaves and of bark, so that by sheer necessity the count, scarcely delaying, was obliged to come there to defend his land.[18]

Edward was well aware of the invasion in Champagne, and his son-in-law's need for support against the French. On 4 June he wrote to Adolf of Nassau, urging him to assist Henri:

> Since our son, the count of Bar, has begun war against the King of France and, furthermore, given that none of our other allies are in this region, and because he is under greater attack by our enemies than any other, we pray and earnestly entreat your highness that you will it that the said count be given aid by those of your men who are nearest him and who can best act in such manner as may protect [him] against our common enemy; this until we are able to provide other assistance there.[19]

Adolf was unable to dispatch any immediate military aid, but he did set about enlisting nobles to do military service.[20] Between July and September he recruited several German nobles to his army, and sealed contracts of financial aid with a number of German towns. In the short term, however, all he could do was send 600 *livres*, via the Count of Flanders, to aid the Sire de Blâmont.[21]

Henry of Bar's chevauchée may have been an effort to divert the French from the invasion of Flanders. Other members of the alliance were unable to take action. Count John of Holland was deterred by powerful opposition in his own country. They appealed for aid to the Count of Hainault, who raised troops to hold John in check.[22]

However, a number of the German princes on Edward's payroll did cross into Flanders to help repel the French. These included Count Eberhard von der Mark and Otto, Count of Waldeck: 'The same Count Eberhard, with a company of chosen allies, knights and squires, chief amongst whom was the Count of Waldeck, brought aid to Edward, King of England and Guy, Count of Flanders, and entered Ypres and held it, not without considerable peril to themselves.'[23]

The French launched their invasion on 15 June.[24] King Philip advanced towards Lille and summoned Charles d'Artois from Gascony to assist in the siege. A number of skirmishes were fought around the city, and on 16 July the French defeated a force of Germans and Flemish at the bridge of Comines.[25] These included several of the German lords who had entered Flanders shortly before the invasion started. They retreated back to Ypres, where they burnt the suburbs to prevent the French capturing the town.[26]

From an English (if not Flemish) perspective, the removal of Charles and his field army from Gascony was a blessing. Almost as soon as he was gone, Henry de Lacy led out his troops from the ducal fortresses and embarked on another chevauchée into the Toulousaine countryside. The marauders burnt towns and villages, 'ravaging with fire and sword' up to the feast of St Katherine (29 September). They also broke the siege of St-Quiterie, a loyalist town, conducted by the men of Toulouse.[27] Lacy's presence at St-Quiterie is verified by a letter patent dated there on 28 August, in which one Amauri de la Zouche acknowledged a loan from the king. The agreement was witnessed by

Lacy and Hugh de Vere and the money spent on the 'sustenance' of Sir Robert Fitz-Neal, a knight serving in Amauri's company.[28]

Afterwards Lacy and his troops returned to winter quarters at Bayonne, laden 'with much booty'.[29] The threat of Edward's arrival in Flanders effectively created a second front, forcing Philip to weaken the French position in Gascony. This in turn enabled a boost to English morale before the end of the campaign season.

While Edward's men in Gascony gained much-needed respite, his allies in Flanders struggled to repel the concentrated French onslaught. Count Guy was in urgent need of support from England, and Edward would ideally have set sail in July or early August. This proved impossible: his Welsh infantry had not yet reached the departure point of Winchelsea, in East Sussex, and the king himself was still wrangling with his subjects over taxes raised for the war.[30]

17

SURROUNDED WITH PERILS

On 14 July Edward staged a remarkable piece of public theatre, appearing on a raised platform outside Westminster Hall in front of a large crowd. Here the king publicly admitted his mistakes, acknowledged the suffering of his subjects and insisted he was acting for the good of the realm and the defence of his people. The central theme of his speech, if Langtoft is to be trusted, was the recovery of Gascony:

> I am castle for you, and wall, and house,
> And you the barbican, and gate, and pavilion;
> My land of Gascony is lost through treason,
> I must recover it, or lose my process.
> I have undertaken the expedition, I have finally made the vow;
> It is the duty of each of you by name to pass with me,
> Of that not a soul has excuse by evasion.[1]

Edward followed this up by issuing a proclamation at Udimore in Sussex on 12 August. Much of it was concerned with explaining his arguments with the earls of Norfolk and Hereford, who had refused to serve in Gascony, and the king's oppressive exactions for the campaign in Flanders. The first part of the text reiterated his motives for going overseas, stating that 'because the king desires always the peace and quiet and welfare of all the people of his realm and in particular desires that, after the journey he now proposes to make for the honor of God and to recover his rightful heritage [Gascony] of which he has been most deceitfully defrauded by the King of France and for the honor and common profit of his realm'.[2]

The proclamation goes on to mention the Count of Flanders as the king's ally, and that the king and his 'good people' had undertaken to cross the sea to help 'the king's friends over there', another reference to the Flemings.[3] In context this was a secondary motive, and Edward's prime concern was clearly the salvation of Gascony.

The king finally sailed from Winchelsea on 23 August. For all his delays and mishaps over the past three years, Edward missed his best chance of victory by just a few days. On 20 August a pitched battle had been fought at Veurne in the west of Flanders.[4] A combined Flemish and German force was assembled under the command of William of Jülich the elder, a grandson of Count Guy. It also included the Count of von der Mark, who had joined Edward's alliance for a subsidy of £500, and Waleran of Valkenburg, whose fee was 300 *livres tournois*.[5] Also presented was the Sire de Blâmont, the Count of Bar's lieutenant, and Jan de Cuyck.[6] Thus a considerable number of Edward's allies had combined to face the French under the Count of Artois.

The German princes were acting independently of their king, Adolf of Nassau, who at this point was in peace talks with Philip. On 30 July Philip authorised a commission to meet with German envoys, and talks were still ongoing on 31 August, when Adolf informed Count Guy of the possibility of his reaching agreement with France. A peace was not, in the end, concluded, but the negotiations further prevented Adolf from assisting his allies.[7]

If Edward had joined his allies in time, the Battle of Veurne (also called the Battle of Bulskamp, since it was fought on the plain of Bulskamp south of Veurne) might have turned out differently. Instead, it was decided by treachery. When the armies were engaged, two Flemish nobles, the Viscount of Veurne and the Sire de Ghistelles, defected to the French. William of Jülich was advised to retreat but insisted on continuing the fight. After heavy casualties on both sides, the German–Flemish army was forced to flee. The survivors burnt Veurne and then retreated to Lille. Eighteen knights and squires were taken prisoner at the battle, including Blâmont, and at least five Flemish nobles slain.[8]

It is unknown when Edward learned of the defeat. Even if the news reached him before he left England, the king was too committed to change his plans. He ran into difficulties as soon as the English fleet arrived at the Zwin estuary on the north-east coast of Flanders. There was a bitter, age-old feud between the sailors of the Cinque Ports and Yarmouth, and they chose this moment to attack each other. Edward took hostages from both sides to keep the peace, but the damage and loss of life was severe. The most reliable account states that seventeen ships were burned, twelve looted and 165 men killed, with damages estimated at £5,000.[9] The records of the Wardrobe and its equipment aboard the *Bayard* of Yarmouth were in danger, and only saved by the quick-witted action of one Philip de Hales, who cut the mooring cable and enabled the ship to drift clear.[10]

After this unpromising start Edward marched up the coast to join Count Guy at Bruges, one of the few cities still held by the Flemings. According to the Bury chronicler the king's army was in grave danger, threatened on all sides by French troops: 'The king was surrounded with perils: behind him he saw danger, by which he was troubled, since his troops were closely engaged; in front of him he saw the enemy in open country, which ought to frighten him; as for his flanks, they were almost bare of troops.'[11]

Edward adopted a ruse, sending some of his Welsh infantry in advance of the army, 'with lances erect and pennons attached', to deceive the enemy into thinking his army was much larger than it seemed. The ruse worked, and Edward safely linked up with Count Guy at Bruges.[12] Here the king had his first direct experience of the political divisions within Flanders. Edward noted the town magistrates showed little desire to defend the town, even though a loan for this purpose had been collected in June. When the king offered to contribute money to the fortification, it was refused.[13] Edward suspected treachery and quickly left for the safer refuge of Ghent.[14] One English source claims the provost of Bruges was plotting against Count Guy, and meant to kidnap King Edward and hand him over to the French.[15] These suspicions were justified when the Brugeois formally surrendered the city to the French on 18 September, along with the port town of Damme.[16] Edward's hurried departure from Bruges is shown by the large amount of supplies his army left behind, including thousands of quarters of wheat as well as meat carcasses, beans, peas and oats.[17]

On the march from Bruges to Ghent, the king's army was again tracked by the French. This time they were reluctant to attack due to the number of archers in Edward's host.[18] Since most of his infantry were Welsh, this could be an indirect reference to the bow of Gwent described by Gerald of Wales, which had a short range but was capable of pinning an armoured man to his saddle.[19] It could even refer to the longbow. Modern archaeological digs on castle sites in Wales have discovered narrow armour-piercing arrowheads, specifically crafted for use in warfare against mailed or armoured opponents. These arrowheads are too long and heavy to have been fitted with short bows, the longest with socket (discovered at Dryslwyn) being over 16 centimetres in length. They date from the mid- to late thirteenth century and suggest that 'true longbows' were in use among the Welsh in this period.[20]

Ghent was a heavily fortified city, 'an impregnable fortress and an invincible place of refuge, surrounded by remarkable walls, ditches, palisades and moats'.[21] When Edward reached the city, he initially kept his army behind a fosse or defensive ditch, constructed with the help of Flemish labour.[22] One beneficial consequence of his stay was a temporary boost to the ailing Flemish economy due to the extra supplies he bought locally and the alms and oblations distributed by his almoner.[23] Meanwhile Philip marched to Ingelmunster, some 21 miles (as the crow flies) south-west of Edward's base at Ghent, where the patricians of Bruges offered him the keys to their city.[24]

Even at Ghent, Edward and his men were not safe. Soon after his arrival he and Count Guy left the city on a sortie. While they were gone, the citizens barred the gates and began to slaughter the English, who were trapped inside. The English rallied and managed to drive off the Flemings; one of the Welsh infantrymen earned a bounty from the king for swimming the river to save a comrade.[25] Edward and his party were only able to re-enter the city thanks to the services of more Welshmen, who contrived to get inside via one of the streams by which the city was intersected and burn down the gates. The Welsh then ran riot and set fire to part of the city.[26] On another occasion Edward was nearly killed when a Flemish crossbowman tried to shoot him in the street. The bolt missed and hit one of his retinue. In a rage, Edward ordered the street to be fired.[27] From this it seems the king was struggling to control his Welsh infantry. Edward's own lack of self-control scarcely helped matters, though his anger at being shot at is understandable.

His mood cannot have been improved by news of the disaster of Stirling Bridge in Scotland, where on 11 September the Earl of Surrey was routed by the Scots led by William Wallace and Andrew de Moray.[28] When the king became aware of the defeat is uncertain, though it was known in London by 24 September. It made no immediate difference to his plans, and the task of recovering the English position in Scotland was initially given to Surrey, who was instructed 'not to leave that land in any way until its state be assured'.[29]

The situation in the empire was scarcely less confused. Edward was relying on his ally, Adolf of Nassau, to bring a German army into Flanders. Some of Adolf's subjects had arrived, and played a vital role in the defence of Ypres, but there was no sign of the emperor.

Adolf was embroiled in troubles at home. On 18 September he was at Sélestat, near the borders of the Rhine. From there he sent a letter to Count Guy, stating he could not come to Flanders to 'rescue' him from King Philip, because a revolt had broken out against Adolf in Germany. While at Sélestat, Adolf was warned that the Bishop of Strasbourg had defected to the French and was planning to ambush him. The emperor was obliged to quickly board a ship with his family and sail down the Rhine to Germersheim, narrowly evading the trap.[30]

In these dangerous circumstances, Adolf made an effort to send all the help he could. Shortly before his flight from Sélestat, he appointed one of his nobles, Graf Theobald von Pfirt, to the post of 'Landvogt' of Alsace, near the Franco-German border. Theobald's task was to defend the German frontier and attack the French. The graf immediately obeyed and launched an invasion of French territory: 'Having assembled a strong army, he fell upon the French and did them great harm. At last his relatives in the country came and begged him not to strip them of their possessions and offered him a ransom of 5000 *livres tournois*. He accepted their prayers and returned to Alsace.'[31]

Theobald was also on Edward's payroll, so here was another member of the 'grand alliance' who honoured the terms of his contract. However, the king's own situation in Flanders remained difficult. The only fighting had occurred between his own sailors and against the Flemings, whom he was supposed to be helping. At least he had avoided defeat and his army was still intact, which was something.

In early October the allies in Flanders finally went on the offensive. Damme, the port town of Bruges, had fallen to the French in late September.[32] The loss of Bruges and Damme cut off Edward's forces in Flanders from the most direct route to the Channel, which probably explains the motive for the allied counter-attack. Damme was also an important harbour for extra supplies sent via Winchelsea in August and September.[33]

On 6 October an allied army led by Robert of Béthune, Count Guy's eldest son, appeared before the walls of Damme. The *Chronique Artésienne* claims the action occurred on 10 October,[34] four days later, but this dating is contradicted by a payment to Robert de Scales, a banneret in the English army:

> To lord Robert de Scales, knight, for his wages from the sixth day of October when he first raised his standard before Damme and for his one knight made a knight on the same day and six of his squires, until the eleventh day of November, each of whom are credited for 37 days; with the aforesaid Robert at 4 shillings per day, his knight at 2 shillings per day, and for all the squires 12 pence per day by his own hand.[35]

A later enquiry from 1304 reveals split loyalties within the town in 1297. It was divided into two parties, one for the King of France, the other for Count Guy. The leaders of the pro-French party, 'the party of the Lily', were named as Guillaume and P. de Speye and J. le Cosere; the leaders of the opposition as Cl. li Leus, Dierkin son of Dierk, G. le Blank and P. Winne. These factions vied for the support of the general populace, the 'floating mass', whose loyalties swayed back and forth. After the Battle of Veurne they held to the pro-Philip party, only to switch their support to the pro-Flemish after suffering oppression by the French garrison.[36]

In fact the defenders of Damme were a mix of French and Flemish. Philip had won the support of the guilds in Bruges with a subsidy of £1,000, and they subsequently sent crossbowmen and artisans to help garrison the town. By 3 October these Flemish troops consisted of 131 crossbowmen and 24 helpers, 69 weavers, 62 fullers and 34 shearers.[37] According to the annalist of Ghent there were also at least 400 French nobles and commoners.[38] In early October work began on refortifying the town, and iron chains stretched across the narrow streets as a means of protection.[39]

The fortifications were still incomplete when Robert arrived at the head of an Anglo-Welsh-Flemish army on 6 October. A bloody action followed when his men stormed the walls. An account written by a Minorite of Ghent takes up the story:

> Robert, the count's eldest son, with many Flemish, English and Welsh, attacked the town of Damme where encirclement with a ditch and walls had begun, and slew in it many French, both nobles and common people, to the number of four hundred, and captured others, and entered into possession of that town, and, as a result, of the port of Bruges. And he would have secured Bruges itself, had not the victorious English and Flemings disagreed among themselves and fought each other over the division of spoils.[40]

Another account of the sack of Damme is a dispatch from Gerard le Moer, one of Count Guy's knights. His report to Guy contains some interesting details:

> To his most honourable lord, honour and reverence. Know that we came before the town of Dam yesterday [or recently], last Sunday. And the French surrendered the fort which the Welsh fortify against them; and know that the town is taken. And while we were in the town the garrisons of Bruges came here to aid [them], and they have returned to attack you. Command us your

> will, and trust the bearer of these letters. By monsieur Gerard le Moer.[41]

Gerard was thus in the town shortly after it was taken, and records a failed counter-attack by the French garrison at Bruges. This gives some credence to the Minorite's claim that the allies planned to follow up the victory by recapturing Bruges itself. If they had succeeded, this might have turned the tide against the French. Any such plans were scuppered by the indiscipline of the allied infantry, who once again fell to brawling among themselves.

The chaos at Damme is recorded by another eyewitness account, this time anonymous, sent to Edward I at Ghent:

> Sire, on the Tuesday that we left you, we went to Aardenburg, and on the next day we went to Damme, and when we stayed there, there was a fight between a German valet and a Fleming, a taverner in the town. Our footmen ran there and assembled in large numbers, so that houses were broken where the Flemings were, and a good thirty or forty of them were killed, as far as we know, and not a soul of our men was killed, thanks to God. And as soon as we knew about it we went there and calmed it down, so that before Vespers all was at peace, honour be to God.[42]

The 1304 enquiry reveals that the leaders of the anti-French party inside Damme were made aldermen after the town was recaptured.[43] Edward would later pay the expenses of two friars, John of Wrotham and William of Pickering, going on royal business to Damme throughout the month of October.[44]

Edward must have been angry at the behaviour of his infantry at Damme, which had ruined a promising combined assault. It seems curious that he did not lead the allied army, but stayed at Ghent and entrusted his men to Robert of Béthune. However, he and Count Guy still had their eyes fixed on the German border, waiting in vain for the arrival of Adolf of Nassau.

Some good news did arrive from another quarter. Two days after the capture of Damme, Edward's allies in Burgundy went into action. On 8 October Jean de Chalon-Arlay and his associates attacked the castle of Ornans, a formidable stronghold perched upon a rocky ledge above the Loue valley in Franche-Comté. The castle was taken and destroyed, and on the same day Jean wrote to Edward, informing him of the success:

> Most dear sire, this is to inform you, that on Tuesday, the eve of the feast of Saint Denis, myself and my companions of Burgundy captured and razed the castle of Ornans, which was held by Burgundy of the King of France and was the strongest castle in the whole of Burgundy. And know that, I and my other comrades broke down the walls of the castle and forced our way inside, and secured the castle, and took nine prisoners and put a large number to the sword, apart from those who threw themselves down below the rock.[45]

On 9 October Jean was moved to write a second letter to the king. This included the same details of the capture of Ornans 'for the glory of your cause', and the Frenchmen taken prisoner or slain. He added that the French were sending a force to recover the castle, though Jean hoped to 'come soon (without delay) and to serve you for a term without excuses'.[46]

The attack on Ornans was probably symbolic as well as strategic, since it was the birthplace of the pro-French Count of Burgundy.[47] The castle was levelled to the ditches and the town looted and burned.[48]

The Truce of Vive-Saint-Bavon

On 9 October, a day after the fall of Ornans, representatives of the kings of England and France agreed a truce at Vive-Saint-Bavon.[49] Philip's decision to agree to the truce, since he apparently had Edward at his mercy, has been questioned.[50]

Edward's situation in Flanders was certainly difficult, but his rival also had problems. His presence on Flemish soil had turned Philip's flank, obliging him to siphon off forces from Gascony to meet the threat. The loss of Damme was a blow to the French. Philip must have been aware of the war in Burgundy, though news of the fall of Ornans would not have reached him until after the truce. More significantly, he was also aware of Henry de Lacy's chevauchée in August and September, which left its mark on the Toulousain.

On 8 October, the day before the truce, Philip's officials in Paris granted exemption from war taxes to certain inhabitants of the Languedoc. The details of this grant may refer to the castles and vills targeted by Lacy's troops. It states:

> We inform you that the representatives of the men of the see of Albi, of the vills of Marsac and of Rouffiac, of the bishop of Albi's Bastide, of Denat, Puyfaucon, Montsalvy, Cambon and Montille, and of the other castles and vills of the bishop of Albi and of the monastery of Saint Salvi in the seneschalcy of Carcassonne, have objected to a decree made, so it is said, in the said seneschalcy by master Jehan de Foret, the lord King's clerk, for the raising of eight small sous Tournois from each hearth as an aid for the present war, and maintain that the aforesaid men have been repeatedly and unendurably burdened by this war.

The order goes on to state that the collectors of subsidies in Carcassonne, Beaucaire and Rodez were to set no precedents in the levy of subsidies in the Languedoc.[51] Interestingly, it also states the men of Languedoc had suffered 'grievous burdens' on account of the current war against England, and the previous war against Aragon (1284–85). Petitions from other communities in the Toulousain, notably the vill of Laurac, show that Philip's officers were employing violent and extortionate methods of raising tax.[52] Edward's captains in Gascony appear to have realised the Toulousain was vulnerable, and repeatedly targeted it: John de St John had led a similar chevauchée into the region at the end of the campaigning season for the previous year.[53]

There is also the actual size of the opposing armies to consider. One complete account exists for mounted French men-at-arms under Charles of Valois, when he invaded Flanders after the expiration of the truce in 1300. The scribe records a total of 1,563 men with armour. This is the only sure figure for French armies of this era, since records are otherwise fragmentary and numbers given by chroniclers cannot be relied on. A rough estimate is that Philip generally maintained a force of 5,000 to 10,000 men when on campaign.[54] Though precise figures are a matter of conjecture, it seems that French armies in this period did not raise large numbers of foot to complement the men-at-arms. For instance, the army of Charles d'Artois at Bellegarde has been estimated at 900 men-at-arms and 700 foot.[55] Modern historians have estimated the size of the French army at Courtrai in 1302 at some 3,000 knights and 5,000 infantry. Many sources cite the large number of French knights at Courtrai, implying this was unusual.[56]

If the above calculations are correct, then Philip's army at Ingelmunster may not have greatly outnumbered Edward's army of some 8,000 infantry and 800 cavalry. There were also Count Guy's troops. At the start of 1297 he had raised 602 men-at-arms from the Rhine area and Brabant and hoped to increase this figure to 732. He tried to engage another 480 horse from the same region as well as Luxembourg and Namur.[57] The number of Flemish infantry is unknown. Despite losses at Comines and Veurne, it is reasonable to suppose that Guy still had a significant force.

Therefore it is possible the opposing armies were of roughly equal size. This in turn could explain the reluctance of either king to risk a battle. Philip's forces twice failed to attack the English army in the open, when Edward marched from the Zwin estuary to Bruges and from Bruges to Ghent. The situation in October 1297 was finely balanced. At this point Philip was faced with a stalemate in Flanders, ongoing war in Burgundy and Gascony and the effects of severe ravaging in Champagne and the Toulousain. There was also the potential threat of other members of Edward's alliance, and Philip had to take into account the state of his finances. The French war effort in Gascony had been running at a chronic deficit since the previous year, and the war in Flanders did nothing to ease that burden. French troops in Gascony were still owed large outstanding payments in the summer of 1298.[58] Overall, a truce may have seemed preferable to Philip than fighting on several fronts at once.

Edward, of course, would have wished to heap far more pressure on his enemy. His allies were supposed to attack Philip from all sides. Instead they arrived piecemeal and in many cases not at all. The most important absentee was Adolf of Nassau, whose actions and motivations shall be discussed later. His failure to join Edward did not discourage some of the lesser German princes, who joined the ill-fated army defeated at Veurne on 20 August. In one case failure to attend was unavoidable: the Archbishop of Cologne had died at Bonn in April, still waiting for Edward's arrival.[59]

After the recapture of Damme, Edward once again called upon the services of his son-in-law Henri, Count of Bar. On 8 October, Henri sent a reply to Edward's summons excusing his non-appearance. The count claimed he was away from his estates when the king's letters arrived and did not receive them until the Sunday after the feast of St Remy (1 October). He assured his father-in-law that he would soon have his men ready, and expected to set off on the Tuesday next after the Feast of Saint Luke the Evangelist (18 October).[60] Therefore the count did not take part in the campaign until at least nine days after the truce, probably later.

An account of Henri's actions is given by Langtoft:

> King Edward remains, and eat and drinks;
> His Welsh often issued forth for plunder.
> The warlike Count of Bar often rode out with them,
> And invaded and plundered the territory of the king of France;
> Robbed his markets and fairs of their chattels,
> Spared not to do evil everywhere;
> And King Philip did as much to him.[61]

Since the Count of Bar did not set off to join Edward until 18 October, Langtoft's verse would imply the allies broke the truce and kept on attacking the French. However it is possible that some of Bar's knights were already in Flanders and had joined Edward when he first arrived at Ghent in September. These men in turn could be those described by Langtoft as raiding French territory alongside Edward's Welsh troops, probably before the truce was struck on 9 October.

Edward continued to wait in vain for the arrival of Adolf of Nassau. His hopes were dented on 15 October when Jan de Cuyck wrote to Edward informing him that Adolf had not gathered enough troops but expected reinforcements.[62] The king was not entirely discouraged. On the 16th he wrote to the Exchequer asking for more money for subsidies to the Duke of Brabant and the King of Germany, for without it the alliance might fall through.[63]

When Adolf still failed to appear, Edward gave up hope of a military victory and reverted to arbitration. The initial terms of 7 October had afforded only a little breathing space, with the truce to last just two months in Flanders and three in Gascony.[64] Further negotiations were held in November at Groningen Abbey near Courtrai, conducted on the English side by William Hotham, an experienced diplomat and archbishop-elect of Dublin. A further armistice was agreed.[65] On 23 November the truce was extended another three months. The following day writs were dispatched to England to summon more knights to perform military service in Flanders.[66] Edward's intentions are revealed by a letter of 27 November, to his son and the council in London, asking for reinforcements. These were required so he could impress the French and gain better terms.[67]

18

TRICKS AND PLOTS

The truce held until the end of January 1298, when two papal legates, the generals of the Franciscan and Dominican orders, arrived to repeat the Pope's request that both Edward and Philip submit their dispute over Gascony to arbitration before the Holy See. On 31 January, the English envoys once again met with their French counterparts, this time at Tournai, and agreed to a more permanent armistice to last until 7 January 1300.[1]

Edward had achieved a three-year peace with France, lifting the intense pressure placed on his strongholds in Gascony after Lacy's defeat at Bellegarde. This was a tangible gain, though the victory he had hoped and paid for proved impossible. He also gained a respite for Count Guy and Flanders, albeit a temporary one. It is wrong to state that Edward 'shamefully abandoned' Guy at this juncture.[2] Along with the rest of Edward's allies, the count was included in the initial truce of Vive-Saint-Bavon.[3] One of the terms of the treaty between England and Flanders was that Edward would not make peace with France without Guy's knowledge and consent.[4] This was given on 10 October, when he formally accepted the truce.[5]

Guy was also included in the further armistice agreed at Groningen on 23 November, and in the final round of peace talks at Tournai in February 1298.[6] The Tournai agreement preserved what remained of independent Flanders until the expiry of the truce in January 1300. Philip kept his territorial gains, including Lille and Bruges, while

Guy was left with Douai, Ypres, Ghent, the Waas country between Antwerp and Ghent, and the region of Quatre-Métiers.[7]

The success of these peace talks caused tensions to melt away. At this time, says Lodewijk van Velthem, there were great celebrations. Edward staged a magnificent feast at the city of Vive-Saint-Bavon, where many nobles were gathered. Count Guy and the Duke of Brabant joined in the festivities, though none could rival the brilliance of Edward's feasts.[8] He had certainly come prepared to entertain. The accounts for the Flanders expedition show he brought a well-equipped squadron of minstrels and dancers. Two were from the household of the Earl of Lincoln, while one was an acrobatic dancer or *saltatrix* with the intriguing name of Matilda Makejoy.[9]

Edward was not simply engaged in merrymaking. Van Velthem records that the king left Ghent to visit his daughter and her husband, the Duke of Brabant:

> Not long after this was done,
> the King travelled to Brabant,
> to visit his daughter [*wife of the Duke*] and also the country.
> He came in Brussels with much honour.
> There he received the Lords well.
> He closely inspected the town
> and amused himself and conversed.
> There were certainly many Counts,
> who all were vassals of the Duke;
> the King marvelled very much
> that so many a Lord held his lands from him [*the Duke*].
> About this the King was much pleased,
> because before he had not thought.[10]

This was far more than a social visit. While in Brabant, Edward was granted the port of Antwerp and adjoining towns of Lier, Hérenthals and their dependencies by his son-in-law, Duke John. This may have been done in secret, since the duke held these towns as fiefs of the Holy Roman Empire, and had no authority to grant them away, even on a temporary basis. This was a remarkable concession by the anglophile duke, and may have reflected Edward's desire to secure the

English monopoly of the wool trade.[11] The king also kept abreast of events at home, and ordered counter-operations in Scotland against William Wallace, who had invaded Northumberland over the winter months before withdrawing.[12]

Perhaps distracted by these affairs, Edward seems to have been oblivious to fresh trouble brewing in Ghent. In February 1298 another rising occurred in the city, whose inhabitants had brawled with Edward's soldiers the previous September. It has been suggested the riot was caused by anger among the Gantois, when they realised Edward was deserting them.[13] None of the English or Flemish chronicles give this as a motive. One English source claims the Gantois planned to betray Edward:

> Moreover the men of Flanders had planned to hand over the king of England, to whom they had allied themselves, to the king of France. They attempted to deceive him by various tricks and plots, because it is said, their wives, daughter and maidservants had been debauched by the English. So on the feast of St. Blaise [11 February] they attempted to carry out the wicked plan they had conceived against the English.[14]

The Flemings, it was said, rang bells inside the town as a pre-arranged signal for the entire country to rise against the English. Edward's men were trapped inside and exposed to fire from ballistae and war machines placed on the battlements. Fortunately, some of his English and Welsh troops were quartered in the suburbs. These men managed to burn their way through the gates to help their comrades, who turned on the Flemings and routed them. Edward himself joined in, charging the Flemings at the head of his household knights and trampling down a chain stretched across the street.[15]

A different version of events is found in the pro-Flemish account of the aforementioned Minorite of Ghent. This claims the English started the riot by setting fire to parts of the city. The Gantois then marched out to defend their families and property, and 'strongly and courageously resisted the English'. If not for the intervention of Count Guy, the annalist claims, King Edward and all his men would have been killed or captured.[16] In all, it seems more likely the violence was caused by tensions between Edward's infantry and the citizens of Ghent, rather than political factors.

It is difficult to assess casualties suffered by the king's army. The Minorite gives precise figures and claims the Gantois slew thirty of Edward's 'noble knights' and about seventy of his infantry. Of the citizens, he claims twelve were burnt by the English and twenty-five killed in the fighting.[17] The figure of thirty English knights must be an overstatement, if not outright fabrication. This would have represented the worst loss of English nobles in a single engagement since the Battle of Evesham in 1265, and the names of the dead would almost certainly have been listed. For instance, the names of sixteen English knights drowned at the Battle of Moel-y-Don in Wales in November 1282 were carefully recorded by the annalist of Chester.[18] The casualties suffered among English knights in the war in Gascony are recorded in various chronicle sources: Adam de Creting, killed at Rions in May 1295;[19] Philip of Matersdon and Alan of Twitham, killed at Bellegarde in January 1297;[20] James de Beauchamp, killed at the same battle;[21] and so on. No slain knights are mentioned by name in any source for the Flanders campaign.

Casualties among the infantry are less certain. One constable of Welsh infantry, Llywelyn Goly, was paid his expenses by the king on 28 September so he could return home on account of infirmity.[22] Unfortunately the Wardrobe Book only gives extracts rather than full accounts for the infantry, and records no other certain losses before the account ends in autumn 1297, when the regnal year closed. The only other potential reference to casualties is a payment of £20 16*s* 8*d* by Edward's almoner on 2 November for the souls of the faithful departed ('*animarum fidelium defunctorum*').[23]

Even less information can be gleaned for the second rising in February 1298. On 24 February Privy Seal writs were drawn up in Ghent, to be sent to England to request safe-conduct for Welsh troops who had already been shipped back to England. On 11 March the Chancery issued letters for the men of Glamorgan, with further letters on 15 March for the men of north and west Wales. One final batch of letters, for a group of five stragglers, was issued on 27 March.[24] Unfortunately little can be gleaned from these routine orders, save that the Welsh infantry appear to have been transported home more or less intact. Their officers or 'conductors', Robert le Veel, Gruffudd Llwyd and Morgan ap Maredudd, were certainly alive and well. The accounts are silent on the condition of Edward's English and Irish troops.

Whatever the truth behind these events, it is clear that Ghent was not a safe refuge. On 4 February 1298 commissions were issued for ships 'suitable for carrying men, horses and other necessaries' to be collected in Norfolk and Suffolk, for the purpose of sailing to Sluys and carrying the king and his army home.[25]

Sometime between 23 February and 1 March Edward moved from Ghent to Aardenburg, near the Zeeland border and the territory of another son-in-law, the Count of Holland.[26] From this new base Edward tried to salvage the wreckage of his expedition. First, he made amends to the injured citizens of Ghent. On 2 March he issued a charter to the Gantois, confirming their mercantile privileges in England.[27] He also, according to Guisborough, paid a large sum of money in damages.[28]

Edward also had to attend to his financial difficulties. The king had been obliged to borrow 4,000 *livres* from a group of merchants of Asti, back in October, at an exorbitant interest rate. Emergency loans were obtained from Italian banking firms, notably the Frescobaldi. In early February, Edward wrote to the Exchequer demanding money to pay off his Burgundian allies and deliver him and his army from Flanders.[29]

Some of the Scottish knights in Edward's army, who had agreed to serve in exchange for their release, slipped away en route to Aardenburg.[30] The Scots supposedly went to Paris, where they begged King Philip to attack Edward. Philip angrily refused and dismissed them, saying the Pope had forbidden him to break the truce.[31]

Edward, however, was not done yet. On 7 March the king drew up a new treaty with his allies in Franche-Comté. Given his situation at this time, its terms are remarkable and worth quoting in detail. An agreement was made with eighteen nobles of Burgundy, headed by Renaud de Burgoyne, Count of Montbéliard, and Jean de Chalon, sire d'Arlay. It was stated that these men had 'promised and sworn to us that, in order to have our financial assistance to defend their rights against the King of France, they should assist us in good faith and help us in the war that we and our allies have against the King of France and his heirs'.[32]

This referred to the activities of the Franc-Comtois on Edward's behalf to date. The next section reveals his intention to continue the war, saying, 'The said nobles should make and continue lively and open war against the same King of France, and against his allies and accomplices, in the county of Burgundy and its neighbouring places, for as long as the war which we have against the said King of France should continue; and they should continue to do so until a final peace should be made, just as is most plainly contained in the said promise and in other agreements, according to the letters made concerning those aforesaid agreements.'[33]

This is followed by the terms of payment, reading, 'And know that we have promised to the said noble men that we shall give and pay to them and their heirs, or at their command, in aid of the costs which they shall endure in making and continuing the said war, according to what is contained in the said agreements, 30,000 small *livres tournois*, or the same value in other money, beyond the sum of 60,000 small *livres tournois* which they have already had and received of our gift, in order to make and continue this said war for this year, ending on the first day of June, to be paid at Brussels in Brabant each year afterwards, for as long as the war should last and continue.'[34]

It was then stipulated that the first payment of 15,000 *livres* would be made on the first day of June, and the second on the first day of December. If there was a delay, payments would be made within ten weeks of these dates. Edward promised to provide this assistance for as long as the war lasted, and in return the nobles would 'make and continue' their war against Philip. If, for whatever reason, the payments could not be made at Brussels, the nobles would receive their money either at Ghent in Flanders, or some other suitable place in Flanders or Brabant.[35]

In February Edward had insisted on paying the Burgundians before he left Flanders, but that was for their service to date. They did not receive full satisfaction until 10 May 1306, so the money Edward promised in March 1298 was not paid over for several years.[36]

The king's strategy is not easy to interpret. He had no intention of remaining in Flanders for any longer than necessary, and landed at

Sandwich on 14 March, just seven days after the above treaty was struck at Aardenburg.[37] At the same time there was little point in renewing the war in Burgundy, at such extra cost, if Edward didn't intend to salvage something from his overseas campaign. Perhaps the most likely interpretation is that he wanted to keep the French occupied and prevent them sending aid to the Scots. Alternatively, he may have hoped to defeat the Scots with relative ease – just as he had in 1296 – and then turn about to deal with the French. As it was, the Falkirk campaign proved difficult and Edward was unable to return to the Continent.

The lords of Burgundy did indeed resume their war against the French. Unfortunately the chronology of this campaign is vague. The fall of Ornans can be securely dated, thanks to Jean de Chalon-Arlay's letters to Edward in early October 1297 (see above), but there is some confusion over his other activities. Jean and his comrades, the Count of Montbéliard and the Sire de Joux, were still in arms in 1299. In September of that year Philip IV engaged Geoffroi d'Aucelles, knight, to deliver these men to the king if they fell into his hands.[38]

The league enjoyed other successes, though the dating is imprecise. A number of skirmishes were fought against Philip's knights, some of whom were captured and imprisoned in the castle of Roulans, another stronghold in Franche-Comté. Among the captives was Girard Flote, bailiff of Mâcon. His loss was a serious blow to the French, since Philip had previously made him second-in-command of royal forces in the region.[39] Funck-Brentano states these knights were captured after Edward's treaty on 7 March, but the source is unreliable.[40]

At Pentecost 1301, when Jean finally made peace with Philip, he and his companions agreed to pay to repair the castles of Ornans and Clerval (Clairvaux, some 25 miles north-east of Ornans), as well as the '*sale de* Pontalié' (the hall or palace of Pontarlier, 23 miles south-east of Ornans), all of which the league had destroyed during the war.[41] The attacks on Clairvaux and Pontarlier cannot be dated precisely, though they probably occurred between the sack of Ornans in October 1297 and the cease of hostilities in Burgundy in 1301.[42]

Overall, the barons of Franche-Comté served their paymaster well, and inflicted serious damage on Philip's cause in Burgundy. Edward in turn appreciated their efforts; hence his insistence on paying the

Franc-Comtois in February 1298, and the renewal of his alliance with them in March.

The actions of Adolf of Nassau, King of Germany, were vital to the outcome of the war. He had pledged to aid the league of Franche-Comté and accepted offers of massive subsidies from King Edward. Both of his allies waited in vain for him to appear. A later French memorandum, possibly drawn up in the 1330s, states the King of Germany accepted a 'bribe' from Philip to desert the English. The document is riddled with inaccuracies and Adolf is not actually named in the text. It may be that the author was confused between Adolf and his enemy Albert of Hapsburg, who was in French pay.[43]

With regard to the English alliance, it has been pointed out that Adolf did not receive all the money owed to him. It was agreed he should receive a subsidy of £60,000 in three instalments, the first two of which were paid by Christmas 1294. The third was to be paid when Edward landed on the Continent. Adolf had to wait another three years for this last instalment, and it seems he never got it. When the barrels of coin finally arrived in Flanders, Edward needed them to pay his troops and purchase supplies. In this respect the English king certainly failed his ally, and the truce he made with Philip at Vive-Saint-Bavon was in breach of his earlier treaty with Adolf, whereby neither party was to negotiate a peace or truce separate from the other.[44]

Not that Adolf's behaviour is above reproach. He failed in his obligations to Edward, the Count of Bar and the league of Franche-Comté. Moreover, he used the English subsidies that did reach him to purchase the lands of Albrecht 'the Degenerate', Landgrave of Thuringia. These were joined to other territories to create a substantial power base for Adolf in the middle of Germany.[45] Two bloody campaigns against the people of Thuringia followed, again funded with English money.[46] This was all to Adolf's advantage, but hardly in the spirit of the alliance with Edward. The subsidies were supposed to help the German king fund an army to lead against the French, not destroy his enemies at home.

19

WE PRAY YOU TO MAKE PEACE

The immediate result of the war in 1297 was complex. Neither side had gained everything they desired. From a French perspective, Philip succeeded in removing Edward and his army from Flanders. The price of this advantage was a lengthy truce that prevented an almost certain French victory in Gascony, and left Edward free to move against Philip's allies in Scotland. It also prevented, for the moment, the final French conquest of Flanders.

Philip's attitude towards his Scottish allies is revealed by talks held at Provins in the diocese of Sens between 6 and 15 June 1298, a few weeks before the Battle of Falkirk. Here, King Edward's envoys agreed to another truce, this time proposed by the King of France, and an exchange of prisoners.[1] Thus, even as Edward's army hunted William Wallace in Galloway (Falkirk was fought on 22 July), the French showed no desire to come to the aid of the beleaguered Scots.

In June 1298 both sides submitted their claims to Gascony to the Pope, Boniface VIII. Philip brought against his vassal, Edward, a charge of treason for having waged open war against him, his liege lord. As a result he demanded Gascony, his vassal's fief, as a forfeit. The English lawyers responded that Gascony had always been held of the French Crown as *allod* (freehold), not a fief, and that Philip had failed to uphold his side of the feudal contract as set out by the Treaty of Paris. Therefore he had forfeited his lordship.[2]

Count Guy's three sons, Robert de Béthune, Jean de Namur and Philippe de Thiette, were also at Rome to argue their father's case before the Curia. Their father wrote a letter to his sons, warning them what to expect, stating, 'You should know that the Roman court is very grasping, and that anyone who wants to do business there must make many gifts and promises and pledges.'[3]

Boniface initially welcomed the Flemish, but soon made it clear he did not favour them. On 11 June they asked for their rights under the Treaty of Tournai to be respected, and for their sister Philippa to be sent back to Flanders so her long-delayed marriage to Edward of Caernarfon could take place. Boniface merely replied they should leave the whole matter in his hands. Guy's sons asked for a day's grace and met with the English envoys the next morning at their lodgings. They received a brusque response: the King of France already occupied much of Flanders, and King Edward had enough to do in England, Scotland and Gascony. He could offer no more aid. The English would never willingly return to Flanders. Finally, they owed no money to Count Guy, as the treaty specified this was only due in time of war, not truce. Therefore it was better for the Flemish to agree to the Pope's suggestion, since it would be even worse to turn it down.[4]

The English did not entirely withhold assistance. On 25 June Guy's sons had another audience with the Pope, this time in the company of Edward's diplomats. They described what followed in a letter written to their father:

> Then, turning to the plenipotentiaries of the King of England, one of the Count's representatives added: 'We pray you that you speak with the Holy Father, as we do not wish to renounce our alliance between your master the king and our lord the count of Flanders, nor have we ever given you licence to make peace without us.' Then the archbishop of Dublin addressed the pope: 'Sir, we pray you to make our peace along with the peace with the count of Flanders.' These words were repeated by the other English envoys. But Boniface VIII became angry and answered sharply that he would not abandon bringing his intentions to a good conclusion solely for the count of Flanders, and that, moreover, if the count regretted entrusting his affairs to him, then he would release him from his oath.[5]

Then, turning to the plenipotentiaries of the King of England, one of the count's representatives added:

> We pray you that you speak with the Holy Father, as we do not wish to renounce our alliance between your master the King and our lord the Count of Flanders, nor have we ever given you licence to make peace without us.

Then the Archbishop of Dublin addressed the Pope:

> Sir, we pray you to make our peace along with the peace with the Count of Flanders.

These words were repeated by the other English envoys. But Boniface VIII became angry and answered sharply that he would not abandon bringing his intentions to a good conclusion solely for the Count of Flanders, and that, moreover, if the count regretted entrusting his affairs to him, then he would release him from his oath.[6]

This reveals the English tried to have Count Guy included in the final peace between England and France, but their appeal was rejected by the Pope. Since Edward's diplomats presumably acted in the knowledge their master would approve, this can also be taken as a reflection of the king's attitude. Indeed, on 24 January, at Ghent, Edward had given full power to Hotham and his envoys to negotiate and affirm an armistice between himself and King Philip, and their respective allies and subjects.[7] Boniface, however, was not prepared to risk anything for the sake of Flanders alone.

The final conference took place on 30 June. Here the English at first declined to accept the Pope as arbiter, except with the consent of the counts of Flanders and Berry and certain Burgundian nobles. This was meant to uphold Edward's composition with Count Guy. As agreed beforehand, Guy's sons declared they would accept the Pope's authority, which released the English from their obligation.[8] Confusingly, Boniface presided over the case as Benedict Gaetano, the name he went under before his ascent to the throne of St Peter. This was due to French influence. Philip had previously informed the Pope's envoys that he acknowledged no superior in the government of his realm and would submit to no living man in temporal affairs. He absolutely declined to accept the Pope as arbiter, but was willing to permit him as a private individual to broker peace between France and England.[9]

The Pope's award, published the same day, satisfied neither the English nor the French. Boniface wished for a perpetual peace, sealed by the marriage of Philip's sister Margaret to King Edward, and his daughter Isabella to Edward's heir, Edward of Caernarfon. This meant the annulment of the previous contract to marry the English prince to one of Guy's daughters. Both parties would pay war damages. The crucial issue of Gascony was left undecided. Instead Edward would remain in possession of those parts of the duchy he already held, 'on terms to be fixed by the pope, so that no new right shall accrue to either party'.[10] This was so displeasing to the French that Philip's brother, Charles d'Artois, seized the award, tore it to bits and trampled it.[11]

The Flemish had even less cause for celebration. Boniface reluctantly included them in the award, but only in a short additional clause that extended the time limit of Count Guy's appeal.[12] On the same day Robert of Béthune and his brothers had another meeting with the English, in which they denied uttering harsh words against the Count of Savoy, one of Edward's envoys. They did not, they said, wish to do anything to endanger the alliance between England and Flanders. It appears they blamed Savoy for not arguing their case to Boniface with sufficient zeal.[13]

Boniface's attitude was coloured by his own dealings with the French. Philip IV had waged war on Count Guy as a rebellious vassal, and the Pope was using the same argument against rebels in the papal states. He badly needed French support to press on with his war against Frederick III in Sicily. In these circumstances he could not afford to be anything but harsh with the Flemish envoys.[14]

Edward's grand alliance was a dead letter. His envoys had persuaded Boniface not to cut Guy adrift completely, but that was as far as they got. Guy himself was under no illusions. He sent an emotional letter to Edward, describing the dangers that faced him and imploring the king to have pity:

> Sire, I send to you, as to he in whom, after God, I placed my supreme hope; but the news from Rome is hard and has greatly astonished us, us and our friends. Sire, the pope has apparently

> pronounced peace between you and the king of France, marriage plans concluded between your two houses, and I remain outside treaties. Yet the king's people, breaking truces, seize our towns, kill our people, take their property from fields and houses, throw the aldermen of our towns into prison, and, through fear and constraint, make our subjects take an oath of loyalty to the king. Certainly, Sire, it would not be proper that I add to my words, because I cannot believe that I will not find help and aid in you, that you be not decided to stand in my favour, according to the treaties between you and me. I therefore beseech you, dearest Sire, by God's mercy, to wish to have compassion on me and my State, to aid me, you in whose hands I have placed my patrimony and my honour.[15]

Robert of Béthune added a further entreaty. On 1 December 1298 Edward replied to Robert, assuring him the Pope had extended the Anglo-French truce for one year. The king added that he was grieved to hear the truce was badly kept in Flanders. It was a matter for the Pope to deal with, but Edward would gladly do what he could, if Robert thought a request from the king might be helpful.[16]

While Edward was still prepared to try and exercise his influence on Guy's behalf, it was clear that no further material support would come from England. Or, for that matter, anywhere else. Guy went to increasingly desperate lengths to procure support. He renounced the territory of Zeeland to Count John of Holland and appeared in person at the coronation of Duke Albert of Austria as King of Germany. Neither had any effect: the count died young in 1299, and Albert made an alliance with King Philip. Within Flanders, the pro-French elements refused to support Guy, and the patricians of Douai actually called upon Philip's support.[17]

20

THE GOLDEN SPURS

Edward's diplomats moved on. In May 1299 the English and French envoys met again to hammer out peace terms at Montreuil. Shortly after the deliberations were concluded on 19 June, the Court of Appeals in Paris decided in favour of Edward's claim to Ponthieu. The comté was handed back to the English after French administrators had spent five years harvesting its revenues.[1] Philip's decision to permit Anglo-French talks to take place at Montreuil, which lay inside the borders of Ponthieu, represented another concession to English interests. Such meetings were usually held in Paris.[2]

In August 1300 Boniface privately assured the king's envoys he favoured their argument for Gascony, and that Philip was guilty of 'wrongful detention' of the land. Yet he could not give the English an award, since the French would simply ignore his decision. Nor could they be compelled to surrender Gascony. The Pope claimed to have exerted all the pressure at his disposal by excommunicating Philip for levying taxes on the clergy and on French prelates for granting them.[3]

The key point, with regard to these negotiations, is that Edward had only retained part of Gascony due to his presence in Flanders in 1297. Otherwise he would have had nothing to bargain with. This was especially important given Philip's subsequent refusal to hand over his share of Gascony to the Pope. He was probably influenced by Boniface's desire for a return to the pre-war status quo, which would have required Philip to restore the duchy to Edward.[4]

Philip adopted draconian measures to suppress resistance at Bordeaux. In all, 165 leading citizens were taken hostage and imprisoned in poor conditions; 29 of them died in captivity.[5] In November 1297 the mayor and jurats threatened to rise in arms unless their kinsmen were released from prison.[6] Over 100 Bordelais nobles chose to quit the city in disgust and go into exile in England.[7] Bordeaux's commerce fell into a state of crisis as Anglo-Gascon ships blocked the Gironde and wine exports to London fell dramatically.[8] Thanks to the armistice, Philip could take no action against the remaining ducal enclaves.

The king's tenuous hold on Gascony was further threatened by his conflict with the papacy. Philip had already quarrelled with the Pope over the taxation of clergy in France. In 1301 he reignited the feud by arresting the Bishop of Pamiers, Bernard Saisset. His inquisitor, Pierre Flote, accused the bishop of stirring up treason against the king in the Languedoc. He alleged that Saisset 'thought, spoke, negotiated and, as far as was able, acted during the Gascon war between the kings of France and England, to the end that men might be sooner incited to treason, and aroused against the king of France, and to subvert the whole Kingdom'.[9]

Pope Boniface summoned French bishops to Rome to discuss Philip's actions. In December 1301, as if to confirm Flote's suspicions, he sent his legate to Agen to preach against the king. Philip wrote a furious letter to the consuls of Agen, expressing his displeasure that that the legate had been sent 'to the parts of Gascony' without his knowledge or consent. They were ordered not to believe anything the legate said and to rest assured that Philip would respect their liberties, privileges and franchises. The practical effect of Boniface's action was to whip up local resentment against the French occupation and, to an extent, legitimise resistance.[10]

How much longer Philip could have held onto Gascony is a moot point, for his hand was forced by an astonishing military reversal in Flanders. When the truce of Tournai expired, on 6 January 1300, the Flemish were overrun. First the town of Douai surrendered to Philip's forces, and then Charles of Valois captured Damme and most of the other towns along the Zwin river. The surrender of the last two strongholds, Ghent and Ypres, marked the effective conquest of Flanders. Count Guy, his son Robert of Béthune and more than 100 Flemish noblemen surrendered and were imprisoned in French castles.[11]

The French triumph was illusory. In 1301 the commoners and guildsmen of Bruges staged a revolt against the French, remembered as the Matins of Bruges. The response of the Count of St Pol was disproportionate, and in May 1302 the French garrison was driven out. Open war erupted again in Flanders, and Philip sent an army to restore order.

On 11 July the Count of Artois mustered his host on the marshy plain of Groeninge, near Courtrai. He had the flower of French chivalry under his command, about 5,000 knights arranged into ten divisions or *batailles*. Facing him, positioned behind a long and marshy waterway, was the Flemish army. Only a few nobles were among the Flemish troops: Guy de Namur, Willem van Jülich the younger and Jan de Renesse. The majority of the army consisted of militia on foot, artisans from the towns and peasants from the countryside.[12]

The French held a council of war. They were supremely confident of victory: after all, how could a rabble of men on foot hope to defeat mounted knights? As their commander, Artois, declared, 'What can such common people do against us? Even if there were many of them, one hundred knights are worth a thousand men on foot! The more vigorous the enemy defends himself the more honour shall fall to us on the battlefield. We have not advanced here to kill and pursue defenceless men!'

It was decided to send the crossbowmen forward first, to break up the dense ranks of Flemish infantry. The French knights would then finish the job. At first all went well, as the Flemish missile troops were forced back. Artois ordered his crossbows to withdraw and sent his cavalry across the stream. The impetus of their terrible charge was slowed as they picked their way across three metres of water. To the bitter surprise of the French, their knights failed to pierce the thick Flemish hedge of pikes, lances and *goedendags* (a type of spiked club). The handful that did break through were dragged from their horses and killed. Others tumbled into the deep Groeninge stream.

The decisive moment came when Jan de Renesse threw his reserve into the fray. His counter-attack split the French ranks and enabled the townsmen to advance. Artois launched a desperate charge to save the day. He almost reached Guy de Namur and seized his banner with both hands, ripping away the flag, but Flemish soldiers swarmed around the French commander until he was struck down by a *goedendag*. With his last words, Artois begged for his horse to be spared. He was then surrounded and beaten to death. The victor of Bellegarde and Veurnes, the finest French captain of his day, was slaughtered in the mud by Flemish weavers and craftsmen.

His death signalled the collapse of the French army. The usual rules of warfare were suspended. Hundreds of French nobles were massacred. Apart from Robert d'Artois, the butcher's bill included Raoul de Nesle, Geoffrey de Brabant, the Count of Eu, the Count of Aumale, the lord of Tancarville and Pierre Flote, that clever French lawyer, who had put on armour for the day. Only one of the French commanders, Mathieu de Trie, was taken prisoner.

Courtrai was not a only terrible shock (especially to the French) but a game-changer. It altered the political landscape completely. After the devastating loss of his field army, Philip IV was in a dire position. He could no longer aid the Scots against King Edward, and his already fragile hold on Gascony started to crumble away. When they heard of the miracle in Flanders, the citizens of Bordeaux started to plan their own liberation.[13]

In England news of the battle was greeted with hilarity. The Flemish had done what the English could not, and inflicted a shattering defeat on Philip's forces. A popular song, called the 'Song on the Flemish Insurrection', was composed to celebrate the downfall of the French:

> Seven counts and forty barons in number
> fifteen hundred knights proud and very bold
> sixty thousand squires what with young and old
> to take the Flemings.
> The Flemings boldly came against them;
> these proud French comtes, their knights, and their men
> they killed and slew over the hills and the plains
> all for their King's sake.

These French came to Flanders light as the hare;
before it was midnight there fell upon them with care;
they were caught in the net as a bird is in the snare,
with horse and with steed.
The Flemings dab them on the bare head;
they will take for them neither ransom nor pay;
they dod off their heads, happen what may,
and thereto have they need.[14]

From Edward's perspective, the Flemish victory was as unexpected as it was glorious. His erstwhile allies had done him the most incredible favour. At a stroke, the French politicos and generals who had tormented him for years – Pierre Flote, Robert d'Artois, Raoul of Nesle, John of Aumale – were swept off the board. Now Edward had to make the most of this unlooked-for gift.

His first move was on 11 August, a few weeks after the battle. On that date he issued a charter to the merchants of Aquitaine, granting them exclusive trading rights and liberties in England. The ancient toll or prise on wine exports to England, whereby the king would take two tuns from each loaded ship at a fixed sum, no matter the current price, was lifted. Instead a new tax of 2 shillings pen tun was imposed, but all others dropped. Merchants of Aquitaine could not be impleaded or accused of crimes at merchants, fairs or boroughs in England (save the crime of murder), unless enough of their colleagues were present to see justice done. They were also permitted to lodge at will in any city or town in England for three months instead of the customary forty days, and store goods there with the consent of the owner.[15]

These were startling concessions, and look like a deliberate attempt to curry favour with the merchants of Aquitaine. Edward must have been aware of the damaging effect the war had wrought on the wine trade, especially at Bordeaux. By offering this charter, so soon after Courtrai, he dangled a lure before the eyes of the impoverished mercantile community. If the Bordelais revolted against the French, and came back to his allegiance, they stood to profit.

His second move, on 26 August, was to appoint John de Hastings as Lieutenant and Seneschal of Gascony. Hastings arrived in the duchy on 30 November and may have entered into secret talks with pro-English elements in Bordeaux. Their ringleader was one Arnaud Caillau, who in January 1303 led a popular uprising against the French. He was assisted by Bernard Cliquat, a bourgeois who advanced money for the security of the city during the rising. By 15 January 1303 the French garrison had been ejected and Arnaud installed as mayor.[16] It was not accomplished without violence; when a French lawyer attempted to remonstrate, Arnaud tore out the man's tongue and killed him on the spot.[17]

The revolt at Bordeaux finally swung the tide in Edward's favour. On 14 February his envoys the Count of Savoy, Henry de Lacy and Othon de Grandson crossed the Channel to 'expedite certain affairs'. In March he hired ships to convey the Bordelais exiles and their companies back to their city.[18] They brought retinues ranging from a handful of men to fifty or more, so the army that landed at Bordeaux was quite a considerable one.[19] Their appearance put an end to any pretensions towards republicanism, on the Flemish or north Italian pattern, held by the burgesses.[20]

Even in his moment of triumph, Edward was not minded to renew the Flemish alliance. On 25 March he dined with Flemish envoys, including Jean de Namur, at Ogerston. The king informed them that no further alliance on equal terms could be concluded between England and Flanders, since there was so much disparity between their respective strengths and their positions vis-à-vis the King of France.[21] In any case, Edward had empowered his envoys to affirm the treaty of alliance with the French on the 22nd, just three days earlier.[22]

A final peace was negotiated. In May 1303 a treaty was agreed in Paris, and Gascony handed back entire to the King of England. Nine years of strenuous warfare and diplomacy had resulted in a return to the pre-war position.[23]

Philip had political and financial reasons to restore Gascony to the English. The first was the sheer cost of maintaining a permanent occupation. French expenditure in Gascony between 1296–98 has been calculated at a monthly average of 29,500 *livres tournois*.[24] Edward's military expenditure in Scotland for the regnal year 1299–1300 was £29,198.[25] Such a massive outlay could not be sustained for long. Complete figures do not survive, but in July

1298 only 8,000 *livres tournois* had been received from the king's treasurer at Paris to pay off debts from the Gascon war. These debts were increased by loans contracted with the Italian banking house of Scotti and individual creditors.[26]

To add to Philip's woes, there were the consequences of his manipulation of the currency. After his first debasement in 1295, the value of French currency depreciated by 15 per cent in relation to English pound sterling and the Florentine gold florin. When the county of Flanders declared independence from France in 1296, Philip's finances were even further constrained. His desperate need for funds to sustain military expenditure led to further debasements and more borrowing. In the short term this was beneficial: French accounts between Christmas 1296 and Christmas 1299 show receipts of over 2 million *livres tournois* to offset war costs of 1,066,266 *livres tournois*. It appears that very little of this money went to pay off debts in Gascony, which may cast a different light on Philip's priorities. The impact of his policy can be shown in the steady depreciation of the French currency in relation to silver. In 1295 the *gros* was exchanged for an equivalent of 3.21 grams of silver, but by October 1299 the exchange was made at 2.57 grams.[27]

The impact of debasement started to bite after the French defeat at Courtrai: in the fifteen months after the battle, the French currency depreciated by 37 per cent, and new decrees were issued forbidding the export of gold and silver from the kingdom. Such was Philip's desperation, French officials and citizens were ordered to send their silver vessels (all of them in the case of officials, half in the case of civilians) to the mints to be melted into coin. His subjects resorted to investing their wealth in non-monetary assets to take them out of the country. This in turn obliged Philip to issue another decree, in 1303, which forbade the export of any merchandise without royal permission. The result was further depreciation, which forced him to formally recognise the devaluation. On 22 August, new coins were issued with just a third of the silver of the coins issued by Louis IX in 1266. Shortly afterwards the bishops of France issued a declaration, asking the king not to devalue the currency any further without the permission of the high clergy and nobility.[28]

There was another consideration. In 1302 Philip was in a similar position to Edward in 1297: his army had suffered a heavy defeat, and he had to juggle priorities. Philip's priority was to reverse the disaster of Courtrai and recover his position in Flanders. Given the state of his finances, it was no longer possible to fight simultaneous wars in Flanders and Gascony. He therefore cut his losses and chose to restore Gascony to Edward. By doing so he acknowledged his initial mistake in provoking a war over the duchy in 1294: 'Philip IV changed his plans: he realised that he had made a big mistake. The King had not been told that his policies were wrong.'[29]

Such an interpretation might imply that restoring the duchy was Philip's own decision, made without the influence of counsellors. Pierre Flote, after all, had been slain at Courtrai.

It was a canny strategic move. Philip was quite aware that Edward's only reason for going to war was the recovery of his inheritance. Once Gascony was handed back, he might turn Edward into a useful ally. Technically the English king was once again a French vassal, liable to do military service, but circumstances had changed. In March 1304 Philip requested Edward's military aid against Flanders. This was not interpreted as obligatory feudal service, but as a friendly gesture; a product of the treaty of alliance concluded between the two sovereigns. It was not to set a precedent.

Edward reverted to his former policy of evading service by any plausible means. He promised to assemble a fleet of twenty ships for the war in Flanders, but they were never dispatched. A letter of excuse was sent to Philip, carried by three messengers including Roger Savage and Peter of Dunwich.[30]

He was not entirely able to slide out of his obligations. One of his nobles of Ponthieu, the lord of Varenne, served in Flanders between 20 November 1301 and 19 November 1302.[31] It may be that Philip had decided to change his policy towards Edward as early 1299, when Ponthieu was restored to the English. Instead of fighting an expensive and unwinnable war against his cousin, it made far more sense to use Edward's resources against Flanders. However, until his hand was forced at Courtrai, Philip would not admit his mistake over Gascony.

The war was every bit as expensive for Edward. Almost 60 per cent of his war expenditure between 1294–99 was spent on wages to

Gascon troops, while another 10 per cent went to English troops.[32] The overall cost of his wars in Flanders and Gascony was in the region of £750,000.[33] These budgetary constraints alone might have influenced Edward's attitude towards the Flemings after 1297. Such was the implication of the statement made by his envoys to Count Guy's sons at the Curia. Philip also had to spend very large sums on the war, and unlike Edward was unable to fall back on a tradition of taxation.

Edward's 'grand alliance' hardly justified the vast financial outlay, though it wasn't completely ineffectual. He got good service from the Count of Bar, who twice went into action on his behalf. The barons of Franche-Comté caused the French a deal of trouble in Burgundy and continued the fight even after Edward's return to England. Several of the German princes on his payroll fought in Flanders. The Duke of Brabant, Edward's anglophile son-in-law, joined the king at Ghent with his knights. In light of the above, it is incorrect to state that Edward's diplomatic preparations 'brought no military assistance from his hoped-for allies'.[34] Any hopes of victory were dashed by the non-appearance of Adolf of Nassau.

Edward has been criticised for 'incompetent military planning' in Flanders.[35] Yet, unlike his earlier scheme for the reconquest of Gascony, there is no direct information for the king's tactical plans. He probably intended to join with the combined German and Flemish army but was unable to sail in time before they were defeated at Veurne. This must have severely disrupted any plans the king had in mind. Afterwards he remained at Ghent, waiting for Adolf. The king did not, however, keep his army entirely static behind a defensive fosse. English and Welsh troops were despatched to assist Robert de Béthune in the sack of Damme, and Welsh infantry accompanied the Count of Bar on raids into French territory. When it became clear his German allies were not going to arrive, he switched to a realistic policy of arbitration backed up by military force. Edward also benefited from the actions of Henry de Lacy, his *capitaneus* in Gascony, whose ravaging of the Toulousaine lands applied more pressure to the French.

The contemporary opinion of the Flemish on Edward is perhaps best summarised by the Minorite, who described the king's death in 1307 as 'the just judgement of God'.[36] Such harsh statements do not (understandably) take into account Edward's circumstances. His efforts to get to Flanders in 1297 have been described as 'frenzied'[37] and 'almost superhuman',[38] but this wasn't his only military option. As we have seen, the Earl of Norfolk had refused to serve in Gascony except under the king's personal command. Norfolk declared he was quite willing to go to Gascony with the king and march before his face in the first line of battle, as was his hereditary right.[39] Therefore Edward might have chosen to abjure his oath to Count Guy in February, and sail to Gascony with a larger army than the one he took to Flanders. For Edward to let slip such an opportunity, along with his evident resolution to sail to Flanders, can only mean he was initially determined to uphold his oath to Guy.

The details of the negotiations at Rome after the campaign reveal Edward's changed attitude. He would not offer any further material assistance, since he had none to spare. The wars in Gascony and Scotland were devouring his resources. His envoys did, however, attempt to include Flanders in the peace between England and France. This was in line with the terms of the Tournai armistice, which Edward may have hoped to prolong. When the Pope rejected this appeal, there was nothing more to be done. Peace with France, and good relations with the papacy, were more important.

Edward gained two advantages from his difficult sojourn in Flanders. At great risk and expense, he retained a portion of Gascony and the freedom to pursue his interests in Scotland. The former gave him a vital stake in the tortuous negotiations that followed, which resulted in a marriage alliance with France and the recovery of Ponthieu. It is possible the English would have recovered Gascony eventually, given the rising tide of local discontent at French occupation and Anglo-Gascon command of the seas. Yet the stand-off might have continued for years, and in the end Edward owed a debt of gratitude to the Flemish triumph at Courtrai. He certainly exploited it to the full.

21

AFTERMATH

The immediate result of the peace in 1303 was beneficial to both kings. Finally released from their hopeless duel, they could now turn on Flanders and Scotland: 'A tacit, and surely cynical, part of the peace process was that Edward I and Philip I were both left free to pursue their designs upon their northern neighbours.'[1]

Philip focused on wiping out the humiliation of Courtrai. He ordered a general levy of troops for 1302–04, from which his subjects could only be exempted by paying the 'Flanders subsidy'. In addition he hired a great number of foreign mercenaries, mainly Genoese archers.[2]

At first his renewal of the war went badly, as a French army was defeated by the Flemings at Arques on 4 April 1303. Philip redoubled his efforts, and on 10–11 August 1304 his fleet won a naval victory at Zierikzee.[3] On 18 August he led a French army to a victory of sorts at Mons-en-Pévèle. Philip was almost killed in his tent when the Flemings attacked unexpectedly, but led a counter-attack that forced his enemies to withdraw.[4] After some further skirmishes, Philip entered into negotiations. He had won his face-saving victory, but a continuation of the war was impossible. Another tax, after the heavy subsidies he had levied already, would have provoked serious disorders.[5]

The terms of the Treaty of Athis-sur-Orge, settled in June 1305, were favourable to Philip. Count Guy of Flanders had died in a

French prison in March and was succeeded by his son, Robert of Béthune. As the price of holding Flanders from the French Crown, Robert agreed to pay a rent of 20,000 *livres tournois* per year. Until this was paid, Philip was to hold the cities of Lille, Douai and Béthune. The people of Flanders were to pay an additional indemnity of 400,000 *livres tournois* in four years, with exemptions for those who had sided with the French. Some 3,000 inhabitants of Bruges were to go on pilgrimage (1,000 to the Holy Land) to expiate the Matins. The fortifications of Flemish towns were to be destroyed. The new count, his nobles and the town governments were to swear to observe these terms.[6]

It was one thing to agree a set of terms, quite another to enforce them. Many of the Flemings were unhappy with the arrangement, and disputes rumbled on to the end of Philip's reign and beyond. A determined effort at settlement in 1312, when much of western Flanders was ceded to Philip in exchange for cancellation of the rent, failed to bring peace. In 1315, Philip's successor, Louis X, was assembling another French army to invade Flanders. Further armies were raised in 1319 and 1325. Robert of Béthune and his heirs continued to nurse resentment, until finally the counts of Flanders threw in their lot with the English in the Hundred Years War. The wheel had turned full circle.[7]

Away from the military front, Philip took drastic measures to stabilise his finances. To salvage the French currency, he needed to issue new coins with a greater concentration of silver. The problem lay in finding that amount of silver. His solution was to arrest the Jews, on 22 July 1306, and confiscate their goods on 24 August. Their silver was used to provision the mints, a measure which probably raised upward of 2 million *livres tournois* for the Crown. This revaluation of the coinage had the perverse effect of forcing debtors to repay in the stronger currency debts which had been incurred in the weaker. The position of debtors was further impoverished by lease payments made on the new, strong currency.[8]

The king's financial policy caused riots in Paris. He was forced to take refuge in the Templar fortress, while crowds outside refused to allow supplies to be brought in, or anybody to go in or out, until the king agreed to talk to them. Philip, who had planned to flee in secret, loosed his soldiers on the mob. Many were killed in the street fighting, or captured and hanged. Victims included the innocent as well as the guilty, while others fled Paris. There was also much violence and unrest in the provinces.[9]

Finally, Philip turned on the Templars. There isn't sufficient space here to discuss this hugely controversial subject, except with regard to Philip's financial difficulties. One recent argument is that the financial motive for his persecution of the Templars was just a side-effect. Rather, it should be seen in the context of the confrontation between the king and Pope Boniface VIII.[10] Another argument is that the Templar treasury was the only remaining source of silver available to Philip, after he had taken all he could from the Jews and exhausted the silver mines in Saxony. By way of comparison, James II of Aragon and Edward II of England exploited Templar silver reserves in their kingdoms to obtain funds. On balance, it seems likely that Philip plundered the silver found in the Paris Temple to restore his currency.[11]

The accounts are fragmentary, but it appears Philip made very little out of his seizure of Templar assets. Possibly he overestimated their wealth. While Philip managed to stabilise the currency, he remained short of cash. Pope Clement V, Boniface's successor, stated flatly that this was the result of Philip's wars. He had once been rich, Clement remarked in December 1309, but war had impoverished him, and now his kingdom was emptied of money.[12]

For Edward, the agreement of Paris was no less of a release. In May 1303, while talks were still in progress in France, he marched north to prepare for his final all-out attempt to conquer Scotland. The lack of distractions on the Continent meant he could focus all his resources on the Scots, but there were still problems to overcome. His garrisons on the border were short of money and provisions, and the situation threatened to repeat the failures of previous campaigns.[13] After their defeat at Falkirk in 1298, the Guardians of Scotland had adopted a policy of avoiding battle, secure in the knowledge that Edward's army would fall apart due to lack of supplies.

This time the king was determined to get results. Emergency supplies of money and food were rushed up from England, and his administration performed miracles to keep the army in the field.

For the first time since 1296, Edward was able to cross the Forth and ravage Scottish heartlands. The Scots were faced with a choice of risking battle or submission on terms. They chose the latter, and by 9 February 1304 agreement had been reached between Edward's diplomats and Sir John Comyn, the head of the Guardians.[14] On 24 July Stirling Castle, the last Scottish stronghold in arms, surrendered to the king. After eight years of warfare, his conquest appeared to be complete.[15]

In the aftermath Edward drew up a new instrument or ordinance for the government of Scotland. This was a surprisingly lenient arrangement, in which he included the Scottish magnates in a revamped administration. There was no doubt, though, who was really in charge:

> We should not take this apparent foray into sensitivity too far, however; the bottom line remained that Edward I now ruled Scotland in deed as well as in name, and if he regarded any current practice as detrimental to his royal rights, or contrary to his overriding vision of how Scotland was to be run, then it would not be allowed to continue.[16]

While Edward hammered out the details of the ordinance, his agents were no less busy in Gascony. Othon de Grandson and Henry de Lacy were faced with an unenviable task. Almost a decade of war had left Gascony in a state of considerable disorder, in which royal revenues were badly affected and many royal rights of jurisdiction usurped.[17] There was also the physical damage to lands and property, financial deficit and the smouldering ill will between Gascons and Frenchmen. Arguments over dispossessions would continue for years, and inquiries into the usurpation of ducal rights were still being conducted in 1311.[18]

Edward and his officers did their best to attack these problems. At the parliament of February 1305, the king heard and responded to hundreds of petitions from Gascony. The details of these give a vivid impression of the chaotic state of the duchy. There were pathetic appeals for back pay from veteran soldiers such as Vigorous de Gascoyne, who had lost a limb in the king's service.[19] The merchants of Gascony begged for repayment of loans they had made to the king during time of war.[20] Similar appeals of debt were made by Gascon nobles who had served in the king's garrisons.[21] There were disputes between lords and tenants, such as that of the lord of Estibeaux, who complained that the king's lieutenant in Gascony prevented him from doing justice on three runaway villeins.[22]

The above is just a sample of the 1,592 surviving petitions.[23] Edward's responses were usually generous: he could scarcely be otherwise, given the loyalty and suffering of his Gascon subjects.

Inevitably, in the chaotic aftermath of war, there were all kinds of territorial disputes to resolve. Many nobles had exploited the conflict to seize lands belonging to their neighbours, or to recover lost estates. One of these was Augier, the aged former Viscount of Mauléon whom Edward had disinherited back in 1261 (see chapter 3). Upon the outbreak of war in 1294, Augier was summoned to arms along with the rest of the Gascon gentry. Instead he defected to the French and used the situation to seize his lost viscountcy of Soule, along with the castle of Mauléon. After the end of the war, Augier refused to give up his lands, despite repeated protests from Edward I. He finally agreed to exchange them for lands in Navarre, and the King of Navarre in turn sold them back to Edward II. Thus ended the long saga of Augier de Mauléon.[24]

Amid these difficulties, one bright spot was the recovery of the wine trade. Edward had identified this as a key driver of Gascon loyalty, and the years after 1303 witnessed a swift return to prosperity. At its peak in the early fourteenth century, the duchy annually exported nearly 103,000 tuns of wine. The average level of exports between 1305 and 1330 was 85,000 tuns, which meant considerable revenues for the English Crown. A sizeable percentage of exports went directly to England, and the king benefited from a custom on wine landed in England.[25]

In other respects, however, the recovery of Gascony meant a return to the same old problems. Just when it seemed as though the English administration had a grip on affairs, private wars erupted all over the duchy. In April 1305 Edward ordered the new seneschal, John de Havering, to protect Bidau Brane, lord of La Mote de Villenane, as a war had broken out between the gentry of Brassenx near St-Sever.[26]

Another local war erupted in the Agenais, and yet another in Landes between Amanieu d'Albret and the Sire de Caumont.[27] The latter conflict threatened to spread to Poitou, Saintonge, Périgord, Toulouse and Comminges. Havering acted swiftly. He raised a ducal army, captured d'Albret and Caumont and imprisoned them at Bordeaux and La Réole respectively.[28]

The counts of Foix and Armagnac chose this moment to renew their feud, which had gone into abeyance during the war. They had both defected to the French, but reverted to Edward's allegiance after the restoration of Gascony. The king may have wished he could leave them in Philip's care. On 12 August the Count of Foix invaded the lands of Armagnac. He also seized the royal castle of Rivière-Basse and other places belonging to the king-duke. Edward's officers again reacted swiftly and decisively. Within weeks Foix had sued for peace.[29] Yet the damage of these wars undid the work of the past two years, and threw the administration back into a state of paralysis.[30]

Apart from feuds between rival houses, there was the never-ending controversy of Gascon appellants. The king's strongman in Bordeaux, Arnaud Caillau, had a straightforward attitude towards this problem. After the French defeat at Courtrai, he was said to have regularly threatened fellow citizens in Bordeaux who wished to appeal to Paris:

> Why do you appeal from us to the French? We will kill you, and the king of France has so many things to do with the Flemings that he will not help you; and if a war begins and you are appellants, the English king will conquer Normandy and we will kill you and you will gain nothing unless you give up your appeal.[31]

Arnaud's view that Edward was in a position to conquer Normandy is of interest, though scarcely realistic. Nor was the problem of appellants likely to be resolved by threats and menaces. The resumption of Edward's vassal status brought with it all the old legal difficulties of the Treaty of Paris. In 1306 one of Edward's lawyers, Philip Martel, spoke the plain truth in a bad-tempered conference with French envoys at Montreuil:

> Of what use is it for Englishmen to go to law against the king of France in his kingdom, against his whole council, and against

> you who are our co-judges? Certainly none! Further, for that reason we and the king of England and his council ought to act likewise against your plaintiffs. God forbid, for such a situation would have no solution![32]

By this stage the English regarded the Treaty of Paris as a terrible blunder, and Crown lawyers devised all kinds of stratagems for wriggling out of it. In about 1306 a secret document was drawn up, listing the 'principal and secret aims' of English diplomacy. These were to 'withdraw with impunity and honesty towards God and man' from the accursed treaty of 1259. One suggested method of achieving this was to postpone homage by asking such enormous war damages that the income of France in three years would not be able to pay it. Other tactics included taking complete control of the English Channel, or refusing to pay war compensation to the French.[33]

None of these ideas came to anything. The English were trapped in a legal bind, and Edward's trials were not over. On 10 February 1306 the fragile peace in Scotland was shattered by the assassination of John Comyn by Robert de Bruce, Earl of Carrick. Bruce went into revolt against the English regime, and the war resumed. Gascony's contribution was 200 tuns of wine sent from Bordeaux to Scotland – a far cry from the thousands of Gascon troops Edward had once raised to spearhead his conquest of Wales.[34]

There was no resolution to the Scottish war. Edward died on 7 July 1307 at a barren outpost in the Cumbria marshes, still convinced he could do what his captains could not. His heir, Edward II, inherited a difficult legacy that he wasn't remotely capable of redeeming. While he struggled to contain the resurgent Scots, Gascony slid further into chaos. The situation was summed up by the mayor and jurats of Bordeaux, who in 1311 wrote to the king:

> Be it known that since the last war all your land of Gascony, and above all your city of Bordeaux, whether by an insufficiency of your officials, or by the presumptuous insubordination of the nobles and the powerful men of the country, has endured a government not only bad but detestable.[35]

22

TROPHIES AND DEAD THINGS

The peace treaty of Paris in May 1303 declared that the marriage alliances between England and France would encourage a state of mutual love. Edward and Philip would be better friends and 'all rancours, injuries, ill-will and hatreds be put away, remitted and pardoned on one side and the other'.[1]

This was optimistic, to say the least. There was little love lost between the two kingdoms, and the following decades would see relations sour even further. Edward I had recovered his inheritance, but was otherwise unable to halt the tide of French expansion in Europe. After the ceasefire in 1297, most of his allies fell under French influence. The new King of the Germans, Albrecht, was a French ally. Holland was lost when its young count, John, died in 1299. The pro-French Count of Hainault, John d'Avesnes, moved in and took over the regency. The Burgundians under Jean de Chalon-Arlay were forced to submit and do homage to Philip in 1301.[2]

Special treatment was meted out to Count Henri of Bar, Edward's son-in-law and the most loyal of his allies. In June 1301 he was forced to sign the Treaty of Bruges, whereby much of the county of Bar was ceded to Philip. He was also made to pay compensation for the damage he had committed during the war. Finally, Henri had to agree to go on pilgrimage to the Holy Land. The crusader states had ceased to exist after the fall of Acre in 1290, so he set off to Cyprus instead. He died in Naples in September 1302, two months after his enforced departure from the *Barrois*.[3] Henri's fate was remarkably similar to that of Prince Dafydd of Wales and Gaston de Béarn, both of whom had been required to swear an oath to go to the Holy Land. It seems that this form of exile was a favoured strategy of the kings of France and England; a convenient way of disposing of their enemies.

Edward managed to claw back some of his influence in Bar. After Henri's death, the king intervened on behalf of his grandsons, and in 1307 Philip agreed to restore certain castles and lands to the late count's heir, named Edward after his royal grandsire. In 1313, at the entreaty of Edward II, Philip restored more territory to the Count of Bar. Thanks to English influence, the most painful consequences of the Treaty of Bruges were reversed within twelve years.[4]

This was a minor consolation. Philip IV had shown the way to his successors, and the French exploited the troubles of Edward II's reign to gnaw away at the borders of Aquitaine. The treaty of 1303 had re-established Capetian feudal supremacy, and their policy afterwards was thoroughly consistent. They continued Philip's strategy of using cases and appeals to affirm their rights and put pressure on the English. Such methods were chosen for the simple reason that war costs more than a lawsuit.[5] Nor were the English ever allowed to forget their inferior status. Charles IV (r. 1322–28) spelled this out to the ambassador of Edward II in 1324:

> How can you have the audacity to offer on behalf of the duke of Guyenne to make amends for wrongs done to the king of France, his sovereign? The king, being emperor in his kingdom, has no other superior but God, and the law will not suffer a sovereign to be judged by his subject.[6]

Where cost and opportunity served, the French were prepared to use force. In 1324 they seized upon another dubious pretext, a conflict of jurisdiction over a bastide built on French territory, to invade Saintonge and the Agenais. The War of St Sardos, as it was known, ended in disaster for the English as their army was forced to surrender at La Réole. Once again, as in the previous war, the king-duke was rescued by the loyalty of the Gascons. More than 100 Gascon nobles, sons and grandsons of those who had fought for Edward I, rallied to the Plantagenet banner. They had no wish to repeat the experience of 1294–1303, and ensured that none of the major towns and castles of Gascony fell into French hands.[7]

In 1303 it was hoped that the marriage of Edward II to Philip IV's daughter, Isabella, would bring a lasting peace. After the deposition of her husband in 1327, Isabella strove to postpone the impending conflict with France. With the aid of the papacy, she managed to persuade Charles IV to accept the homage of her son, Edward III. War broke out again when Charles insisted on retaining the Agenais as an indemnity. The French planned another full-scale invasion of Aquitaine: a budget for a proposed conquest of the duchy survives from 1327, estimating the costs of supplies and provisions.[8] A truce followed, but it was merely delaying the inevitable.

Edward III decided he might as well fight as be nibbled to death. He lit the fuse by laying claim to the throne of France via his mother, Isabella. His claim was dubious, to say the least, and relied on questionable interpretation of laws of succession in France. The strategy was possibly inspired by Edward II, who had contemplated a claim to the French throne in a letter of 1317.[9]

Edward III's decision to go to war was really driven by the catch-22 that had bedevilled his father and grandfather:

> It was not the dynastic question that brought about the war, though, war being inevitable, Edward might well, as he himself said, use his claims as a buckler to protect himself against his enemies. The fundamental difference between the two nations lay in the impossible position of Edward in Gascony. He could not abandon his ancient patrimony, and Philip [VI] could not give up that policy of gradually absorbing the great fiefs which the French kings had carried on since the days of St Louis. The support given to the Scots, the Anglo-imperial alliance, the growing national animosity of the two peoples, the rivalry of English and French merchants and sailors, all these and many similar causes were but secondary.[10]

The final step on the road to war was taken in 1337, when Philip VI confiscated Gascony. Over a century of intermittent conflict followed.

This was the era of the longbow and the famous English victories of Crécy (1346), Poitiers (1356) and Agincourt (1415). Edward III's capture of Calais in 1348 gave the English a foothold in northern France that would not be lost until the Tudor era. The French, under inspired leaders such as Bertrand de Guesclin and Jeanne d'Arc, fought back and eventually triumphed. In 1453 the last English field army in Gascony was blown away by French cannon fire at Castillon. The surrender of Bordeaux soon afterwards triggered the final conquest of Aquitaine. Almost two centuries after the Treaty of Paris, Edward I's beloved duchy fell to the French.

The English and their Gascon subjects did remarkably well to hold off the French for so long, but the seeds of their defeat were already sown. Henry III's conversion to a French vassal in 1259 had left him and his heirs brutally exposed. The aggressive policy of Philip IV, coupled with the inadequate peace arrangements of 1303, sealed the fate of Aquitaine. Edward I and his successors would never admit it, but they were pre-ordained to fight a losing battle.

> Vain the ambition of kings, who seek by trophies and dead things to leave a living name behind, and weave but nets to catch the wind.
>
> John Webster (*c.* 1580–1632)

APPENDICES

1. The Treaty of Paris, 1259; *English Historical Documents 1189–1327*, edited by David Charles Douglas and Harry Rothwell (Routledge, 1996) pp. 371–374

Henry, by God's grace king of England, lord of Ireland and duke of Aquitaine. We make known to all and to all who are to come that we by God's will have made peace with our dear cousin, the noble king Louis of France in this manner: namely that he give us and our heirs and our successors all the right that he has and holds in these three bishoprics and in the cities, namely, of Limoges, Cathors and Périgueux, in fief and domain, saving the homage of his brothers and if they hold anything there for which they are his man, and saving the things that he cannot alienate owing to letters granted by him or his ancestors, which things he must take steps to acquire in good faith from those who hold these things so that we may have them within a year next All Saints day or give us a suitable exchange, in the opinion of men standing nominated by either side the most suitable for the interests of both parties.- The aforesaid king of France shall also give us in money each year the value of the land of the Agenais according to the assessment to be made of it on the proper value of the land by men of standing nominated on either side, and payment shall be made at Paris at the Temple each year, half on the quinzaine of the Ascension and the other half of the quinzaine of All Saints. And should it happen that this land escheats from the countess Joan of Poitiers to the king of France or his heirs, he or his heirs shall be bound to surrender it to us or our heirs and when the land has been surrendered they shall be relieved of the payment. And if it comes in domain to us, the king of France shall not be bound to render this payment. And if it is decided by the court of the king of France that, to have the land of the Agenais, we ought to put down or hand over some money as security, the king of France shall return this money or we shall hold and have the payment until we have had what we have put down for this security.- Again, it shall be enquired in good faith and without impediment, at our request, by men of standing of either side chosen for the purpose, whether the land that the count of Poitiers holds in Quercy on behalf of his wife was given or granted by the king of England with the land of the Agenais as marriage portion or as security, either wholly or in part, to his sister, who was the mother of the last count Raymond of Toulouse. And if it is found that it had so been and this land escheats to him or his heirs on the death of the countess of Poitiers, he shall give it to us or our heirs, and if it escheats to another and it be found by this inquest however that it had been given or granted in the way said above, after the death of the countess of Poitiers, he shall give the fief to us and our heirs, saving the homage of his brothers, if they hold anything there, while they live.- Again, after the death of the count of Poitiers, the king of France or his heirs, kings of France, shall give to us and our heirs the land that the count of Poitiers holds then in Saintonge beyond the R.Charente in fief and in domain that are beyond the Charente, if it escheats to him or his heirs. And if it does not escheat to him, he shall take steps in good fashion to acquire it, by exchange or otherwise, so that we or our heirs shall have it, or he shall give us, in the opinion of men of standing who shall be nominated by either side, a suitable exchange. And for what he shall give us and our heirs in fief and in domain, we and our heirs will do him and his heirs, kings of France, liege homage, and also for Bordeaux, for Bayonne and for Gascony, and for all the land that we hold beyond the English Channel in fief and in domain, and for the islands, if there are any, that we hold that are of the kingdom of France, and we will hold of him as of a peer of France and as duke of Aquitaine. And for all these things aforesaid we will do him our appropriate services until it be found what services are due for these things and then we shall be bound to do them just as they have been found. About homage for the county of Bigorre, for Armagnac and for Fezensac let what is right be done about them. And the king of France absolves us if we or our ancestor ever wronged him by holding his fief without doing him homage and without doing his service, and all arrears.- Again, the king of France shall give us what, in the opinion of men of standing who shall be nominated by either side, 500 knights ought to cost to maintain reasonably for two years and shall be bound to pay this money at Paris at the Temple in six payments over the period of two years, namely the first payment, that is to say a sixth, on the quinzaine of next Candlemas, another payment on the quinzaine of the Ascension following and another on the quinzaine of All Saints and likewise with the remaining payments on the following year. And for this the king of France shall give the Temple or the Hospital or both of them together as surety. And we ought not to spend this money except in the service of God or of the church, or for the benefit of the kingdom of England, and this by view of men of standing of the land chosen by the king of England and by the magnates of this land.- And in making this peace we and our two sons have renounced and do renounce completely all claim upon the king of France and his ancestors and his heirs and successors, and his brothers and their heirs and successors, for us and our heirs and successors if we or our ancestors have or ever had any right in things which the king of France holds or ever held, or his ancestors held or hold, namely in the duchy and the whole land of Normandy, in the county and the whole land of Anjou, or Touraine and of Maine, and in the county and the whole land of Poitiers, or elsewhere in any part of the kingdom of France or in the islands, if the king of France or his brothers, or others from them, hold anything of them, and all arrears.- And likewise we have renounced and do renounce, we and our two sons, all claim upon all those who hold anything, by gift, exchange, sale, purchase, elevation or other similar way, from the king of France or from his ancestors or his brothers in the duchy and the whole land of Normandy, in the county and the whole land of Anjou, or Touraine and of Maine, and in the county and the whole land of Poitiers, or elsewhere in any part of the kingdom of France or in the islands aforesaid, saving to us and our heirs our right in the lands for which we ought to have by this peace, as set out above, to do liege homage to the king of France, and saving that we can ask for our right if we believe we have it in the Agenais, and have it there if the court of the king of France decides it, and likewise in respect of Quercy.- And we have pardoned and renounced all claim upon one another and we pardon and renounce all animosity over disputes and wars, all arrears, and all issues which have been had or which could have been had in all the aforesaid things, and all losses and expenses incurred on either side in war or in any other ways.- And so that this peace may be kept firmly and stably, without any infringement, forever, the king of France has had an oath sworn on his soul by his proxies specially appointed for this and his two sons have sworn to keep these things as long as it concerns each of them, and they have bound themselves and their heirs to keep it by their letters pendant. And that we will keep these things we are bound to give the king of France such surety from the knights of the aforesaid lands that he gives us and from the towns as he will require of us.- And the form of the surety for us from the men and towns shall be this: they shall swear that they will give neither counsel nor support nor aid whereby we or our heir may contravene the peace, and if it should happen, which God forbid, that we or our heir should contravene it and be unwilling to make amends on being requested to do so by the king of France or his heir, the king of France, those who have gone surety shall, within three months of being required by him to do so, be bound to help the king of France and his heirs against us and our heirs until this thing is sufficiently amended in the opinion of the court of the king of France. And this surety shall be renewed every ten years at the request of the king of France or his heirs, the kings of France.- And we promise in good faith for ourselves and for our heirs and successors, to the aforesaid king of France and his heirs and successors, loyally and firmly to keep this peace and this composition established between us and the aforesaid king of France and every one of the things aforesaid just as they are contained above, and we promise that we will not contravene them in any way either personally or through another, and that we have not and will not do anything whereby any or all of the aforesaid things, in whole or part, may be less firm. And so that this peace may be kept firmly and stably, without any infringement, forever, we have bounds ourselves and our heirs to this and have had an oath sworn on our soul in our presence by our proxies to keep the peace, just as it is set out and written above, in good faith as long as it concerns us, and not to contravene it either personally or through another.- And in witness of all these things we have made for the king of France these letters pendant, sealed with our seal. – And by special commandment our sons Edward and Edmund have in our presence sworn to keep and hold firmly this peace and all the things which are contained above and not to contravene them either personally and through others.- This was given at London, the Monday before the feast of St Luke the Evangelist in the year of our Lord's incarnation one thousand two hundred and fifty nine, in the month of October.

2. **Henry Knighton, *Chronicon***, ed. J. R. Lumby, RS, 92 (London, 1895), I, pp. 265–266 (translated by Richard Price)

When he drew near to France and the fame of his glory spread amongst the people, many envied his renown, especially the valiant count of Chalons, who sent to him and asked him to tourney with him in his land; Edward was unwilling to have the praise of his prowess diminished, even though he could have justified and excused himself by reason of his pilgrimage; he did not wish it so, and gladly agreed. It was publicly proclaimed that Edward and his pilgrims would hold their own in a tourney against all those who wanted to participate. And so, many men from all parts of that region came together, amongst whom were many men on foot as well as horsemen, all sworn to despoil the English, and, before the event, offering English horses and arms for sale and drinking wine in celebration of the plunder [they would take] from their future prisoners.

Edward sent to England for some of his magnates, and earls and barons came to him. When the day finally came, there were nearly a thousand men at arms and many footmen with Edward; the other side had twice that number in men and horses. The two sides clashed and the men on foot who had sworn to plunder and kill began [the fight]. Our men held out against them with slings and bows, and, after killing a great many of them, pursued the rest to the city gates. They chased many of them to the river, where a great number drowned.

Meanwhile, the count himself entered the fray with his fifty chosen knights, who followed him to Edward's squadron. The count joined battle with him, and they fought it out with sword blows for a long time. Both of them fought hard but the count saw that he could not overcome him with the sword, so he put his arm around Edward's neck and forcibly choked him. Edward said, 'What are you trying to do? Do you think you can take me?' The count answered, 'Most surely. I will have you and your horse.' Enraged by this, Edward pulled himself upwards and, striking [the count's] destrier, attacked with such force that the other man was pulled off his own horse, still clinging to Edward's neck, who beat him to the ground when he could hang there no longer. Edward, stunned, withdrew immediately to get his breath back and to revive his spirits.

When he saw the wickedness of the French and that they had slain many of his men, behaving as if they were at war not at tourney, he said to his men, 'Spare no-one you set eyes on now, and do the same to them as they are doing to us.' So they began killing the other side, savagely attacking them everywhere with the sword. The men on foot had retreated from the slaughter of their fellows when they saw many of their people fall, but boldly joined the combat of the mounted men; they gutted many of the horses and cut their girths, so that their riders fell to the ground.

Edward set upon the aforesaid count, who had by now been lifted back onto his horse by the hands of his men, and they again traded blows for some time. Edward urged him to yield, which he would not agree to at first, but when at last his strength failed, he surrendered himself on Edward's command to a low-ranking knight. Many of the others fled and a great number of them fell in that place. The victory gained, our men withdrew.

When our men thought it was safer to rest, a message was brought to Edward that his men were being killed by the citizens of the town as they went from house to house. He immediately summoned the mayor and the chief men of the town and ordered them to rebuke and punish their people, otherwise he would burn and raze their city to the ground on the morrow. They went away and stationed guards in all parts of the city, and it settled into peace.

Much blood was spilled in this tournament, and, as a result, its name was changed so that it became commonly called the Little War of Chalons, not a tournament. Edward went on from there to Paris and was received honourably by the French king. A few days later, he set out for Gascony and stayed there until after his father's death.

3. C 47/25/1/4; charges made by the king's subjects in Gascony against Gaston de Béarn, 20 Nov. 1273–19 Nov. 1274 (translated by Dr Shelagh Sneddon)

Item, 77(?) sheep were captured from Goyenetted and Santii of/from ... In seu ... Arcuytz 25 sheep and one ram belonging to Enetus Dunalant'i. Item, 613(?) sheep of the same ... Item, 100 head, between sheep and ... at Laparabere in Bigorre. Item, 13 sheep and 13 goats at Capidos.

Item, up to 3000 oaks were felled and chopped up from the woods of the Lady of ... of the Lord of Laurfontan.

Item, at Barcuyt in Seula, casks full of cider were broken and the cider spilt.

Item, chevauchées took place: one at Salas, another at Rupem Fortem de Cheursano, and animals were seized to the value of

20 pounds. Item, another at Seula, and another at Salas; and the church plundered. Item, another at … and damage done to wine, hay, oats, cloth, and other things, to the value of 30 pounds. Item, another at Lonso, another at … [another] at Big in Bigorre, another at La Parabere, likewise in Bigorre; and among other things ?150 shillings were taken. Item, another there. Item, another at ?Guilliagos in Bigorre, another at Sordua, another at Bonut, another at Saltus, another at Salas, another at Lonso, another at Arzas, another at Cabidos, another at Falhonde, another at Lobinher, another at Sevir, another at Lonson, another at Lobinh, another at Mirus Mons, another at Lana Longa, another at Petra, another at Saltus. Item, another and another there.

Item, ~~your~~ \the King's/ messenger was captured, who was carrying ~~your~~ \the King's/ letters in Seula ~~for~~ \after/ the prohibition of the lord King of France was to be observed, and when he was held many bad things were done to ~~your~~ \the King's/ people of Seula. Item, two … of Sordua were captured, and beaten, and 10 shillings were taken from them. Item, the ?miller of the same place was captured and a rouncey was taken from him … that is, from/of Betres. Item, four pack-horses, loaded with fish and per…, belonging to the Marquise of Verdaisse of Sordua were seized and taken. Item, 1[1] ?whiting were taken from a certain man of Bayonne in the port of Fons Mar. Item, two packhorses belonging to Raymond do Daus and ?150 shillings in money. Item, Bernard dou Ga and Arnold deu Ga of Saltus were captured and 6 pounds 2 shillings taken from them. Item, 100 shillings were taken from Peter del Berart of Saltus. Item a ship belonging to Peter de Casah of Tartacium was broken and the ship's equipment and 80 conches of millet taken from it, at the command or with the consent of Gaston, who was then present at Mons Marciani – that is, this year on the eve of the Lord's Ascension. Item, another ship then, belonging to Dominic de Saubola of Tartacium, and the ship's equipment and 10 and a half conches of wheat taken from it. Item, they kept back from the same Dominic the corn he had bought: that is, 60 conches of wheat. Item, 60 conches of millet. Item 11 pounds of Morlaix

in money. Item, after this ten packhorses from Sordua were captured. Item, four from Castrum Novum.
Item, the place (probably meaning a town or village) of Vineis (the Vines), the castle (or fortified town) of Garros and the place of La Réole were captured and taken wrongfully and by force.

Item, Alberis of Sordua's men are prevented from making their homes at Cussaver (?). Item, the lord of Sancto Quirico [is prevented from] enjoying his woods. Item Alte Rippe [are kept from] possession of the oats owed to them from Ancia by the men of Carressa. Item, Alberis de Sordua likewise. Item, the lady of Fanars [is prevented from] enjoying her woods of Fanars and of Pleys. The lord of Laurfontan likewise [is prevented from] enjoying his woods. The lord of Salas [is prevented from] enjoying the woods and devoirs/duties which he has at Poncii. Item, those which he has at Castens. Item, you and your subjects [are prevented from] enjoying the open and uncultivated land (possibly in the sense of Les Landes?) which is called Lo Gert, the woods of Bonac (?), the lands and woods of the parishes of Beyria, of Milhos, of Sevir, of Fixos, and of Sonson. Item, and the wood of Garda. Item, and the woods and ?property which lie between Salva Terra and Boloscar.

The places, within *fueros*, in the power of Gaston, from which the aforesaid are/were done, and to which they afterwards return/returned, are these: Orchesium, Salias, Salva Terra, Sanctus Martinus de Guaranhon, Mons Guiscardus, Sauboeys, Sevinhac, Milsens, Lemveya, Gauarret, Pau, ?Lanacaube, Sadirac, Lescar, Oléron, Mont Gaston, Castet Puogo, Morlana, Faget Aubin, Gironce, Bac, Camo, Ausa, Artunitz do Ussa, Mons Marciani, Larce, Castanh, Domyn Monstrorum and Pietz; and others.

The names of those who did the aforesaid, together with others whose names are at present unknown, are these: Assimius [or Assumus] de Bauall' [or Biauall'?], Garcias Arnold de Tilh, Arnold de Naualhas, bastard of the lord of Naualhas, Bernard de Bello Loco, Garcias Loup de Campo, Peter, Gerald, and Raymond William de Campo, brothers, Peter de Campo, their uncle, Sans Aimery de Cernerest, Peter Arnold de Balensu, Bernard de Castretis, Bernard Lo Tort, Raymond William de Na

Flos, Peter Arnold Dalaman, son of Arnold de Payou, Raymond Dossenx, ordo of Lana, Garcias de Clauaria, Raymond Arnold, lord of Las, Bernard and Arnold his brothers, Peter Longus, Arnold William Loter and the bastard of Saudum – who were in the garrison of Orchesium. Item Bernard William, bastard son of Gaston Guilhegaut Targuetus, Vidal de Cassauer, Auger, Gerald, and Arnold, [his?] brothers, William de Famos – who were at Salias. Item Vidal of Toulouse and his son Ros, Peter Arnold de Fossis, Gerald de Carressa, Arnold William de Malo Leone, Peter Darboet, Peter Bernard, Fortis Amoravy and Otho de Sadiraco – who were at Salua Terra. Item Arnold Dones, B(er)nard Sine Terra, Arnold William his brother, and Arnold William Despis – who were at Sanctus Martinus de Guaranh. Item Estius Arnold de Sal', and William Bohord his son, and Odo de Lana – who were at Mons Guiscardus. Item Arnold Raymond Dasped and Raymond Arnold Daspet, Talhafer de Lana Plaa, Menaldus de Bello Videre, Sans de Sancto Albino and Arnold, his son, Arnold de Bedo, W. de Agremont, Ayquelmus de Samadet, Peter Raymond de Salias, William Raymond deu Leu, Simon deu Leu, Garcias Arnold de Bordes, Arnold Daugar, Auger de Talh, Auger the bastard of Saut, son of Navarrus de ?Puydomencte, Vidal de Cumpanhos, Garcias de Portas, Lubat de Lana Plaa, Raymond Arnold de Bello Videre and Jordan de Portas – who were at Sauboes. Item Vidal, lord of Sevinhac and the bastard of Peter de Maloleone – who were at Sevinhac. Item Raymond de Millescins, lord of Millescins Auger de Teysa, Galhard de Theysa and Sansol Dalaman – who were at Millescins. Item William Raymond de Doazit and Raymond Bernard de Labatut – who were in Judie(?). Item William Arnold de Pau, Navarrus de Seint Saudun and Auger Danhos – who were at Oleyron. Item Galhard de Paul at Paulum. Item Anerius de Gerzerest and Arnold de Brocas. Item Odo, lord of Sadiracum and his bastard son at Sadiracum. Item Lescarre. Item Arnold Raymond ?Badango at Mont Gaston. Item Galhard de Castet Puogo, Fortaner de Berochis, Bernard de Lannes, Bernard de Burest, Sans Agini de Laniota, Odo de Arrac, Bernard de Balirac – who were at Castet Puogo.

Item ... de Morlana, Raymond Filh, Raymond de Fageto, Arnold de la Garda, Garciot de la Hite, Peter ..., Bernard ..., Arnold de Aichesto(?) – who were at Morlana. Item Turnaber Bassetus and Raymond de ... at Faget' Albinum. Item ... de Naualhes, Bernardus de Bello Loco, Naualhon and Furon(?) at Osbat. Item Jordan de Camo, William Arnold de Camo and Bernard de Begorra – who were at Camo. Item Alaman, son of Alaman Dausa, Perrot de Clavaria of Feus, Doden de Feus, the young lord of Anvila d'Ausa and Arnold de Seint Saudanh at Ausa. Item ?Cocoa de Labada d'Aramitz at Bat... Item Garcias William de Lana, Fortet de Carrera d'Aramitz, Guilhamot de Metuytz, Peter Arnold de Lana, Motetus de Lana, Garcias Arnold de Contura, Senebrun de Sancta Maria at Aramitz. Item Galhard de Pau William Arnold Danhatz Arnold Danhatz, W. Basset at Doosa in Aspa. Bernard de Deu ... Lan Vesada at Mons Marciani. Raymond ... Deinz at Deunz. Raymond Dunhidi de Mostrer at Mostrer. Item ... Andonii, Auger de Fageto, lord of Artigalobe, Arnold de ?Pomar Longo and his bastard brother, Gascias de Luxa, Peter de Gravilhon and William Arnold his brother, Otho de Arrac, bastard of Balansun and bailli of Ordenh. Item Raymond de Morlane, Auger de Miromonte, Bernard de Pantenhan, Bernard Lacay, Raymond Arnold, brother of the lord of Hernede, Amaneu de Sal', Bernard Dosse, Benedict Despereben, Hispanus de Notz, Garcias Arnold ?d'Anbila and W. de Casa Nova. Item Adam de Lescuiz at Gironte. Item Raymond Garcias de Labad and Arnold de Labad of Ripparia Gavaris. Item Fortis Sans de Lados, Peter de Pirra and Bidotus de Gavarreto.

The expenses, costs and injuries are virtually inestimable. But insofar as they can be estimated, they are estimated, for Bordeaux, at 20 thousand pounds of Tours, for Bayonne, ?Dax (Aquis) and the land beyond the Landes, 10 thousand pounds of Tours, for Bazas (Vasatum), La Réole (Regula) and other lands, 5 thousand pounds of Tours. Item, for wages given by you and your other expenses, 65 thousand pounds of Tours and more.

Total of damages and expenses after the King's crossing: 100 thousand pounds of Tours.

4. Letters from officers of Edward I to the king. Taken from *Philip III the Bold, King of France, 1270–85: The Evolution of Royal Power in Medieval Europe* by Charles Victor Langlois, based on his *Le Régne de Philippe III de Hardi* (Paris, 1887), translated by Frank H. Wallis, p. 169

a) Ebles, son of the Viscount of Ventadour, wrote Jean de Grailli, married Gallience, daughter of the late G. de Malemort, with the approval of the friends of the aforesaid Galiennce, but against the wishes of his uncles, the Bishop of Limoges and the Count de Périgord, who endeavour to disinherit him and who gave to understand the King of France and his council that this marriage, if it was not broken, would turn to black favours and their confusion. The King ordered the aforementioned Galienne under his protection; condescend to request he not disturb the marriage of even a faithful vassal.

b) Knowest thou, that Inquisitors of the faith want to force me, me and your bailiffs of Gascony, to lead to Toulouse certain Jews from your domains that they know to be relapsed. I explained to them that I am not held to lead anyone out of your duchy, being ready to carry out their sentences there. One of them warned me he would abstain from very coercive justice until you are informed, but I do not know nevertheless if they will want to await your answer. The business is extremely serious and I beg you to treat with the aforementioned brothers, or even, if need be, with the Pope.

c) I came to Paris, at the Parlement, said Lucas de Tani, for your affairs of Gascony; I proposed to go from there to find you in England, according to your orders, when your secretaries, Maurice de Craon and Othon de Granson, said you return to Gascony. I hesitate: I beg you to enlighten me. Knowest thou that your subjects of Gascony are about to send a solemn message to you; I have many things to say t you on the state of your domains on this side of the sea; the situation is good, in spite of the annoyances of the French.

5. **TNA SC 1/13/3, Edward I to Philip III, king of France, the lack of agreement between Philip and the king of Castile; his difficulties because of wars in Ireland and Wales (translated by Simon Neal)**

To his magnificent leader, lord and kinsman, the very dear lord P., by the grace of God the illustrious king of France, E., by the same grace king of England, lord of Ireland and duke of Aquitaine, greetings and sincere affection of devotion always. Joy has gone far away from us, since, by the relation of our messengers, we have learnt that no form of peace has been begun or found between you and the king of Castella, clearly noticing therefore from the discord that has arisen between you how many Christians are being subjected to dangers, whereby a harmful obstacle is being prepared to the business of the land being made, how great confusion will be imminent for Christians, ... of your belovedness ... our wars of Ireland and Wales, which now ... anew, not without serious loss to our men at the time ... our journey to the parts, in which you are carrying on, the state of our realm having been arranged as swiftly as we can, ... If only he directs more intently ... in the meantime thereupon from here ... to your honour it can be ended or laid to rest more advisedly. Witnessed by me, myself, at Westminster on the ?13th day of November in the fourth year of our reign.

6. **TNA SC 1/19/6; Letter from Gerard de Moer to Count Guy of Flanders (translated by Dr Shelagh Sneddon)**

To his most honourable lord, honour and reverence. Know that we came before the town of Dam yesterday (or 'recently'), last Sunday. And the French surrendered the fort where the Welsh attack/fortify against them; and know that the town is taken. And while we were in the town the garrisons of Bruges came here to aid [them], and they have returned to attack you. Command us your will, and trust the bearer of these letters. By monsieur Gerard le Moer.

7. SC 1/14/184; letters from Jean de Chalon to Edward I; the fall of Ornans in Burgundy (translated by Richard Price)

Most dear sire, this is to inform you, that on Tuesday, the eve of the feast of Saint Denis, myself and my companions of Burgundy captured and razed the castle of Ornans, which was held by Burgundy of the King of France and was the strongest castle in the whole of Burgundy. And know that, I and my other comrades broke down the walls of the castle and forced our way inside, and secured the castle, and took nine prisoners and put a large number to the sword, apart from those who threw themselves down below the rock.

Most dear sire, this is to inform you, that on Tuesday, the eve of the feast of Saint Denis, myself and my companions of Burgundy captured and razed the castle of Ornans, which was held by Burgundy of the King of France and was the strongest castle in the whole of Burgundy. And know that, I and my other comrades broke down the walls of the castle and forced our way inside, and secured the castle, and took nine prisoners and put a large number to the sword, apart from those who threw themselves down below the rock. And know, my very dear Sire, that we are committed to the business of...of Burgundy, I will come to join your company, if you desire it...that I think...took. May God guard you sire...and grant you victory against your enemies, which is our dearest desire.

8. TNA SC 1/15/9; Count of Henry of Bar to Edward I; his forces are ready (translated by Richard Price)

To the most excellent prince, his most dear lord and father Edward, by the grace of God king of England, lord of Ireland and duke of Aquitaine; Henri count of Bar awaits his will and his command.

Sire, though you commanded us that we should go to you with all our men at arms in such fashion and so ordered that we would incur no risk, for you would not have it otherwise, we are letting you know that we are not able so to do, for we were away from our estates, to our great detriment. And do not distress yourself lest any loss befall us, Sire, be certain that we would bear it but lightly, so long as we might do your will or whatever might turn to your honour and your profit. And know, Sire, that it was the Sunday after St. Remy that your letters came to us, when we were all alone with the count of Savoy in another of our towns, but our orders [from you] were at Bar; the which we found when we returned there, and we left Bar this Tuesday after Saint Remy, and, though it wrong the king, there was no man ready to come with us to go to you, for we had not yet informed them. May it not displease you, Sire, that we will be a little late in coming to you, though [the men] will leave us as soon as we can hasten/expedite their muster to go to you; we fully expect to be with all our men at arms at our castle of Sathenay, to set off toward you on the Tuesday next after the feast of Saint Luke Evangelist, If we can do it sooner, we will hurry to you the sooner. Sire, inform us of your bidding, as you would to one ready to do his devoir.'

9. Count Guy of Flanders agrees to the truce, 10 October 1297; Manchester, University of Manchester Library, MS PHC/.146 (translated by Richard Price)

To all those who will see these letters, Guy, count of Flanders and marquis of Namur, gives greeting. We inform you that since an armistice has been made under fixed terms until a set date between the most high princes the King of France and the King of England on behalf of them and their allies in all the wars between them, we, bound to the said armistice in the form it has been made, agreed and sealed with the seal of the said King of England, do assent and promise in good faith, and have so sworn on the holy gospels on behalf of ourself and of our children, that we will keep and will ensure the said armistice is kept loyally and in full, in such wise that all our people of Flanders and of all our power, like ourself, shall henceforth be included in that armistice and may come and go, trade and work throughout all the land of the kingdom of

France and throughout all the lands of the allies of the King of France, in safety and in peace insofar and for so long as the terms of the above mentioned armistice shall last. In witness of which we have made these present letters, sealed with our seal, made and given in the year of grace twelve hundred and ninety-seven.

10. **Privileges granted to the Gantois by Edward I (translated by Simon Neal); *Messager des sciences et des arts, publ. par la Société royale des beaux-arts et des lettres, et par celle d'agriculture et de botanique de Gand.* [Continued as] *Messager des sciences historiques de Belgique* 1839–96; pp. 411–12**

a) Edward, by the grace of God king of England, lord of Ireland and duke of Aquitaine, to all his bailiffs, ministers and other faithful men, appointed both by land and by sea, to whom these present letters will come, greetings. We make known to you that we, hearing about the services which we know that the burgesses of Gantois have laudably exhibited to us up to now, and also about the misfortunes which they endured on behalf of our honour, while we were once staying with them, and therefore wishing that we are found to be helpful towards promoting their condition, we have undertaken the same burgesses, men and their servants into our special protection and defence, and also into our safe and secure conduct, while going with their merchandise, property and other goods into our realm of England and to our other lands, staying there and doing business about the same things, just as they see to be expedient, and then returning at their own pleasure. And therefore we command you, as regards the aforesaid burgesses, their men and servants, while going into our aforesaid realm, or to our other lands, staying there and then returning, just as is aforesaid, you do not inflict or, as far as in your power, you do not permit damage, impediment, trouble or grief to be inflicted upon their persons or property, but rather, if anything will be forfeited by them, you cause without delay compensation to be made to them in due manner. But in such a way that they examine lawful merchandise and make customs that are thereupon due and usual in our aforesaid realm and do not communicate with our enemies. In testimony of which matter, we have caused these our letters to be made patent, as long as it will be pleasing for them to last.

b) Edward, by the grace of God king of England, lord of Ireland and duke of Aquitaine, to all men, to whom these present letters will reach, greetings in the lord. We make known to you that we, hearing about the services, which have been exhibited by the beloved to us the burgesses of Gantois with ready devotion and which they can exhibit in the future more devotedly, considering the inconveniences, which they kindly tolerated, while we were staying with them at one time, on behalf of the name of our honour, and therefore wishing to take provision for the indemnity of the same man and to promote their benefits, we have considered that it should be granted out of our special grace to the aforesaid burgesses by the tenor of these presents, for us and our heirs, that, if their men or servants, whom they will appoint [to travel] with merchandise, property and other goods into our realm of England, or to our other lands, to do business and trade there from henceforth, commit any felony or crime or offence, on account of which goods, found in their hands or in their possession or holding, ought to be applied to us, as if forfeited, committed or liable according to the custom of our said realm and that of our other lands, on this account no prejudice is to be created to the same burgesses, as regards the recovery of those chattels and goods, which they can lawfully prove to be theirs, notwithstanding any contrary use upon this. In testimony of which matter, we have caused these our letters to be made patent.

Dated at Erdenburgh on the second day of March in the year of the lord 1297, and in the 26th [year] of our reign (1298).

11. ***Les Sires de Faucogney, Viscomtes de Vasoul: Notice et Documents publiés par Jules Finot*, Archiviste du Nord, Ancienne Archiviste de la Haute-Saone (Paris, H. Champion Libraire, 15 Quai Malaquais, 15, 1886), pp. 270–73 (translated by Kathy Love)**

Letters by which John II of Faucogney undertook, together with the other lords of the Franche-Comté, formerly allied against Philippe le Bel, to make good the losses caused by them to the partisans of the king of France during the war that they had fought in the county of Burgundy, and specially to have rebuilt the chateaux of Ornans, Clairvaux and la Salle (the state-owned palace) of Pontarlier, which were destroyed during the aforesaid hostilities. (31 May 1301)

To all those who will see and hear these present letters, We Symon de Monbéliart, lord of Montron, Jehanz of Vianne, lord of Mireber, Pierres, lord of Marnay, Estenes d'Oyseler, lord of the Vilenove, Girars d'Arguel, knights, and Estevenat, lord of Oiseler, and Guillame d'Argueil, esquire, greetings in our Lord, we make known that with the noble barons Jehanz de Chalom, lord of Arlay, Renaut, count of Monbéliart, Jehanz de Bourt, Jehanz and Gautier de Monfalcom, Jehanz, lord of Faucoigney, Thiébault, lord of Neufchestel, Humbert, lord of Clerevaux, Guachier de Chastelvilein, Huedes, lord of Monferrant, Guillames, lord of Corcondray, Jehanz d'Oiseler, lord of Flaigé, knights and Johanz de Jou, esquire, are bound [or have undertaken] by their letters sealed with their seals, toward the very high and very excellent prince our dear lord Philippe, by the grace of God king of France, to hold, keep and accomplish the promises [or covenants] contained in the said letter relating to the aforementioned war [which] we energetically pursued and made in the county of Burgundy contrary to the will of the very excellent prince our dear lord the king as above, we who always ['on all days'] desire to have and to keep the grace [or favour] and the good will of our aforesaid lord the king, are at his will and his good favour ['good accord'] and at his mercy and he has received us and has ordained and declared his will in the following manner: It is to be known that we are bound to keep, hold and accomplish all the promises [covenants] contained in the letters sealed with the seals of the noble barons above, having promised and promising before our lord the king to enter, we and our heirs, into his faith and his homage, as the king of France and to his successor kings of France, to take up again and resume toward him as sons the things which follow. It is to be known we, Symon de Monbéliart, lord of Montrom, forty livrées de terre from our borderlands near Rovre; We, Johanz de Vianne, in the manner stated above, thirty livrées de terre, situated at Fronthenay; We, Pierres, lord of Marnay, three hundred pounds in coin; We, Estenes d'Oiseler, lord of the Vile Nove, thirty livrées de terre, lying at Charmoille, and a little way d'iellue; We, Girar d'Arguel, two hundred pounds in coin; I, Estevenant, lord of Piseler, two hundred pounds in coin; I, Guillaume d'Arguel, two hundred pounds in coin. It is to be known that all these things stated above, we ought to undertake in faith and homage for us and for our heirs of our dear lord the king of France stated above, and his successors, kings of France, before the next feast of All Saints. As part of our return to fealty we render and have rendered, we reestablish and have reestablished, together all the barons named above, all the inheritance that we have taken in the country of Burgundy stated above, since the time that it came into the hand of our aforesaid lord the king. As part of our return to fealty we together all the other barons aforesaid will have repaired, at our own cost and expense, the chateaux [or castles] of Ornenes, and of Clerevaux, and the palisade of Pontarlie, and we will remake them into a sufficient state, in the judgment au dit et à l'esgart of the noble men our well-beloved my lord Guachier, lord of Chastillon and constable of Chapaigne, my lord Pierre, lord of Chambry, and my lord Pierre, lord of Veinnes, his son, knights, and chamberlain [or steward] [of] our dear lord aforesaid the king; as part of our return to fealty we will restore and repair all the damage and losses which we and our followers ['aides'] have caused in the said county of Burgundy, from [the time of] the truce up to the day on which these letters are made, whether by imprisonment, in lands, or in chattels [movable goods], or by fire, or in any other way whatsoever. And we have prayed and pray on the holy gospels that we will do and accomplish all the things aforesaid well and loyally. And every one of them. And when the aforesaid things have been done and accomplished, we together with all the other barons in manner which is contained in their letters sealed with their seals, have pledged and pledge one for the other and we bind ourselves and our goods and our heirs, and have given pledges dou roialme sufficient for all the things set out above, to loyally hold, keep and accomplish, in the manner which follows. It is to be known, We, Symond de Monbéliart, have given as surety [or guarantor] Jehanz lord of Cusel, holding land in the kingdom, being the castle of Bart upon [or over] Soigney; We, Jehanz de Vianne my lord Gauthier of Monfalcom; We, Pierres, lord of Marnay, the said Jehanz lord of Cusel; We, Estèes d'Pyseler, lord of Villenove, Girars lord of Chauviré; We, Girar d'Arguel the noble baron my lord Jehanz of Chalom, lord of Arlay; Ik, Estevenat, lord of Oiseler, my lord Jehanz of Oiseler, my uncle; I, Guillame d'Arguel, my lord Vathier de Monfalcon. And so these things will be forever firm and established, We have put our own seals on these present letters. Given and made at Besancon, the Wednesday after the octave of Pentecost in the year of our Lord 1301.

NOTES

Introduction

1. Strayer, *The Reign of Philip the Fair* (Princeton University Press, 21 August 1980) p. 319
2. Strayer, 'The costs and profits of war: The Anglo-French Conflict of 1294–1303' in *The Medieval City*, ed. H. A. Miskimin, D. Herlihy and A. L. Udovitch (New Haven, London, 1977) p. 271
3. Malcolm Vale, *The Origins of the Hundred Years War: The Angevin Legacy 1250–1340* (Clarendon Paperbacks, Oxford University Press, 1996), p. 201
4. *Ibid.*
5. *Rôles Gascons, transcrits et publiés*, ed. Charles Bémont (Paris: Imprimiere Nationale, 1906), vol. 3, 1290–1307

1 Fall of Empire

1. The term 'Angevin Empire' is a misnomer. None of these Angevin rulers referred to themselves as 'emperors' and the term itself was coined by Kate Norgate in the late nineteenth century (see Norgate, *England under the Angevin kings* (London, 1887), vol. 2, p. 491). Nor did they refer to themselves as Plantagenets until their descendants started to use the term as a family name in the fifteenth century. The story that the name came from a sprig of broom (*planta genista*) that Geoffrey of Anjou wore in his hat is another nineteenth-century

anachronism (see John Gillingham, *The Angevin Empire* (Oxford University Press, 2001; 2nd edn), p. 3).

2. Vale, *Origins*, p. 11
3. *Ibid.*
4. Gillingham, *Angevin Empire*, p. 36
5. John Richard Green, *A History of the English People 449–1214*, vol. 1 (Barcelona-Singapore: Athena University Press, 2004) p. 233
6. Gillingham, *Angevin Empire*, pp. 44–45
7. *Ibid.*, pp. 48–49
8. Gillingham, *Richard I* (New Haven and London: Yale, 1999), p. 321
9. W. L. Warren, *King John* (University of California Press, 1978; revised edn), pp. 55–56
10. *Ibid.*, p. 71
11. Gillingham, *Angevin Empire*, p. 94
12. J. F. Verbruggen, *The Art of Warfare in Western Europe During the Middle Ages from the Eighth Century (Warfare in History)* (Boydell Press, 2002 edn), pp. 251–255
13. Gillingham, *Angevin Empire*, p. 107
14. *Ibid.*
15. *Ibid.*, p. 112
16. Vale, *Origins*, p. 13
17. *Ibid.*, p. 15

2 *The Land of* Oïl *and* Òc

1. Margaret Wade Labarge, *Gascony: England's first colony 1204–1453* (Hamish Hamilton, 1980), p. 1; what follows, unless stated otherwise, is taken from Labarge's background to the history of Aquitaine
2. Linda M. Paterson, *Medieval Occitan Society c.1100–1300* (Cambridge University Press, 1993) p. 92
3. J. Beverley Smith, 'Adversaries of Edward I: Gaston de Béarn and Llywelyn ap Gruffudd', in *Recognitions: Essays presented to Edmund Fryde*, edited by Colin Richmond and Isobel Harvey (Aberystwyth, National Library of Wales, 1996), pp. 56–57
4. *Ibid.*, p. 82, f. 25
5. *Ibid.*, p. 61
6. Robin Studd, 'The marriage of Henry of Almaine and Constance de Béarn', *Thirteenth-Century England III: Proceedings of the*

Newcastle upon Tyne Conference 1989, edited by P. R. Coss and S. D. Lloyd (Boydel Press, 1991), p. 164
7. Vale, *Origins*, p. 98
8. *Ibid.*, p. 102
9. Prestwich, *Edward I*, p. 303
10. *Ibid.*, p. 103
11. *Archives Municipales de Bordeaux, vol. v, Livre des Coutumes*, edited by H. Barckhausen (Bordeaux, 1890), p. 609
12. Vale, *Origins*, p. 84
13. Labarge, *Gascony: England's first colony 1204–1453*, p. 10
14. Michael Prestwich, *Edward I* (Yale English University Press, 1997) p. 15

3 *A Taste of Power*

1. *Ibid.*, p. 11
2. *Ibid.*, p. 16
3. J. R. Studd, 'A Catalogue of the Acts of the Lord Edward, 1254–1272', thesis presented for the degree of Doctor of Philosophy in the University of Leeds (May 1971), act 128
4. *Ibid.*, act 145
5. *Edward I: New Interpretations*, edited by Andy King and Andrew M. Spencer (York Medieval Press, 2020), pp. 12–13
6. Studd, A Catalogue, act 194; *Edward I: New Interpretations*, p. 13
7. Studd, A Catalogue, Act 340; *Ibid.*, p. 13
8. J. R. Maddicott, *Simon de Montfort* (Cambridge University Press, 1994), p. 112
9. Marc Morris, *A Great and Terrible King, Edward I and the Forging of Britain* (Windmill Books, 2009), p. 20
10. Studd, A Catalogue, p. 385, f. 3
11. Studd, A Catalogue, act 390
12. Studd, A Catalogue, act 408.
13. Studd, A Catalogue, p. 396, f. 2
14. Studd, A Catalogue, act 216
15. 'L'administration anglaise et Gascogne sous Henri III et Édouard Ier de 1254 a 1307' by Jean Paul Trabut-Cussac in *Économies, Sociétés, Civilisations Année*, 30 (1975), p. 8
16. Studd, A Catalogue, act 65
17. Prestwich, *Edward I*, p. 15

18. *Ibid.*
19. *Ibid.*, pp. 15–16
20. *La Vasconie Étude de historique et critique sur les origines du royaume de Navarre, du duché de Gascogne, des comtés de Comminges, d'Aragon, de Foix, de Bigorre, d'Alava & de Biscaye de la viscomté de Béarn, et des grands fiefs du duche de Gascogne by Jean de Jauguin* (Pau: Impremerie-Stéréotypie Garet, 1898), pp. 471–72
21. *Ibid.*, p. 473
22. *Ibid.*, p. 475
23. *Ibid.*, p. 477
24. Trabut-Cussac, L'Administration Anglaise, p. 23
25. La Vasconie Étude de historique, pp. 477–78
26. *Royal and other Historical letters illustrative of the Reign of Henry III*, ed. W. W. Shirley (Rolls series 1862–6), ii, p. 162
27. La Vasconie Étude de historique, p. 479; below, see chapter 19
28. Royal and other Historical letters, ii, pp. 161–63
29. Prestwich, *Edward I*, pp. 33–34
30. *Ibid.*, p. 37
31. Darren Baker, *Henry III, The Great King England Never Knew it Had* (The History Press, 2017), p. 285
32. Prestwich, *Edward I*, p. 39
33. Trabut-Cussac, L'Administration Anglaise, p. 35
34. *Ibid.*
35. *Ibid.*, p. 36
36. Prestwich, *Edward I*, p. 60

4 *The Lands I Ought to Hold*

1. Charles Victor Langlois, *Philip III the Bold, King of France, 1270–85, The Evolution of Royal Power in Medieval Europe* (Paris, 1887), p. 42; see Appendix I for a full transcript of the treaty
2. Langlois, *Philip III*, pp. 42–43
3. *Ibid.*, p. 45
4. Prestwich, *Edward I*, p. 79
5. *Chronicon Henrici Knighton vel Cnitthon Monachi Leycestrensis*, edited by Joseph Rawson Lumby, vol. I (London, 1889) pp. 265–266; see Appendix 2
6. Vale, *Origins*, p. 52
7. *Ibid.*, p. 52

8. See Appendix I
9. Vale, *Origins*, p. 53, quoting La Patourel, 'The Origins of the Hundred Years War' in *Feudal Empires*, pt XI, p. 34
10. Langlois, *Philip III*, p. 51
11. *Ibid.*
12. *Ibid.*
13. *Recueil des historiens des Gaules et de la France*, vol. 21, edited by Dom Martin Bouquet (Paris: Imprimerie Royale, 1840–1904), p. 781
14. *Ibid.*; thanks to Richard Price for the translation
15. *Ibid.*; thanks again to Richard Price for the translation
16. Langlois, *Philip III*, p. 51
17. *Ibid.*, pp. 51–52
18. *Ibid.*, p. 52
19. Prestwich, *Edward I*, p. 300; Trabut-Cussac, L'Administration Anglaise en Gascogne, p. 42
20. Prestwich, *Edward I*, p. 300
21. *Ibid.*
22. Gascon Register A, edited by G. P. Cuttino with the collaboration of Trabuct-Cussac, vol. I (London: Oxford University Press, 1975), p. 235. Thanks to Richard Price for the translation
23. Thomas Wykes, *Annales Monastici IV* (London, 1869), pp. 255–56
24. TNA C 47/25/1/4; charges made by the king's subjects in Gascony against Gaston de Béarn; see Appendix 3
25. D. Brissaud, *Les Anglais en Guyenne: l'administration anglaise et le mouvement communal dans le Bordelais* (Paris, 1875), p. 253
26. Trabut-Cussac, L'administration Anglaise en Gascogne, p. 43
27. William of Rishanger, *Chronica et Annales, Regnantibus Henrico Tertio et Edwardo Primo AD 1259–1307*, edited by Henry Thomas Riley (London, 1865), p. 80
28. Gascon Register A, vol. II, p. 625; translation by Rich Price
29. *Ibid.*
30. Langlois, *Philip III*, p. 68
31. For the disorders in England at this time, see Andrew M. Spencer, *Nobility and Kingship in Medieval England: The Earls and Edward I 1272–1307* by Andrew M. Spencer (Cambridge University Press, 2013), pp. 195–200
32. Langlois, *Philip III*, p. 66
33. *Ibid.*

34. Prestwich, *Edward I*, p. 303
35. *Recueil des historiens des Gaules et de la France*, pp. 783–784
36. *Ibid.*, p. 784
37. *Ibid.*
38. Langlois, *Philip III*, p. 67
39. Close Rolls 1279–1279 (London, 1900), p. 247
40. Trabut-Cussac, L'Administration Anglaise en Gascogne, pp. 48–49, f. 33
41. J. Beverley Smith, 'Adversaries of Edward I: Gaston de Béarn and Llywelyn ap Gruffudd' in *Recognitions, Essays presented to Edmund Fryde*, edited by Colin Richmond and Isobel Harvey (Aberystwyth: National Library of Wales, 1996), p. 70
42. Langlois, p. 68
43. Prestwich, *Edward I*, p. 301
44. Langlois, *Philip III*, p. 68
45. Smith, *Adversaries of Edward I*, p. 74, f. 85
46. Champollion, I, p. 312; translation in Langlois, Philip III, p. 69
47. Langlois, *Philip III*, p. 69
48. Smith, *Adversaries of Edward I*, p. 74, f. 86
49. *Ibid.*, p. 88
50. *Ibid.*, p. 75
51. *Ibid.*
52. Langlois, *Philip III*, pp. 71–72
53. *Ibid.*, p. 74
54. *Histoire de la guerre de Navarre en 1276 et 1277* by Guillaume Anelier de Toulouse (Paris, 1856), p. 297
55. Langlois, *Philip III*, p. 75
56. TNA C 47/25/1/4, membrane no. 4
57. Smith, *Adversaries of Edward I*, p. 77
58. Langlois, *Philip III*, p. 69; *Lettres des Rois, Reines et Autres Personages des cours de France et D'Angleterre et publieés* by M. Champollion-Figeac (Paris, 1839), p. 280; translation by Simon Neal
59. Close Rolls 1272–1279, p. 493
60. Smith, *Adversaries of Edward I*, f. 94. Edward's emissaries were commissioned at Dover on 7 February 1278, at the time when he despatched his final letters to Philip on Gaston's case
61. *Ibid.*, p. 78

62. *Ibid.*, p. 78 & p. 87, f. 99 for details of Gaston's service to the king in future years
63. Langlois, pp. 168–69
64. *Ibid.*, pp 168–69
65. *Ibid.*, p. 169; see Appendix 4 for translations of the four letters quoted in this section
66. *Ibid.*, p. 169
67. *Ibid.*, p. 170

5 *The Peace of Amiens and After*

1. Langlois, *Philip III*, p. 70
2. Powicke, *Thirteenth Century*, p. 289
3. *Ibid.*
4. G. P. Cuttino, *English Diplomatic Administration 1259–1339* (Oxford: Clarendon Press, 1971; 2nd edn), pp. 8–9
5. Prestwich, *Edward I*, p. 315
6. Hilda Johnstone, 'The County of Ponthieu 1279–1307' in *The English Historical Review*, vol. 29, no. 115 (July 1914), pp. 436–37
7. *Ibid.*, pp. 437–38
8. Calendar of Patent Rolls 1292–1301 (London, 1895), p. 13
9. Vale, *Origins*, p. 72
10. John E. Morris, *The Welsh Wars of Edward I* (De Capo Press, 1969), p. 188
11. *The Chronicle of Pierre Langtoft*, ed. T. Wright, vol. ii (Rolls Series, 1868), p. 181
12. Calendar of Various Chancery Rolls (London, 1912), p. 214
13. Johnstone, 'The County of Ponthieu 1279–1307', p. 445
14. SC 1/15/34, Gaston de Béarn to Edward I, 3 July 1282
15. Smith, *Adversaries of Edward I*, p. 79
16. Powicke, *Thirteenth Century*, p. 242
17. *Ibid.*, f.1
18. *Foedera, Conventiones, Litteraem*, vol. 1.2 (London, 1816), pp. 576, 580
19. Powicke, *Thirteenth Century*, pp. 242–43
20. Cuttino, *English Diplomatic Administration*, p. 11
21. Langlois, *Philip III*, p. 102
22. *Ibid.*
23. *Foedera*, pp. 625, 638

24. *Chronicle of Alfonso X*, p. 254
25. Labarge, *Gascony*, pp. 46–47
26. *Ibid.*, p. 47
27. Esther Rowland Clifford, *A Knight of Great Renown, The Life and Times of Othon de Grandson* (University of Chicago Press, 1961), p. 78
28. *Ibid.*, pp. 78–79
29. Langlois, *Philip III*, p. 107
30. *Ibid.*, p. 119
31. *Ibid.*, p. 120
32. Prestwich, *Edward I*, p. 321
33. *Ibid.*, pp. 321–22
34. Powicke, *The Thirteenth Century*, pp. 246–47
35. *Ibid.*, p. 248
36. *Ibid.*
37. *Foedera*, 1.2, p. 600
38. *https://epistolae.ctl.columbia.edu/letter/536.html*
39. Powicke, *Thirteenth Century*, p. 249
40. Langlois, *Philip III*, p. 126
41. *Ibid.*

6 *The Pard and the Owl*

1. Quoted in Vatteroni 2013 (LXII) – *Rialto* 11. viii. 2014.
2. Juliet Elizabeth Vale, 'Aspects of Chivalric Culture c.1270–1350: The Context of the Court of Edward III' (D.Phil, University of York, Department of History, January 1981), p. 47; translation by Richard Price
3. Ramon Muntaner, *Chronicle*, translated by Lady Goodenough (Ontario: In Parentheses Publications, Catalan Series, 2000), p. 69
4. *Triveti Annales*, ed. T. Hog (English Historical Society, London, 1845), p. 282
5. Thomas Wright, *The Political Songs of England, from the reign of John to that of Edward II* (London, printed for the Camden Society, 1839), pp. 93–94
6. See, for instance, James Conway-Davies's harsh assessment of the king's dealings in Wales in *The Welsh Assize Roll* (Cardiff: University of Wales Press Board, 1940), pp. 231–32

7. R. R. Davies, *The First English Empire, Power and Identities in the British Isles 1093–1343* (Oxford, 2000), p. 22
8. Strayer, *The Reign of Philip the Fair*, pp. 3–4. f. 5
9. *Ibid.*, p. 3
10. Prestwich, *Edward I*, pp. 380–1
11. Strayer, *Philip the Fair*, p. 3; quoting Yves of St Denis, Geoffroi of Paris and Pierre du Bois
12. *Ibid.*, pp. 3–4
13. Clifford, *A Knight of Great Renown*, pp. 185–86
14. Elizabeth A. R. Brown, 'Philip the Fair of France: Nemesis of Edward I and England' in *Prowess, Piety and Public Order in Society: Studies in Honour of Richard W Kaeuper* (Brill, 2017), p. 263
15. Vale, *Origins*, p. 179; Labarge, *Gascony: England's First Colony*, p. 48
16. Labarge, *Gascony: England's First Colony*, p. 48
17. *Ibid.*
18. *Ibid.*, p. 48
19. Vale, *Origins*, pp. 180–81
20. Powicke, *The Thirteenth Century*, pp. 290–91
21. Labarge, *Gascony: England's first Colony*, pp. 48–49
22. Trabut-Cussac, L'Administration Anglaise en Gascogne, pp. 72–77
23. Beverley Smith, *Adversaries of Edward I*, pp. 79–80
24. Vale, *Origins*, p. 84
25. Beverley-Smith, *Origins*, p. 80; TNA C 47/29/2/ no. 2, a memorandum of the arrangements for a joint crusade
26. Beverley-Smith, *Origins*, p. 80

7 *The Love between You and Me*

1. Prestwich, *Edward I*
2. *Ibid.*, p. 324; Trabut-Cussac, L'administration Anglais en Gascogne, p. 87
3. Margaret Bent, *Magister Jacobus de Ispania, Author of the Speculum musicae* (Ashgate, 2015), p. 101
4. *Ibid.*, p. 102
5. *Ibid.*, p. 186; Edward's name in Catalan was rendered as Audoart, which divided into three - *nau*, *do* and *art* – translated as ships, gifts and art.
6. Vale, *Origins*, p. 178

7. Prestwich, *Edward I*, p. 324
8. Strayer, *Philip the Fair*, p. 369
9. Vale, *Origins*, p. 197
10. Prestwich, *Edward I*, p. 325
11. *Ibid.*
12. *Ibid.*
13. Bent, *Magister Jacobus de Ispania*, p. 89 and p. 110, f. 3
14. Prestwich, *Edward I*, pp. 326–27
15. Vale, *Origins*, p. 192
16. Attila Bárány, *The Last Rex Crucesignatus: Edward I and the Mongol Alliance* (Annual of Medieval Studies at Central European University, 2010), pp. 10–11
17. For instance, he sent 5,000 silver marks to the Bishop of Hebron in 1272 and 7,000 marks to Hugues de Revel. Bárány, *The Last Rex Crucesignatus*, p. 9, f. 59
18. Prestwich, *Edward I*, p. 327
19. *Ibid.*, pp. 329–30
20. Jacques Poviot, 'England and the Mongols (c.1260–1330)', *Journal of the Royal Asiatic Society*, Third Series, vol. 10, no. 3 (Nov. 2000), p. 314
21. Christopher Tyerman, *England and the Crusades 1095–1588* (University of Chicago Press, 1996 edn), p. 230
22. *Ibid.*
23. Jean Richard, *Histoire des Croisades* (Fayard, 1996), p. 485

8 *Casus Belli*

1. Prestwich, *Edward I*, p. 301
2. Marc Morris, 'Edward I's Building Works in Gascony' in *The Impact of the Edwardian Castles in Wales*, edited by Diane M. Williams and John R. Kenyon (Oxbow Books, 2007), p. 170
3. Prestwich, *Edward I*, p. 309
4. *Ibid.*
5. Morris, 'Edward I's Building Works', pp. 172–173
6. Vale, *Origins*, p. 179; Trabut-Cussac, L'Administration Anglaise en Gascogne, pp. 81–101
7. Vale, *Origins*, p. 180
8. *Ibid.*, p. 182; René de Lespinasse, *Bibliothèque de l'École des Chartes* (London, 1887), p. 551

9. Vale, *Origins*, p. 88–89
10. *Ibid.*, p. 89
11. Vale, *Origins*, p. 194
12. Thomas K. Heebøll-Holm, *Ports, Piracy and Maritime War: Piracy in the English Channel and the Atlantic, c.1280-c.1330* (Brill, 2013), pp. 70–71
13. *Ibid.*, p. 81
14. *Ibid.*, pp. 81–82
15. Three almost identical reports from the Portsmen are held at the National Archives: C 47/27/15/1; C 47/31/5/2; C 47/31/6
16. What follows is taken from a summary of the three accounts by K. Heebøll-Holm, *Ports, Piracy and Maritime War*, pp. 86–88
17. *Documents relating to Law and Custom of the Sea vol. 1, AD 1205–1648*, edited by Reginald Godfrey Marsden (New Jersey: The Law Book Exchange Ltd, 1999), pp 54–55
18. Vale, *Origins*, p. 183
19. K. Heebøll-Holm, *Ports, Piracy and Maritime War*, p. 89
20. *The Flowers of History* [*Flores Historiarum*], vol. II, from AD 1066 to 1307 (London, 1853), pp. 495–96
21. *Ibid.*, p. 496
22. K. Heebøll-Holm, *Ports, Piracy and Maritime War*, pp. 90–92. The specific chroniclers are the *Flores*, the *Annals of Oseney* and the *Chronicle of Walter of Guisborough*
23. K. Heebøll-Holm, *Ports, Piracy and Maritime War*, pp. 94–95
24. Prestwich, *Edward I*, pp. 377–78
25. K. Heebøll-Holm, *Ports, Piracy and Maritime War*, p. 87
26. Marsden, *Documents*, p. 20
27. Prestwich, *Edward I*, p. 378
28. Powicke, *Thirteenth Century*, pp. 645–46
29. K. Heebøll-Holm, *Ports, Piracy and Maritime War*, pp. 113–17; this analysis relies on the details of Rostand's report contained in C 47/31/5/1
30. Vale, *Origins*, p. 184
31. Vale, *Origins*, p. 201
32. *Ibid.*, pp. 185–86
33. SC 8/291/14521; dated to c.1305
34. Langtoft, II, p. 200
35. Vale, *Origins*, p. 183

36. *Ibid.*, p. 183
37. Prestwich, p. 378
38. Vale, *Origins*, pp. 186–87
39. *Ibid.*, p. 187
40. Details of his service can be found in TNA E 101/351/25, 26; E 101/154/12; Bémont, Roles Gascon, iii, nos 4529–31
41. *Ibid.*, p. 185
42. *Ibid.*, p. 186

9 *Take Spear in Thy Fist*

1. Marc Morris, *A Great and Terrible King: Edward I and the Forging of Britain* (Windmill Books, 2009), p. 267
2. Vale, *Origins*, p. 188
3. *Ibid.*; the printed text of the treaty is contained in *Foedera*, 1.2, pp. 795–96
4. Vale, *Origins*, pp. 188–89
5. Pierre Chaplais, *English Medieval Diplomatic Practice: Documents and Interpretation*, vol. 1, Issue 2 (Public Record Office, 1982), pp. 428–29
6. *Ibid.*
7. Vale, *Origins*, p. 190
8. *Ibid.*
9. Chaplais, *Diplomatic Practice*, pp. 428–29
10. Morris, *A Great and Terrible King*, p. 269
11. *The Chronicle of Walter of Guisborough*, edited by Harry Rothwell (Camden Series, London, 1957), p. 242
12. Chaplais, *Diplomatic Practice*, p. 249
13. *Ibid.*; Strayer, *Philip the Fair*, p. 318
14. Prestwich, *Edward I*, p. 380
15. Vale, *Origins*, p. 188
16. Elizabeth A. R. Brown, 'Philip the Fair: Nemesis of Edward I of England', p. 244
17. H. Rothwell, *English Historical Documents, vol. 3, 1189–1327* (London, 1975; repr. 1996), p. 508
18. François César Louandre, *Histoire d'Abbeville et du comté de Ponthieu jusqu'en 1789*, vol. 1 (Paris, 1923), p. 211; Hilda Johnstone, *The County of Ponthieu*, p. 448
19. Chaplais, *English Diplomatic Practice*, p. 429

20. *Ibid.*
21. Labarge, *Gascony: England's First Colony*, p. 66
22. *Ibid.*; quoting R. Fawtier, 'L'Europe occidentale de 1270 A 1380, pt. I de 1270 a 1328' in *Histoire de Moyen age* 6 (Paris, 1940), p. 317
23. Trabut-Cussac, L'administration de Gascogne, p. 109 & f. 393
24. Charles Victor Langlois, *Saint Louis, Philippe le Bel: les derniers Capétiens direct: 1226–1328* (Paris, 1978) p. 305
25. *Ibid.*, f. 9
26. See, for instance, G. W. S. Barrow, *Robert Bruce and the Community of the Realm of Scotland* (University of California Press, 1965), pp. 47–49 for Edward's manipulation of the Scottish succession crisis
27. Fiona Watson, 'Traitor, Outlaw, King. Part One: The Making of Robert Bruce' (independently published, 2018), pp. 63–66
28. Morris, *A Great and Terrible King*, pp. 266–67
29. Strayer, *Philip the Fair*, p. 318
30. *Ibid.*
31. Vale, *Origins*, p. 206
32. Morris, *A Great and Terrible King*, p. 269
33. *Ibid.*, p. 270
34. Pierre de Langtoft, *The Chronicle of Pierre de Langtoft in French verse, from the earliest period to the death of Edward I*, ed. Thomas Wright (London, 1868, repr. 1886), p. 203 [hereafter Pierre de Langtoft]
35. J. G. Black, 'Edward I and Gascony in 1300', *The English Historical Review*, vol. 17 no. 67 (July 1902), p. 519

10 The Forces within Our Power

1. Trabut-Cussac, L'Administration Anglaise en Gascogne, Introduction, xvi
2. Reginald Philip Lawton, 'Henry de Lacy, Earl of Lincoln as *locum tenens* at *capitaneus* in the duchy of Aquitaine' (unpublished PhD thesis, University of London, 1974), p. 62
3. Morris, *A Great and Terrible King*, p. 270; Trabut-Cussac, L'Administration Anglaise en Gascone, p. 108
4. Michael Prestwich, 'Edward I and Adolf of Nassau' in *Thirteenth Century III: Proceedings of the Newcastle-Upon-Tyne Conference*, ed. P. R. Coss and S. D. Lloyd (Woodbridge, Suffolk, 1991), p. 127
5. Langtoft, ii, p. 203

6. Hans Patze, 'Erzbischof Gerhard II. von Mainz und König Adolf von Nassau: Territorialpolitik und Finanze' in *Hessisches Jahrbuch für Landesgeschichte*, vol. 13 (1963), pp. 489–90
7. G. Barraclough, 'Edward I and Adolf of Nassau: A Chapter of Medieval Diplomatic History', *The Cambridge Historical Journal*, vol. 6 no. 3 (1940), p. 230
8. Marcel Grosdidier de Matons, 'L'Hommage du duc de Bar au roi de France' in *Memoires de la Sociéte des Lettres Sciences et Arts de Bar-le-Duc*, vol. 43 (Imprimeri Content Laguerre, 1918–21), pp. 473–74
9. *Ibid.*, p. 477
10. *Ibid.*, p. 482
11. Frantz Funck-Brentano, 'Philippe le Bel et la noblesse franc-comtoise' in *Bibliotheque de l'école des chartes*, vol. 49 (1888), p. 20
12. Barraclough, pp. 235–36
13. *Constitutiones et acta publica*, p. 502; translated by Richard Price
14. Patze, p. 507
15. J. R. Verbruggen, *The Battle of the Golden Spurs (Courtrai, 11 July 1302), A Contribution to the History of Flanders' War of Lib eration (Warfare in History)*, ed. and trans. Kelly DeVries and David Richard Ferguson (Woodbridge, Suffolk, 2002) pp. 13–14 [hereafter Verbruggen]; Pirenne, *Histoire de Belgique* I, p. 363
16. Prestwich, *Edward I*, p. 388
17. Pirenne, *Histoire de Belgique* I, p. 369
18. Prestwich, *Edward I*, p. 387
19. Michael Prestwich, *War, Politics and Finance under Edward I* (Totowa, New Jersey, 1972), pp. 172–73.
20. Henri Pirenne, *Histoire de Belgique* I (Brussels, 1903), p. 368
21. *History of the Low Countries* edited by J. C. H. Blom and E. Lamberts (Berghann books, 1999), pp. 57–58

11 The First Expedition, 1294–1295

1. Charles Bémont, *Roles gascons, 1242–1307: 1290–1307* (Paris, 1885); Thomas Rymer and R. Sanderson, *Foedera*, 1.2, p. 805
2. Sir James H. Ramsay, *The Dawn of the Constitution, or the Reigns of Henry III and Edward I (AD 1216–1307)* (London, 1908), p. 408
3. Guisborough, ii, p. 273
4. Prestwich, *Edward I*, p. 381

5. Lawton, p. 127
6. K. Heebøll-Holm, *Ports, Piracy and Maritime War*, pp. 57–58
7. Vale, *Origins*, p. 201
8. *Annales Monastici IV, Annales de Wigornia* (henceforth Annales de Wigornia), p. 519
9. Guisborough, II, pp. 45–46
10. *Flores*, iii, p. 92
11. Vale, *Origins*, p. 204
12. Lawton, p. 45
13. *Ibid.*, p. 46
14. Guisborough, ii, pp. 45–49
15. *Ibid.*
16. *Ibid.*
17. Lawton, p. 174
18. Vale, *Origins*, p. 221
19. Guisborough, II, pp. 45–49
20. Annales de Wigornia, p. 520
21. Guisborough, pp. 45–49
22. K. Heebøll-Holm, *Ports, Piracy and Maritime War*, pp. 57–58
23. Guisborough, ii, p. 49
24. *Ibid.*
25. Vale, *Origins*, p. 204; E 372/160. m. 41 (recto)
26. Guisborough, ii, p. 49
27. K. Heebøll-Holm, *Ports, Piracy and Maritime War*, p. 58
28. Lawton, p. 51
29. Trivet, *Annales*, p. 335
30. Annales of Wigornia, p. 519
31. Lawton, p. 208
32. Prestwich, *Edward I*, p. 382; Vale, *Origins*, p. 204
33. Roles Gascons, iii, p. clxxxiv, 4472
34. Lawton, p. 98, quoting Powicke, *The Thirteenth Century*, pp. 678–679
35. Prestwich, *Edward I*, p. 221
36. Pirenne, *Histoire de Belgique* I, p. 371
37. *Medieval Germany: An Encyclopedia*, edited by John M. Jeep (Routledge Revivals, 2016), p. 7
38. Patze, p. 506

39. Prestwich, *Edward I's Wars and their Financing 1294–1307*, Appendix II, p. 445
40. Patze, p. 508, f.151 (a)
41. See, for instance, Johann Martin Lappenburg and Georg Reinhold Pauli, *Geschichte von England* (Gotha, 1855), pp. 87–88; Patze, p. 503
42. Patze, p. 509
43. Patze, p. 505
44. *Constitutiones et Acta Publica Imperatorum et Regum*, edited by Ludowic Weiland (Hanover, 1893), p. 502; translation by Richard Price

12 In Battle Array with Lances

1. Lanercost, ii, p. 114
2. Vale, *Origins*, p. 202
3. Guisborough, ii, p. 49
4. *The Debate on the Trial of the Templars, 1307–1314*, edited by Jochen Burgtorf, Paul Crawford, Helen Nicholson (Ashgate, 2010), pp. 62–63
5. Nangis, p. 239
6. Guisborough, ii, pp. 49–52
7. *Ibid.*
8. Lanercost, ii, p. 114
9. *Ibid.*
10. Guisborough, ii, p. 51
11. *Ibid.*
12. Lawton, p. 128
13. Guisborough, ii, p. 49
14. *Ibid.*
15. *Ibid.*
16. Trivet, for instance (*Annales*, pp. 336–337) claims that 1,500 French men-at-arms died
17. Lawton, p. 184
18. Guisborough, ii, p. 52; Nangis, p. 295
19. Nangis, p. 295
20. Lawton, pp. 199–200
21. Bémont, Roles Gascons, iii, p. 339; translation by Richard Price
22. TNA SC 1/26/195; petition of Arnald de Gabastan (*sic*) to John Langton for restoration of his wife's lands, May 1297

23. Lawton, p. 199; C 47/24/2/23, claim of Arnald Gaveston for expenses in Gascony, 20 November 1299–19 November 1300
24. SC 1/26/195
25. Malcolm Vale, 'The Gascon Nobility and the Anglo-French War 1294–98' in *War and Government in the Middle Ages, Essays in Honour of J.O. Prestwich* (Woodbridge, 1984), p. 136; Roles Gascon, iii, no. 3374
26. Vale, *The Gascon Nobility*, p. 136
27. *Ibid.*; Lawton, p. 207
28. Vale, *Origins*, p. 205
29. Lawton, p. 208
30. Vale, *The Gascon Nobility*, pp. 96–97
31. Vale, *Origins*, p. 97
32. *Ibid.*, p. 204
33. *Ibid.*, p. 85
34. Lawton, p. 207
35. Vale, *The Gascon Nobility*, p. 138
36. Lawton, p. 200; CPR, 1292–1301, p. 301
37. Vale, *Origins*, p. 100; Trabut-Cussac, *L'administration Anglaise et Gascogne*, pp. 342–470
38. Vale, *The Gascon Nobility*, p. 139 f. 43
39. Rothwell, *English Historical Documents*, iii, p. 508
40. Vale, *The Gascon Nobility*, p. 135
41. *Ibid.*, p. 137; Roles Gascons iii, p. 370
42. Vale, *The Gascon Nobility*, p. 137
43. *Ibid.*, p. 138
44. Vale, *Origins*, pp. 218–219; 'Documents Illustrating the Crisis of 1297–98 in England', edited by Michael Prestwich, Camden Society, 4th series, xxxiv (London, 1980), p. 163
45. Vale, *The Gascon Nobility*, p. 139 f. 44
46. *Ibid.*, p. 139
47. Labarge, *Gascony: England's First Colony*, p. 41
48. Vale, *The Gascon Nobility*, pp. 144–145
49. Trabut-Cussac, L'Administration Anglaise et Gascogne, p. 355 & 361–362
50. *Ibid.*, p. 170; Vale, *The Gascon Nobility*, p. 145
51. *Ibid.*, p. 135, f.11

13 Linguam Anglicanam

1. Joseph P. Huffman, *The Social Politics of Medieval Diplomacy: Anglo-German Relations (1066–1307)* (Michigan, 2000), p. 308
2. *The Staple Court Books of Bristol*, vol. 5, edited by E. E. Rich (Bristol Record Society, 1934), pp. 12–13; Powicke, *The Thirteenth Century*, p. 664
3. Prestwich, *Edward I*, p. 372
4. Barraclough, p. 239
5. Joseph Stevenson, *Documents Illustrative of the History of Scotland*, vol. ii (Edinburgh, 1870), p. 8.
6. *Ibid.*, pp. 8–9
7. Barrow, *Robert Bruce*, p. 92
8. Ranald Nicholson, 'The Franco-Scottish and Franco-Norwegian Treaties of 1295' in *Scottish Historical Review*, vol. 38, no. 126, Part 2 (October 1959), p. 30
9. Close Rolls 1288–1296, pp. 450–451
10. E 372/160, Michaelmas 1314–Michaelmas 1315; translation by Simon Neal.
11. *Flores*, iii, p. 510
12. Ramsay, *Dawn of the Constitution*, p. 416
13. *Foedera*, 1.2, p. 826
14. A. Z. Freeman, 'A Moat Defensive: the coast defense scheme of 1295' in *Speculum*, vol. xlii (1967), p. 446
15. *Ibid.*, p. 454
16. *Ibid.*, p. 446; *Flores*, iii, p. 510
17. Prestwich, *Edward I*, pp. 382–83
18. *A Hundred Years of History*, pp. 181–82
19. Prestwich, *Edward I*, p. 383, f. 21
20. *Ibid.*
21. *https://www.british-history.ac.uk/no-series/london-mayors-sheriffs/1188–1274/pp. 293–295*
22. *Ibid.*
23. J. Beverley Smith, 'Edward II and the allegiance of Wales', *Welsh History Review*, vol. 8 no. 2 (December 1976), p. 142. f. 16
24. Prestwich, *Edward I*, p. 383, f. 22
25. *Ibid.*
26. *Flores*, iii, p. 512
27. *Ibid.*

28. Patze, p. 508
29. Prestwich, *War, Politics and Finance*, p. 76
30. Edwards, *Book of Prests*. Pliii

14 Failing Money and Spirit

1. Prestwich, *Edward I*
2. Lawton, p. 43
3. *Ibid.*, pp. 163–64
4. *Flowers of History*, p. 514
5. *Ibid.*, p. 47; Guisborough, ii, pp. 72–74
6. Rishanger, *Chronica*, p. 154
7. Vale, *Origins*, p. 117
8. *Flowers of History*, p. 514
9. Guisborough, ii, pp. 72–74
10. Rishanger, *Chronica*, p. 154; they included the brother of Lord Peter Mauley and the standard bearers of John of Brittany and Alan la Zouche; *Flowers of History*, p. 515
11. Lawton, p. 48; Guisborough, ii, pp. 72–74
12. Lawton, pp. 57–58, f.1 quoting the *Anciennes Chroniques de Flandre*, p. 356
13. Guisborough, ii, pp. 72–74; Lawton, p. 49
14. Vale, *Origins*, pp. 210–211
15. Guisborough, ii, pp. 72–74; Lawton, p. 50
16. Lawton, p. 56
17. Guisborough, ii, pp. 72–74
18. Lawton, p. 56
19. Guisborough, ii, pp. 72–74; Lawton, pp. 56–57
20. Morris, *A Great and Terrible King*, p. 291
21. Lawton, p. 51
22. A useful overview can be found at https://web.archive.org/web/20080507054240/http://www.nederlandseliteratuur.info/pagina10.html/
23. Prestwich, *Edward I*, pp 388–389
24. The details of Floris's death are contained in a surviving newsletter, circulated in Holland shortly after his death. The letter (in Dutch) can be read at the website footnoted above
25. Prestwich, *Edward I*, p. 388
26. *Ibid.*, pp. 472–74

27. *Ibid.*, p. 475
28. *Ibid.*, p. 477
29. Guisborough, ii, p. 74
30. Lawton, p. 72
31. Bémont, Roles Gascon, pcliii
32. Vale, *Origins*, p. 209
33. Rishanger, *Chronica*, p. 155
34. *Flowers of History*, p. 520
35. Lawton, p. 74
36. *Flowers of History*, p. 520
37. Trivet, *Annales*, p. 341; Rishanger, *Chronica*, p. 154
38. Guisborough, ii, p. 74
39. Lawton, pp. 204–205
40. *Ibid.*, p. 287
41. Rishanger, *Chronica*, pp. 154–155
42. Lawton, pp. 170–172; Prestwich, *War, Politics and Finance*, p. 166
43. Lawton, p. 172
44. *Mémoires de la Société des lettres* (1918–1921), p. 486. See: https://archive.org/stream/MemoiresSocieteBarLeDuc43/Memoires_Societe_Bar-le-Duc_43_djvu.txt [hereafter *Mémoires*]
45. Funck-Brentano, *Les origines*, p. 197
46. Prestwich, *Edward I*, pp. 388–89
47. Verbruggen, *Battle of the Golden Spurs*, p.15
48. Prestwich, *Crisis of 1297*, p. 3
49. *Ibid.*, p. 14
50. *Mémoires*, p. 487
51. Charles Gérard, *Les annales et la Chronique des Dominicains de Colmar* (Colmar, 1854), p. 170; Frantz Funck-Brentano, *Philippe le Bel et la noblesse Franc-Comtoise* (Paris, 1888), pp. 20–21.

15 As the Philistines Exulted Over Sampson

1. Lawton, p. 77
2. *Anciennes Chroniques de Flandre*, p. 356; *Recueil des historiens des Gaules et de la France*, vol. 22, edited by Dom Martin Bouque (Paris, 1840–1904)
3. Lawton, pp. 77–78
4. *Ibid.*, p. 78
5. Anciennes *Chroniques de Flandre*, p. 357

6. Langtoft, ii, pp 282–283
7. *Ibid.*, p. 283
8. *Ibid.*
9. Lawton, p. 85
10. Nangis, p. 243
11. Lawton, pp. 90–91
12. Trivet, *Annales*, p. 354
13. *Flowers of History*, p. 523
14. Lawton, pp. 92–93
15. *Ibid.*
16. Lawton, p. 98.
17. For instance, as seen in Kew, London, The National Archives, TNA E 101/155/5/13; E 101 153/15/11; E 101/152/9/39; Documents relating to the administration of Henry de Lacy, Earl of Lincoln, lieutenant in Aquitaine. 24 to 26 Edw I

16 You Will Go or You Will Hang

1. Guisborough, ii, pp. 121–122
2. Vale, *Origins*, p. 209
3. Prestwich, *The Crisis of 1297–1298*, pp. 3–4.
4. Prestwich, *Edward I*, p. 421
5. J. Morris, *The Welsh Wars of Edward*, pp. 277–78.
6. Michael Prestwich, 'Welsh Infantry in Flanders in 1297' in *Wales and the Welsh in the Middle Ages: essays presented to J Beverley-Smith* (Cardiff, 2011) pp. 6–8
7. *Calendar of the Close Rolls, Volume IV A.D.1296–1302*, Preserved in the Public Record Office (London, 1900), p. 79
8. *Book of Prests of the King's Wardrobe for 1294–5, presented to John Goronwy Edwards*, ed. E. B. Fryde (Oxford 1962), pp. 61 and 135 [hereafter Fryde]
9. Fryde, p. xliii; Henry Richards Luard, *Annales Monastici IV*, 5 vols (London, 1869), pp. 520–21
10. *Calendar of Ancient Correspondence concerning Wales*, ed. J. G. Edwards (Cardiff, 1935), p. 80.
11. Prestwich, *Welsh Infantry in Flanders in 1297*, p. 11
12. *Ibid.*

13. Bryce and Mary Lyon, *The Wardrobe Book of 1296–7: A Financial and Logistical Record of Edward I's 1297 Autumn Campaign in Flanders against Philip IV of France* (Brussels, 2004), pp. 98–100
14. Bryce Lyon, 'What were the expenses of the Kings Edward I and Edward III when absent from their realm?', *Journal of Medieval History*, vol. 29 no. 4 (Amsterdam, 2003), pp. 331–45
15. Bryce Lyon, 'The Failed Flemish Campaign of Edward I in 1297. A case study of efficient logistics and inadequate military planning' in *Handelingen der Maatschappij voor Geschiedenis en Oudheidkunde te Gent Ugent*, vol. 59 (Gent, 2005), p. 41 [hereafter The Failed Flemish Campaign]
16. *Mémoires*, p. 488
17. Joseph Strayer, *The Reign of Philip the Fair, Princeton* (New Jersey, 1980), p. 164
18. Guillaume Guiart, *Branche des royaux lignages: chronique métrique de Guillaume Guiart; publiée pour la première fois, d'après les manuscrits de la Bibliothèque du Roi*, ed. J. A. Buchon (Paris, 1828; 2nd edn), p. 184; translation by Dr Shelagh Sneddon
19. *Foedera*, p. 867; translation by Richard Price
20. *Vincenz Samanek, Studien zur Geshichte Konig Adolfs, Vorarbeiten zu den Regesta imperii VI 2 (1292–1298)* (Holder-Pichler-Tempsky, 1930), pp. 215–16
21. *Mémoires*, p. 488
22. Thomas Tout, *The History of England from the Accession of Henry III to the death of Edward III* (London, New York and Bombay, 1905), p. 210
23. Böhmer, Johann Friedrich [Begründer eines Werks] [Sonstige]: Regesta imperii, Bd.: 6,2, Die Regesten des Kaiserreiches unter Rudolf, Adolf, Albrecht, Heinrich VII. 1273 - 1313; 2, Die Regesten des Kaiserreiches unter Adolf von Nassau 1291 - 1298 (Wien, 1948), pp. 297–298, translation by Richard Price
24. Pirenne, *Histoire de Belgique* 2, p. 379
25. Frantz Funck-Brentano, *Chronique artésienne (1295–1304) nouvelle édition, et Chronique tournaisienne (1296–1314)* (Paris, 1899), pp. 13–15
26. Frantz Funk-Brentano, *Annales Gandenses* (Paris, 1896 edn), p. 4
27. F. Nicholai Trivet, *De ordine frat. Praedicatorum, Annales sex regum*, ed. Thomas Hog (London, 1844), p. 362; Guisborough, p. 264.

28. TNA 101/ 155/2/2, documents relating to the administration of Henry de Lacy, Earl of Lincoln, lieutenant in Aquitaine. 22 to 25 Edw I
29. Trivet, *Annales*, p. 362; Guisborough, p. 264.
30. Prestwich, *Documents Illustrating the Crisis of 1297–98 in England*, pp. 26–32

17 Surrounded with Perils

1. Pierre de Langtoft, p. 289
2. Harry Rothwell, *English Historical Documents, vol. 3, 1189–1327* (London, 1996; 2nd edn), p. 477
3. *Ibid.*, p. 479
4. Prestwich, *Documents Illustrating the Crisis of 1297–8*, p. 32
5. Michael Prestwich, 'Edward I's Wars and Their Financing, 1294–1307' (PhD thesis, University of Oxford, 1968), pp. 5 & 11
6. Funck-Brentano, *Les origines*, p. 251
7. Prestwich, 'Edward I and Adolf of Nassau', p. 130
8. Funck-Brentano, *Chronique Artésienne*, pp. 15–16
9. F. W. Brooks, 'The Cinque Ports' Feud with Yarmouth in the Thirteenth Century', *Mariner's Mirror*, vol. 19 (1933), p. 44.
10. Prestwich, 'War, Politics and Finance', p. 143
11. *Chronicle of Bury St. Edmunds*, ed. Antonia Gransden (London, 1964), p. 143.
12. *Ibid.*
13. Frantz Funck-Brentano, *Les Origines de la Guerre de cent ans Philippe le Belle en Flandre* (Paris, 1860), pp. 259–60
14. *Chronicle of Bury St Edmunds*, p. 143
15. Pierre de Langtoft, pp. 295–96
16. Verbruggen, p. 17
17. Prestwich, *Edward I's Wars and their Financing 1294–1307*, p. 206
18. Guisborough, p. 316
19. Gerald of Wales, *The Journey through Wales and the Description of Wales*, ed. and trans. Betty Radice and Lewis Thorpe (London, 1978, 1st edn), p. 113
20. C. Caple, 'Excavations at Dryslwyn Castle 1980–1995' in *Society for Medieval Archaeology Monograph, London: Society for Medieval Archaeology*, vol. 26 (New York, 2007), pp. 192–206
21. *Chronicle of Bury St. Edmunds*, p. 144

22. Bryce and Mary Lyon, 'The Logistics for Edward I's ill-fated campaign in Flanders (1297–1298)', *Handelingen der Maatschappij voor Geschiedenis en Oudheidkunde te Gent Ser. NR*, 55 (2001), pp. 85–87; Bryce and Mary Lyon, *The Wardrobe Book 1296–1297*, pp. 101–102
23. *Ibid.*, pp. 87–88
24. Pirenne, *Histoire de Belgique I*, p. 379
25. *Ibid.*
26. William of Rishanger, *Chronica et annales, regnantibus Henrico Tertio et Edwardo Primo AD 1259–1307*, ed. Henry Thomas Riley (Cambridge, 1865), p. 413
27. *Ibid.*
28. Prestwich, *Edward I*, p. 427
29. *Calendar of Close Rolls 1296–1302*, p. 132
30. Samanek, *Studien*, pp. 216–218
31. *Ibid.*, p. 217; translation by Richard Price
32. Verbruggen, p. 18
33. Bryce and Mary Lyon, *The Wardrobe Book 1296–1297*, pp. 32 & 54
34. Funck-Brentano, *Chronique Artésienne* (Paris, 1889), p. 17, f. 4
35. Bryce and Mary Lyon, *The Wardrobe Book of 1296–1297*, p. 85
36. Frantz Funck-Brentano, *Les Origines*, pp. 268–69
37. Verbruggen, p.18.
38. *Annales Gandenses: Annals of Ghent*, ed. and trans Hilda Johnstone (Oxford, 1985), pp. 5–6
39. Verbruggen, p. 18
40. *Annales Gandenses*, pp. 5–6.
41. TNA SC 1/19/6; translation by Shelagh Sneddon
42. Prestwich, *Documents*, pp. 152–53. My thanks to Professor Prestwich for supplying this translation via email.
43. Funck-Brentano, *Les Origines*, pp. 269
44. Bryce and Mary Lyon, *The Wardrobe Book of 1296–1297* (Brussels, 2004), p. 19
45. Fritz Kern, *Acta Imperii Angliae et Franciae (1267–1313)* (New York, 1973), p. 85; translation by Richard Price
46. *Ibid.*, pp. 85–86. My thanks to Richard Price for these translations
47. Édouard Clerc, *Essair sur l'histoire de la Franche-Comté*, vol. 1 (Ghent, 1870), p. 504

48. A. Laurens, *Annuaire statistique de département du Doubs* (Lyon, 1830), p. 97
49. Pierre Chaplais, *English Medieval Diplomatic Practice*, vol. I (London: Her Majesty's Stationary Office, 1981), p. 353
50. Prestwich, *Edward I*, p. 394
51. Claude de Vic and Dom J. Vaissete, *Histoire générale de Languedoc*, vol. x, c. 345 (Toulouse, 1872); translation provided here by Richard Price
52. Ch. V-Langlois, 'Les Doléances des Communautés du Toulousain contre Pierre de Latilli et Raoul de Breuilli (1297–1298),' *Revue Historique*, vol. 95 no. 1 (1907), pp. 23–53
53. Guisborough, p. 262
54. Strayer, *The Reign of Philip the Fair*, pp. 376–77
55. This figure is gleaned from a comparison of sources. Guiart: 600 men-at-arms and 700 foot; *Ancienne Chroniques de Flandre*: 700 men-at-arms and 700 foot; Guisborough: 1,500 men-at-arms.; Nangis: 500 French. However, Langtoft and the *Chronica de Melsa* inflate the numbers of French to 1,500 men-at-arms and 5,000 foot. Figures taken from Lawton, [previously cited at n. 38] pp. 112–13
56. Kelly DeVries, *Infantry Warfare in the Early Fourteenth Century: Discipline, Tactics and Technology (Warfare in History)* (Suffolk, Woodbridge, 1996, repr. 2000), pp. 13–14
57. Verbruggen, p. 16
58. Vale, *Origins*, p. 212
59. Joseph Patrick Huffman, *The Social Politics of Medieval Diplomacy: Anglo-German Relations (1066–1307), Studies in Medieval and Early Modern Civilization* (Michigan, 2000), p. 309
60. Fritz Kern, *Acta Imperii Angliae at Franciae*, pp. 84–85
61. Langtoft, pp. 295–96
62. Prestwich, *Documents*, no. 158
63. *Ibid.*, no. 159
64. *Foedera*, pp. 878–79
65. *Ibid.*, pp. 881–82
66. *The Parliament Writs and Writs of Military Summons* (Lyon, 1827), pp. 698, 699, 749, 872, 880, 886
67. Prestwich, *Edward I*, p. 394

18 Tricks and Plots

1. *Foedera*, pp. 885–86
2. Prestwich, *War, Politics and Finance under Edward I*, p. 32
3. *Foedera,* pp. 878–79
4. Pirenne, *Histoire de Belgique I*, p. 378
5. Manchester, University of Manchester Library, MS PHC/.146. Translation by Richard Price; see Appendix 9
6. *Foedera*, pp. 881–92; pp. 885–86
7. Pirenne, *Histoire de Belgique I*, p. 379
8. Funck-Brentano, *Les origines de la guerre*, pp. 272–73
9. Kervyn de Lettenhove, 'Comptes de l'expédition d'Edouard Ier en Flandre' in *Compte-rendu des séances de la commission royale d'histoire*, 2nd series, vol. 13 (1872), p. 198
10. *Lodewijk Van Velthem's voortzetting van den Spiegel historiael (1248–1316)*, 3 vols (Académie Royale de Belgique, Commission Royale d'Histoire, 1906, 1931, 1938), pp. 667–70; 674–79; English translation supplied to me via email by Dr Jan Burgers
11. J. Sturler, 'Les relations politiques de l'Angleterre et du Brabant sous Edouard I et Edouard II Plantagenet' in *Revue belge de Philogie et d'Histoire* (1932), pp. 639–40
12. Prestwich, *Edward I*, pp. 478–479
13. Prestwich, *Edward I*, p. 394
14. *Chronicle of Bury St. Edmunds*, p. 146
15. *Ibid.*, pp. 146–47
16. *Annales Gandenses*, p. 7
17. *Ibid.*
18. Record Society for the Publication of Original Documents relating to Lancashire and Cheshire, *Annales Cestrienses, or, Chronicle of the Abbey of St Werburg at Chester* (Lancashire and Chester, 1879), pp. 112–13
19. Lawton, p. 128
20. *Ibid.*, pp. 129 & 137
21. *Ibid.*, p. 155
22. Bryce and Mary Lyon, *The Wardrobe Book* (Brussels, 2004), p. 77
23. *Ibid.*, p. 7
24. *Calendar of the Patent Rolls 1292–1301* (London, 1895), pp. 334–35
25. *Ibid.*, p. 328
26. Prestwich, *Documents Illustrating the Crisis*, pp. 187–88

27. Funck-Brentano, *Les origins de la guerre*, p. 275
28. Guisborough, ii, p. 173
29. *Ibid.*, p. 35.
30. Fiona Jane Watson, *Traitor, Outlaw, King. Part One: The Making of Robert Bruce* (Amazon Media, 2018), p. 102; Rishanger, *Chronica et annales, regnantibus Henrico Tertio et Edwardo Primo*, p. 185
31. Pierre de Langtoft, vol. II, p. 311
32. *Foedera*, p. 888. Translated by Professor Jonathan Mackman at the National Archives
33. *Ibid.*
34. *Ibid.*
35. *Ibid.*
36. *Calendar of Patent Rolls 1301–1307*, p. 432.
37. Prestwich, *Edward I*, p. 431
38. *Mémoires et Documents Inédits, pour servir a l'histoire de la Franche-Comté publiés par L'Académie de Basencon Volume 3* (Besancon, 1844), p. 165, f.1
39. Funck-Brentano, *Philippe le Bel et la noblesse Franc-Comtoise*, pp. 5–40
40. Funck-Brentano (above, p. 28) quotes Clerc, *Essair sur l'histoire de la Franche-Comté, Volume 1*, p. 504; Clerc provides no reference.
41. *Bulletin des bibliothéques et des archives Paris, au bureau du cabinet historique* (Paris, 1860), p. 72
42. Clerc, *Essair sur l'histoire de la Franche-Comté, Volume 1*, p. 483
43. Prestwich, *War, Politics and Finance under Edward I*, p. 174
44. Prestwich, *Edward I and Adolf of Nassau*, pp. 132–33
45. Abulafia, *The New Cambridge Medieval History*, p. 398
46. Bayard Taylor, *A History of Germany* (New York, 1897), p. 182

19 We Pray You to Make Peace

1. *Calendar of Documents Relating to Scotland, 1272–1307*, vol. II, ed. Joseph Bain (Edinburgh, 1884), pp. 252–54
2. H. Rothwell, 'Edward I's case against Philip the Fair over Gascony in 1298' in *The English Historical Review*, vol. 42, no. 168 (October 1927), p. 575
3. Frantz Kervyn de Lettenhove, *Etudes sur l'histoire du xii siecle, Mémoires de l'academic royale de Belgique, XXIII* (Brussels, 1954), p. 31 [hereafter Lettenhove]

4. *Ibid.*, pp. 41–43
5. Funck-Brentano, *Philip le Bel*, p. 293; Lettenhove, pp. 48–49. Translation by Richard Price.
6. *Ibid.*
7. Chaplais, *English Medieval Diplomatic Practice*, vol. I (Oxford, 1982), pp. 148–49
8. *Calendar of Papal Registers Relating to Great Britain and Ireland, Volume I, 1198–1304* (London, 1893), p. 579
9. M. C. MacInerny, *A History of the Irish Dominicans from original sources and unpublished records, Volume I, Irish Dominican Bishops (1224–1307)* (Cork, 1916), p. 467
10. *Calendar of Papal Registers*, I, p. 579
11. H. Rothwell, 'Edward's case against Philip the Fair in Gascony in 1298' in *The English Historical Review*, vol. 42 no. 168 (October 1927), p. 575
12. Lettenhove, p. 50
13. *Ibid.*, p. 49
14. Jean Dunbabib, *The French in the Kingdom of Sicily, 1266–1305* (Cambridge University Press, 2011), p. 128
15. Funk-Brentano, *Les origins de la guerre*, pp. 325–326; translation by Claire Noble
16. Chaplais, *English Medieval Diplomatic Practice*, vol. 1, pp. 10–11
17. Pirenne, *Histoire de Belgique*, I, pp. 379–80

20 *The Golden Spurs*

1. Francois-César Louandre, *Histoire d'Abbeville et du comté de Ponthieu jusqu'en 1789*, vol. I (Paris, 1844–45), p. 211
2. Vale, *Origins*, pp. 72
3. Black, *Edward I and Gascony in 1300*, p. 521
4. Tout, *History of England*, p. 211
5. Vale, *Origins*, p. 221
6. *Ibid.*
7. *Ibid.*, p. 218
8. *Ibid.*, p. 222; M. K. James, 'Fluctuations of the Anglo-Gascon wine trade in the fourteenth century', *Economic History Review*, vol. 4 no. 2 (1951), pp. 170–82; Renouard, 'Le grand commerce des vins de Gascogne', *Revue Historique*, vol. 221 no. 2 (1959) pp. 284, 288
9. Vale, *Origins*, p. 220

10. *Ibid.*, pp. 219–20
11. Verbruggen, pp. 18–19
12. *Ibid.*, p. 225; my account of the battle is largely taken from Verbruggen's narrative
13. Nangis, p. 261
14. Thomas Wright, *The Political Songs of England from the reign of John to Edward II* (London, 1829) pp. 191–92
15. *English Historical Documents 1189–1327*, edited by David Charles Douglas and Harry Rothwell (Routledge, 1995) pp. 515–17
16. Vale, *Origins*, p. 223
17. Labarge, *Gascony: England's first colony*, p. 83
18. TNA E 101/10/23, Payments made by John of Cockermouth to Gascons being conveyed from Portsmouth to Gascony, March 1303
19. TNA E 101/160/4, m.1, Part of an account of the seneschal of Aquitaine. Pons de Castillon brought two knights and twelve esquires; Bernard Trencaléon brought twenty-three esquires and thirty sergeants, Auger de Pouillon thirty-four foot-sergeants (etc.)
20. Vale, *Origins*, pp. 222–23
21. Chaplais, *English Medieval Diplomatic Practice Volume I*, pp. 116–18
22. Chaplais, *English Medieval Diplomatic Practice Volume II*, pp. 497–98
23. Labarge, *Gascony: England's first colony*, pp. 74–75
24. Vale, *Origins*, p. 212
25. Watson, 'Edward I in Scotland' (unpublished PhD thesis, University of Glasgow, 1991), p. 150
26. Vale, *Origins*, p. 212
27. Nicholson, Crawford & Burgtorf, *Templars*, p. 63
28. *Ibid.*, pp. 63–64
29. Verbruggen, *The Battle of the Golden Spurs*, p. 12
30. Vale, *Origins*, p. 58
31. E 101/10/13; my thanks to Professor Michael Prestwich for informing me of this reference
32. Vale, *Origins*, p. 206
33. *Ibid.*, p. 400
34. Bryce Lyon, The Failed Flemish Campaign, p. 42
35. *Ibid.*, p. 31
36. *Annals of Ghent*, p. 85
37. Prestwich, *Documents Illustrating the Crisis*, p. 26

38. G. Barraclough, 'Edward I and Adolf of Nassau: A Chapter of Medieval Diplomatic History', *The Cambridge Historical Journal*, vol. 6 no. 3 (1940), p. 242
39. Prestwich, *Edward I*, p. 416; Guisborough, pp. 289–90

21 *Aftermath*

1. Prestwich, *Edward I*, p. 396
2. Nicholson, Crawford & Burgtorf, *Templars*, pp. 64–65
3. Verbruggen, *The Battle of the Golden Spurs*, p. 249
4. *Ibid.*, p. 88
5. Strayer, *Philip the Fair*, p. 336
6. *Ibid.*, pp. 336–37
7. *Ibid.*, p. 346
8. Nicholson, Crawford & Burgtorf, *Templars*, p. 65
9. Malcolm Barber, *The Trial of the Templars* (Cambridge University Press, 2006), p. 52
10. Alain Demurger, *The Persecution of the Templars: Scandal, Torture, Trial* (Profile Books, 2018), p. 10
11. Nicholson, Crawford & Burgtorf, *Templars*, pp. 65–66
12. Strayer, *Philip the Fair*, pp. 286–87, f.150
13. Watson, *Edward I in Scotland*, pp. 229–30
14. *Ibid.*, pp. 229–35
15. Michael Brown, *Hearts and Bodies: Edward I and the Scottish Magnates, 1296–1307*, p. 105; *Edward I: New Interpretations* edited by Andy King and Andrew M. Spencer (York Medieval Press, 2020)
16. Fiona Watson, *Settling the Stalemate: Edward I's Peace in Scotland 1303–1305*, p. 143; *Thirteenth Century England VI* edited by Michael Prestwich, R. H. Britnell, Robin Frame (Boydell Press, 1995)
17. Prestwich, *Edward I*, p. 553
18. Vale, *Origins*, pp. 224–25
19. TNA SC 8/291/14531
20. TNA SC 8/292/14577
21. TNA SC 8/292/14570
22. TNA SC 8/289/14410
23. Guilhelm Pepin, *Petitions from Gascony, Testimonies of a Special Relationship* (downloaded from www.academia.edu), p. 125
24. pp. 479–481
25. Labarge, *Gascony: England's first colony*, pp. 84–85

26. TNA SC8/292/14557
27. Trabut-Cussac, L'administration Anglaise en Gascogne, p. 127
28. *Ibid.*, p. 128
29. *Ibid.*, p. 130
30. *Ibid.*, p. 136
31. *Fourteenth Century England*, vol. 7, edited by Mark Ormrod (Boydell Press, 2012), p. 80
32. Cuttino, *English Diplomatic Administration*, p. 80
33. *Ibid.*, p. 26
34. Trabut-Cussac, L'administration de Gascogne, p. 131
35. Labarge, *Gascony: England's first colony*, p. 82

22 *Trophies and Dead Things*

1. *Ibid.*, p. 75
2. Cuttino, *English Diplomatic Administration*, p. 13
3. *Mémoires*, pp. 501–505
4. *Ibid.*, pp. 503–504
5. Cuttino, *English Diplomatic Administration*, p. 24
6. *Ibid.*, pp. 24–25
7. Vale, *Origins*, pp. 238–239
8. *Ibid.*, p. 247
9. Cuttino, *English Diplomatic Administration*
10. T. F. Tout, *England in the Late Middle Ages* (Ozymandias Press, 2016) p. 337

BIBLIOGRAPHY

Primary Manuscript Sources

TNA SC 1/13/3; Edward I to Philip III, king of France, the lack of agreement between Philip and the king of Castile; his difficulties because of wars in Ireland and Wales

TNA C 47/29/2/ m.2; arrangements for a joint crusade between Edward I and Philip IV

TNA E 101/155/5/13; E 101 153/15/11; E 101/152/9/39; E 101/155/2/2, documents relating to the administration of Henry de Lacy, earl of Lincoln, lieutenant in Aquitaine 24 to 26 Edward I

TNA SC 1/26/195; petition of Arnald de Gabastan (*sic*) to John Langton for restoration of his wife's lands, May 1297

TNA C 47/24/2/23; claim of Arnald Gaveston for expenses in Gascony, 20 November 1299–19 November 1300

TNA SC 1/19/6; Letter from Gerard de Moer to Count Guy of Flanders

TNA SC 1/14/184; letters from Jean de Chalon to Edward I; the fall of Ornans in Burgundy

TNA SC 1/15/9; Count of Henry of Bar to Edward I; his forces are ready

TNA E372/160; record of the Exchequer Michaelmas 1314–Michaelmas 1315

TNA E 101/10/23; Payments made by John of Cockermouth to Gascons being conveyed from Portsmouth to Gascony, March 1303

TNA SC 8/291/14531; TNA SC 8/292/14577; TNA SC 8/292/14570; TNA SC 8/289/14410; Gascon petitions to the King and Council, 1305

TNA E 101/160/4, m.1; part of an account of the Seneschal of Aquitaine
TNA E 101/10/13; account of the service of Jean de Varenne in Flanders

Primary Printed Sources

Annales Londonienses, Chronicles of the Reigns of Edward I and Edward II, edited by W. Stubbs, vol. 1 (Rolls Series, 1882)

Annales Monastici, edited by H. R. Luard (5 vols, Rolls Series, 1854–69)

Archives Municipales de Bordeaux, vol. v, Livre des Coutumes, edited by H. Barckhausen (Bordeaux, 1890)

Calendar of Chancery Rolls, Supplementary Close Rolls, Welsh Rolls, Scutage Rolls AD 1277–1326 (Hereford Times Limited, 1912)

Calendar of Close Rolls (HMSC, 1892–)

Calendar of Documents Relating to Scotland, edited by Joseph Bain, vols i & ii, A.D. 1272–1307 (H.M. General Register House, Edinburgh, 1884)

Calendar of Inquisitions Miscellaneous (Chancery) preserved in the Public Record Office, vol. 1 (HMSC, 1916)

Calendar of Liberate Rolls, VI, 1267–72 With Appendices 1220–1267, 1964 (Digital General Collection, University of Michigan)

Calendar of Patent Rolls (HMSC, 1906–)

The Chronicle of Bury St Edmunds, 1212–1301, edited by A. Gransden (London, 1964)

Chronicle of Lanercost, edited by J. Stevenson (Edinburgh, 1939)

The Chronicle of Pierre de Langtoft, edited by T. Wright, vol. ii (Rolls Series, 1868)

The Chronicle of Walter de Guisborough, edited by H. Rothwell (Camden Society, 3rd series, lxxxix, 1957)

The Chronicle of William of Rishanger of the Barons' Wars, edited by J. O. Halliwell (Camden Society, 1st series, xv, 1840)

Chronicles of the Reigns of Stephen, Henry II and Richard I [includes the Chronicle of Newburgh], vol. 2 (University Library, University of North Carolina, 1884)

Chronicon de Lanercost, edited by Joseph Stevenson, vol. 1 (Edinburgh: Impressum, 1739)

Chronique latine de Guillaume de Nangis de 1113 à 1300: avec les continuations de cette chronique de 1300 à 1368, vol. 2 (Paris: J. Renouard, 1843)

Close Rolls, Henry III (HMSO, 1902–38)

Constitutiones et Acta Publica Imperatorum et Regum, edited by Ludowic Weiland (Hanover, 1893)

Documents Illustrating the Crisis of 1297–98 in England, edited by Michael Prestwich (London: Camden Society, 4th series, xxxiv, 1980)

Documents Illustrative of the History of Scotland, edited by Joseph Stevenson, vol. ii (Edinburgh, 1870)

English Historical Documents 1189–1327, edited by David Charles Douglas and Harry Rothwell (Taylor & Francis e-library, 2004)

Flores Historiarum, edited by H. R. Luard, vol. ii (Rolls Series, 1890)

Foedera, Conventiones, Litteraem, vol. 1.2 (London, 1816)

Henry Knighton, *Chronicon Henrici Knighton vel Cnitthon Monachi Leycestrensis*, edited by J. R. Lumby (2 vols, Rolls Series, London, 1889–95)

J. R. Studd, 'A Catalogue of the Acts of the Lord Edward, 1254–1272' (Unpublished thesis, University of Leeds, May 1971)

Lettres de rois, reines et autres personnages des cours de France et d'Angleterre [etc], vol. 1 (University of Toronto, 1839)

Lettres des Rois, Reines et Autres Personages des cours de France et D'Angleterre et publieés, edited by M. Champollion-Figeac (Paris, 1839)

Matthaei Parisensis, Monachi Sancti Albani, Chronica Majora, edited by H. R. Luard (7 vols, Rolls Series 1872–83)

Monasticon anglicanum; a history of the abbies and other monasteries [etc], Sir William Dugdale, vol. VI (London: Bohn, 1846)

Nicholai Triveti ... Annales Sex Regum Angliae, edited by T. Hog (London, 1845)

Pierre Chaplais, *English Medieval Diplomatic Practice: Documents and Interpretation*, Vol. 1, Issue 2 (Public Record Office, 1982)

René de Lespinasse, *Bibliothèque de l'École des Chartes* (London, 1887)

Rôles Gascons, transcrits et publiés, vol. 3, 1290–1307, edited by *Charles Bémont* (Paris: Imprimiere Nationale, 1906)

Royal and other historical letters illustrative of the reign of Henry III, edited by Walter Waddington Shirley, vol. 2 (Cambridge University Press, 2013)

Thomas Wright's Political Songs of England, edited by P. Coss (Cambridge, 1996)

The Welsh Assize Roll, edited by James Conway Davies (Cardiff: University of Wales Press Board, 1940)

Willelmi Rishanger, Chronica et Annales, edited by H. T. Riley (Rolls Series, 1865)

Secondary Printed Sources

'Adversaries of Edward I: Gaston de Béarn and Llywelyn ap Gruffudd' by J. Beverley Smith in *Recognitions: Essays presented to Edmund Fryde*, edited by Colin Richmond and Isobel Harvey (Aberystwyth: National Library of Wales, 1996)

A Great and Terrible King: Edward I and the Forging of Britain by Marc Morris (Windmill Books, 2009)

A History of the English People 449–1214, vol. 1 by John Richard Green (Barcelona-Singapore: Athena University Press, 2004)

'A Moat Defensive: the coast defense scheme of 1295' by A. Z. Freeman in *Speculum*, vol. xlii (1967)

'Aspects of Chivalric Culture c. 1270–1350: The Context of the Court of Edward III' by Juliet Elizabeth Vale (D.Phil, University of York, Department of History, January 1981)

Chronicle by Ramon Muntaner, translated by Lady Goodenough (Ontario: In Parentheses Publications, Catalan Series, 2000)

Documents relating to Law and Custom of the Sea vol. *1, AD 1205–1648*, edited by Reginald Godfrey Marsden (New Jersey: The Law Book Exchange Ltd, 1999)

Edward I by Michael Prestwich (Yale University Press, Newhaven and London, 1997)

'Edward I and Adolf of Nassau: A Chapter of Medieval Diplomatic History' by Geoffrey Barraclough in *The Cambridge Historical Journal*, vol. 6 no. 3 (1940)

'Edward I and Adolf of Nassau' by Michael Prestwich in *Thirteenth Century III: Proceedings of the Newcastle-Upon-Tyne Conference*, edited by P. R. Coss and S. D. Lloyd (Woodbridge, Suffolk, 1991)

'Edward I and Gascony in 1300' by J. G. Black, *The English Historical Review*, vol. 17 no. 67 (July 1902)

'Edward I's Building Works in Gascony' by Marc Morris in *The Impact of the Edwardian Castles in Wales* edited by Diane M. Williams and John R. Kenyon (Oxbow Books, 2007)

Edward I: New Interpretations, edited by Andy King and Andrew M. Spencer (York Medieval Press, 2020)

England and the Crusades 1095–1588 by Christopher Tyerman (University of Chicago Press, 15 Dec. 1996)

'England and the Mongols (c. 1260–1330)' by Jacques Poviot in *Journal of the Royal Asiatic Society*, Third Series, vol. 10, no. 3 (Nov. 2000)

England in the Late Middle Ages by T. F. Tout (Ozymandias Press, 2016)
England under the Angevin Kings, vol. 2 by Kate Norgate (London, 1887)
English Diplomatic Administration 1259–1339 by P. Cuttino (Oxford: Clarendon Press, 1971; 2nd edn)
'Erzbischof Gerhard II. von Mainz und König Adolf von Nassau: Territorialpolitik und Finanze' by Hans Patze in *Hessisches Jahrbuch für Landesgeschichte*, vol. 13 (1963)
Esther Rowland Clifford, *A Knight of Great Renown, The Life and Times of Othon de Grandson* (University of Chicago Press, 1961)
Fourteenth Century England, vol. 7, edited by Mark Ormrod (Boydell Press, 2012)
Gascony: England's first colony 1204–1453 by Margaret Wade Labarge (Hamish Hamilton, 1980)
Geschichte von England by Johann Martin Lappenburg and Georg Reinhold Pauli (Gotha, 1855)
Henry III: The Great King England Never Knew it Had by Darren Baker (The History Press, 2017)
Histoire d'Abbeville et du comté de Ponthieu jusqu'en 1789, vol. 1 by François César Louandre (Paris, 1923)
Histoire de la guerre de Navarre en 1276 et 1277 by Guillaume Anelier de Toulouse (Paris, 1856)
Histoire des Croisades by Jean Richard (Fayard, 1996)
King Henry III and the Lord Edward, The Community of the Realm in the Thirteenth Century (Oxford: Clarendon Press, 1947)
King John by W. L. Warren (University of California Press, 1978; revised edn)
'L'administration anglaise et Gascogne sous Henri III et Édouard Ier de 1254 a 1307' by Jean Paul Trabut-Cussac in *Économies, Sociétés, Civilisations Année*, 30 (1975)
La Vasconie Étude de historique et critique sur les origines du royaume de Navarre, du duché de Gascogne, des comtés de Comminges, d'Aragon, de Foix, de Bigorre, d'Alava & de Biscaye de la viscomté de Béarn, et des grands fiefs du duche de Gascogne by Jean de Jauguin (Pau : Impremerie-Stéréotypie Garet, 1898)
'L'Europe occidentale de 1270 A 1380, pt. I de 1270 a 1328' by R. Fawtier in *Histoire de Moyen age 6* (Paris, 1940)

'L'Hommage du duc de Bar au roi de France' by Marcel Grosdidier de Matons in *Memoires de la Sociéte des Lettres Sciences et Arts de Bar-le-Duc*, vol. 43 (Imprimeri Content Laguerre, 1918–21)

Les Anglais en Guyenne: l'administration anglaise et le mouvement communal dans le Bordelais by Louis-Desire Brissaud (Paris, 1875)

Linda M. Paterson, *Medieval Occitan Society c. 1100–1300* (Cambridge University Press, 1993)

Medieval Germany (2001): An Encyclopedia edited by John M. Jeep (Routledge Revivals, 2016)

Money and its Use in Medieval Europe by Peter Spufford (Cambridge, 1993, repr. 1988)

Nobility and Kingship in Medieval England: The Earls and Edward I 1272–1307 by Andrew M. Spencer (Cambridge University Press, 2013)

Philip III the Bold, King of France, 1270–85: The Evolution of Royal Power in Medieval Europe by Charles Victor Langlois (Paris, 1887)

'Philip the Fair of France: Nemesis of Edward I and England' by Elizabeth A. R. Brown in *Prowess, Piety and Public Order in Society: Studies in Honour of Richard W. Kaeuper* (Brill, 2017)

'Philippe le Bel et la noblesse franc-comtoise' by Frantz Funck-Brentano in *Bibliotheque de l'école des chartes*, vol. 49 (1888)

Recueil des historiens des Gaules et de la France, vol. 21 edited by Dom Martin Bouquet (Paris: Imprimerie Royale, 1840–1904)

Robert Bruce and the Community of the Realm of Scotland by G. W. S. Barrow (University of California Press, 1965)

'Settling the Stalemate: Edward I's Peace in Scotland 1303–1305' by Fiona Watson in *Thirteenth Century England VI* edited by Michael Prestwich, R. H. Britnell, Robin Frame (Boydell Press, 1995)

Simon de Montfort by J. R. Maddicott (Cambridge University Press, 1994)

Simon de Montfort, Comte de Leicester by Charles Bémont (Oxford University, 1884)

The Angevin Empire by John Gillingham (Oxford University Press, 2001; 2nd edn)

The Art of Warfare in Western Europe During the Middle Ages from the Eighth Century (Warfare in History) by J. F. Verbruggen (Boydell Press, 2002 edn)

The Battle of the Golden Spurs (Courtrai, 11 July 1302), A Contribution to the History of Flanders' War of Liberation (Warfare in History) by J. R. Verbruggen, edited and translated by Kelly DeVries and David Richard Ferguson (Woodbridge, Suffolk, 2002)

'The costs and profits of war: The Anglo-French Conflict of 1294–1303' by Joseph R. Strayer in *The Medieval City*, edited by H. A. Miskimin, D. Herlihy and A. L. Udovitch (New Haven, London, 1977)

'The County of Ponthieu 1279–1307' by Hilda Johnstone in *The English Historical Review*, vol. 29, no. 115 (July 1914)

The Dawn of the Constitution, or the Reigns of Henry III and Edward I (AD 1216–1307) by Sir James H. Ramsay (London, 1908)

The Debate on the Trial of the Templars, 1307–1314, edited by Jochen Burgtorf, Paul Crawford and Helen Nicholson (Ashgate, 2010)

'The Failed Flemish Campaign of Edward I in 1297: a case study of efficient logistics and inadequate military planning by Bryce Lyon in *Handelingen der Maatschappij voor Geschiedenis en Oudheidkunde te Gent*, vol. 59 (2005)

The First English Empire, Power and Identities in the British Isles 1093–1343 by R. R. Davies (Oxford, 2000)

'The Franco-Scottish and Franco-Norwegian Treaties of 1295' by Ranald Nicholson in *Scottish Historical Review*, vol. 38, no. 126, part 2 (October 1959)

'The Gascon Nobility and the Anglo-French War 1294–98' by Malcolm Vale in *War and Government in the Middle Ages: Essays in Honour of J.O. Prestwich* (Woodbridge, 1984)

'The Last Rex Crucesignatus: Edward I and the Mongol Alliance' by Attila Bárány in *Annual of Medieval Studies*, vol. 16 (Central European University, 2010)

'The marriage of Henry of Almaine and Constance de Béarn' by Robin Studd in *Thirteenth-Century England III: Proceedings of the Newcastle upon Tyne Conference 1989*, edited by P. R. Coss and S. D. Lloyd (Boydel Press, 1991)

The Origins of the Hundred Years War: The Angevin Legacy 1250–1340 by Malcolm Vale (Oxford: Clarendon Press, 1996)

The Persecution of the Templars: Scandal, Torture, Trial by Alain Demurger (Profile Books, 2018)

The Reign of Philip the Fair by Joseph R. Strayer (Princeton University Press, 1980)

The Social Politics of Medieval Diplomacy: Anglo-German Relations (1066–1307) by Joseph P. Huffman (Michigan, 2000)

The Staple Court books of Bristol, vol. 5, edited by E. E. Rich (Bristol Record Society, 1934)

The Trial of the Templars by Malcolm Barber (Cambridge University Press, 2006)

Thomas K. Heebøll-Holm, *Ports, Piracy and Maritime War: Piracy in the English Channel and the Atlantic, c. 1280-c. 1330* (Brill, 2013)

Traitor, Outlaw, King. Part One: The Making of Robert Bruce by Fiona Watson (2018)

War, Politics and Finance under Edward I by Michael Prestwich (Rowman and Littlefield, 1972)

Unpublished Theses

'Edward I in Scotland' by Fiona Watson, (Unpublished PhD thesis, University of Glasgow, 1991)

'Henry de Lacy, Earl of Lincoln as *locum tenens* at *capitaneus* in the duchy of Aquitaine' by Reginald Philip Lawton (unpublished PhD thesis, University of London, 1974)

INDEX